CONTRACT LAW IN PERSPECTIVE

Fifth Edition

Contract Law in Perspective complements 'black letter' treatments of contract by looking at legal doctrine and statutes in their social, political and economic contexts. It increases students' understanding of the law of contract as well as explaining its importance to us all.

In addition to describing the key doctrines in the field, this book explains the ideology behind them and considers the extent to which they serve the needs of the business community and consumers. By taking the 'big ideas' in contract theory and relating these to practice, the book helps to broaden students' understanding and appreciation of the subject.

This fifth edition:

- Includes a new section on privity, discussion of the Rights of Third Parties Act, as well as an examination of the Law Commission's Unfair Terms in Contract Bill
- Includes clear diagrams and illustrations to help students identify the key points within each chapter and reflect on what they have learnt
- Advice on further reading is included at the end of each chapter to point students towards sources for more detailed study
- Additional self-test questions enable students to consolidate and practise their knowledge and understanding of the subject at regular intervals.

Linda Mulcahy is Professor of Law and Society at Birkbeck College, University of London.

CONTRACT LAW IN PERSPECTIVE

Fifth Edition

Linda Mulcahy
Birkbeck College
University of London

Routledge·Cavendish
Taylor & Francis Group
LONDON AND NEW YORK

First published by Butterworths Ltd.
The third and fourth editions of this book were published by Cavendish Publishing Limited.

Fifth edition published 2008 by Routledge-Cavendish,
2 Park Square, Milton Park, Abingdon, Oxon, OX14 4RN

Simultaneously published in the USA and Canada
by Routledge-Cavendish
270 Madison Ave, New York, NY10016

Routledge-Cavendish is an imprint of the Taylor & Francis Group, an informa business

© 2008 Linda Mulcahy

Typeset in Palatino by Keyword Group Ltd
Printed and bound in Great Britain by TJ International, Padstowe, Cornwall

British Library Cataloguing in Publication Data
A catalogue record for this book is available from the British Library

Library of Congress Cataloging in Publication Data
Mulcahy, Linda, 1962–
Contract law in perspective / Linda Mulcahy. – 5th ed.
p. cm.
1. Contracts–England. 2. Contracts–Wales. I. Title.
KD1554. M85 2008
346. 4202–dc22
2007050662

ISBN 13: 978-0-415-44431-6 (hbk)
ISBN 10: 0-415-44431-4 (hbk)

ISBN 13: 978-0-415-44432-3 (pbk)
ISBN 10: 0-415-44432-3 (pbk)

CONTENTS

PART ONE: INTRODUCTION

PART TWO: BIG IDEAS IN THE LAW OF CONTRACT

PART FOUR: BARGAINING NAUGHTINESS AND FORMATION PROBLEMS

PREFACE

In 1981, when Tillotson's first edition of *Contract Law in Perspective* was published, I was in my first year at university studying for my LLB. I spent a considerable amount of time in the library trying to understand the intricacies of the 15 or so contract cases which we were asked to read each week. The weighty 'black letter' texts my lecturers directed me to in order to help me understand the cases failed to stimulate and were insufficiently critical of formal rules for my liking. They dealt with the detail at the expense of the big ideas. I stopped going to seminars and spent some time in bookshops looking for an approach to contract law that would inspire me to return to the cases. I was saved by the publication of the first edition of *Contract Law in Perspective*, written by John Tillotson, which moved away from doctrinal intricacies to reflect on the function of contract law, its relevance to my life and the reasons why it was an important and stimulating field of scholarship. At the time it was first published, the book was a breath of fresh air for those of us who wanted to place what we were learning within a historical, political and sociological context. I gave up all thought of abandoning the law and stuck to it.

Twenty-six years later as a law professor I am able to direct my students to a burgeoning number of socio-legal and critical texts on the subject. Within the academy, we talk more readily of the importance of understanding contracts from a range of different perspectives, but there is also a growing sense of the challenge to find a coherent theory of contract law. As I have grappled with doctrine alongside studies of the lived experience of contract, relational contract theory, feminist theories of contract, notions of reliance, good faith and inequality, I have been made patently aware of what an exciting time it is to study the subject. It goes without saying that I feel extremely honoured to follow in the steps of John Tillotson in introducing students to some of these big ideas and to introduce a range of different perspectives to them.

In this fifth edition, I have sought to take account of recent developments within the topics covered as well as rewriting and reorganising many topics within the book. In response to reviews I have now included a section on privity of contract. I have added more text boxes and illustrations in the hope that these will help readers to understand key issues.

I am extremely grateful to a number of people who have helped with the gestation of this project. In particular I would like to Cathy Andrews for her insights on relational contract theory. I have been privileged to teach courses on contract and the commercial relationship to some really first-rate mature students at Birkbeck, University of London. At times it has become clear that they know much more about the lived world of contract than I, and I have enjoyed the fact that they are always prepared to stand up to me and argue their point. Alice Rutter has done a first-rate job tracking down missing references for me and updating statutes and cases. Valerie Kelley has provided excellent proofreading services and my thanks also go to Josie Lloyd for her support with updating the text. Finally, I would like to thank Richard, Connor and Sam for their ongoing tolerance of my many inadequacies, and Dylan for keeping me company in the final stages of the edits.

Linda Mulcahy
Anniversary Professor of Law and Society
Birkbeck College
December 2007

TABLE OF CASES

TABLE OF BILLS STATUTES AND LEGISLATION

LIST OF FIGURES AND BOXES

PART ONE:

INTRODUCTION

CHAPTER 1

INTRODUCTION, AIMS AND GENERAL PRINCIPLES

What does looking at contract in perspective mean? Whose perspective is being referred to and why does it matter? In my view, the first perspective we should start with is yours. By the time you finish reading this book you will probably have made tens, if not hundreds, of contracts. Each time you buy a pair of jeans or a CD, go to a nightclub, get on a bus, rent a DVD, order a book from Amazon or register for your latest course, you are entering into a contract. Few people in a modern society could survive without exchanging their labour for money, and their money for goods and services. Moreover, each exchange you make is probably only possible because of earlier exchanges between, for instance, the music store and the distributor, the distributor and the record company, the record company and the artist, and the artist and his or her manager. It should soon become clear to you that the law of contract is not a remote and archaic body of rules but a living area of law with which you engage on a daily basis.

The second perspective from which you are encouraged to look at the law of contract from is that of the business community. A number of historians have highlighted the fact that it was this community that the law of contract was developed to serve during the industrial revolution. But in the twenty-first century we are still debating the extent to which the needs of the business community are served by the law of contract. A host of empirical studies now inform our understanding of how law works in practice and its relevance to those who use it on a regular basis. At one level, the message of these studies is depressing. We have had to accept that the law of contract is frequently ignored and that it is often seen as irrelevant within the commercial sector. It would seem that contract law is in serious danger of becoming irrelevant or lacking in legitimacy if it continues to focus on the 'paper deal' at the expense of the 'real deal'. This raises important issues for students of contract law. Should the law reflect the practice and needs of the business community or should it impose standards which lawyers think are appropriate regardless of whether these are of practical use? In the course of considering this very issue Lord Wilberforce has argued:

> If I am faced with the alternative of forcing commercial circles to fall in with a legal doctrine which has nothing but precedent to commend it or altering the doctrine so as to conform with what commercial experience has worked out, I know where my choice lies. The law should be responsive as well as, at times, enunciatory, and good doctrine can seldom be divorced from sound practice. *Miliangos v George Frank* at para. 3

The lawyer's view of contract tends to focus on the legal implications of contractual breakdown, on rights, obligations and the consequences of litigation, but the lawyer's preoccupations by no means occupy the forefront of the businessperson's mind. For someone in business the contract is primarily a facilitative device within an economic cycle, which turns on such processes as the acquisition of materials, the production of finished goods, marketing and sales, finance and payment. Business people and economists are most often concerned with the cost of contracting. For example, standard form contracts are less expensive to produce than 'tailor-made' documents. It is often the case that, for them, insistence on precise contractual performance is expensive in terms of both money and business relationships. It becomes clear that the lawyer, who only knows the law of contract, and little or nothing of the rest of contract, has only a small, incomplete, view of the commercial sector.

A final set of perspectives from which to view contracts are those provided by disciplines other than law. It is naïve to think that contracts are only of interest to lawyers. Contractual relationships are also of relevance to sociologist, anthropologists and economists interested in what fuels co-operation between individuals in society, the norms which emerge from the voluntarily imposed agreements that become contracts and how contracting parties can be given incentives to maximise their own gain and that of the broader economy. Viewed in this way, contract is not an end in itself but is a tool of social order. It is also an intensely political subject. Treatments of contract law that present the subject as a series of neutral rules and doctrines often fail to emphasise this point. Contractual doctrines reflect particular ideologies about how and whether contractual relationships should be governed, and are often hotly contested by those from the left and right of the political spectrum.

The main aim of this book is to present a broader view of the basic features of contract law than that found in the traditional 'black letter' treatments of the subject. The idea of understanding law in context is not new but the aim of looking at and beyond legal rules has been pursued more vigorously in some areas than in others. Most expositions of contract law do not venture beyond the rules. They tell us little or nothing of the social or economic significance of doctrines, or how they relate to the practices of the business community. The result is an unhealthy division between the study of formal law and an evaluation of the needs of the wider community it should be designed to serve. At a level suitable for student readers, this books attempts to remedy those defects.

It is undoubtedly an exciting time to be studying contract. Debate and argument regarding the state of the health of contract law continue more energetically than ever before. In fact, numerous critiques and theories of contract law have been produced over the last 50 years or so. Many of them point to a 'transformation' of contract law. Writers such as Atiyah (1989) have argued that there has been a movement, observable in the case law and statutory interventions from 'principles to pragmatism', from 'doctrine to discretion' or from 'market-individualism to consumer-welfarism'. Indeed, as will be seen from the cases, the nineteenth-century foundations of contract law, built on the concepts of promise and discrete agreement, have been overtaken by an increased emphasis on such open-ended notions as reliance, reasonableness, good faith and fairness. This can lead to situations where it may be said that the 'old' view of the courts would give rise to a certain result but the 'new' approach would produce a different one. A closer examination of cases reveals that a mixture of old and new approaches is still apparent.

This has led some commentators to conclude that the modern law of contract is in a muddle and lacks a set of clear principles to underpin it. For a growing group of academics this crisis relates to the absence of a clear theoretical framework. But the inadequacies of existing doctrine are also made apparent in the work of a number of empirical researchers who have found that the business community often circumvents contractual rules because they fail to facilitate flexible enough agreements. Looking at contract law in perspective allows us to interrogate these claims in ways that are not possible in books which focus on doctrine alone.

GENERAL PRINCIPLES: THE NATURE AND CONTENT OF CONTRACT LAW

In a society where the exchange of goods and services is central to its economic order, as in a developing capitalist society based on free enterprise, a means of supporting the process of exchange of goods and services needs to be found. It is in this context that the foundations of modern contract law were established, and contract became the juristic mechanism for the distribution and utilisation of the goods and services. By the third quarter of the nineteenth century, British society had experienced accelerating industrialisation generated by scientific innovation, economic entrepreneurship, more widespread access to capital and increasingly geographically mobile labour. This gave rise to an unprecedented boom in trade, both at home and in expanding markets overseas. This boom was accompanied by an extensive development of those areas of the law which are designed to facilitate and regulate business relationships. In particular, there was a considerable expansion of contract, commercial and company law.

The general principles of contract law are still, for the most part, of a judge-made character, and many of them emanate from the time of the industrial revolution and the 'classical' period of contract law which accompanied it. The theoretical assumptions underpinning the classical model were heavily influenced by prevailing economic theories of the nineteenth century, which treated contracting parties as economic units assumed to have equal bargaining strength and endowed with complete freedom of decision. Indeed, the key theme underpinning contract law during this period was the idea of *freedom of contract*. It is highly significant that, in this model of contract, the judges saw their role as a minimalist one. The purpose of the law was not to control the terms on which parties might contract, nor would it readily give relief if agreed terms turned out to be harsh or unfair to one party.

Since that time, the principles associated with managed rather than free markets have also taken a hold in this area of law and we have seen a decline in influence of the idea of freedom of contract. In part, this has come about as a result of social change. In the twenty-first century it is no longer the individual entrepreneur but the government or large multi-national enterprises that are primarily concerned with the allocation of resources in the British economy. These facts of modern economic life have served to emphasise the myth of equality of bargaining power, presumed to exist between contracting parties in the classical era. But, then again, as we shall see, many modern commentators have argued that the notion of freedom of contract was never an adequate social tool through which to understand the market.

STRUCTURE OF THE BOOK

Part Two of this book carries on from the introductory section by establishing some key ideas about the notion of contract. Legal and business perspectives are introduced, as are some sociological and economic theories. These 'views' of contract are set within the framework of a shift from what is generally described as a *laissez-faire* to a mixed economy. This shift broadly coincides with the rise and fall of freedom of contract, and hence with a transformation of contract's function and substance. The aim of the section is to introduce students to this historical account of contract in order that they can understand the environments in which different visions of contract have emerged. Students are also introduced to contemporary critiques of contracts. The literature on relational contract theory, feminist perspectives and empirical understandings of the subject provides students with a range of tools with which to critique and interrogate traditional models and current cases. These various themes and perspectives are pursued throughout the remainder of the book.

Part Three focuses on how contracts are formed. It looks at the process by which a contract emerges from negotiations which may be lengthy and protracted. It is in this section above all that students will become aware of the formalistic and 'rule-bound' tendencies of the English common law. These tendencies are discussed with reference to alternative views of the formation process, which draw on ideas about the expectations of the parties, their respect of and need for formality, and their understanding of obligation.

The fourth section is rather loosely labelled 'Bargaining naughtiness and formation problems'. Where Part Three introduces the reader to ideas around what ought to happen before a binding contract can be recognised or enforced, Part Four focuses on the various ways in which contract may be set aside because of behaviour considered to be inappropriate. It moves on to look at what is contained within a contract, and particular emphasis is placed on the trend towards judicial and legislative interference with content. Here, the stress is on the ways in which 'welfarist' approaches to the law of contract have mitigated against the harshness of the market. The tensions that are played out in case law and commentaries about the appropriate rule of the judiciary and legislature in the regulation of 'private' contracts remain significant and many examples of these tensions emerge from this section. Moreover, they will undoubtedly remain a subject for discussion for many years to come. In the final substantive section, we look at what happens when things go wrong in the performance of the contract. The focus here is on what constitutes breach of contract, the remedies that are available for breach and the ways in which disputing parties are most likely to resolve their dispute.

The vast majority of cases to be found in this book are of modern origin and therefore illustrate contemporary business situations. Discussion of many of them is, however, on a modest scale as is inevitable in a work of this nature. Ultimately there is no substitute for the law reports. At the end of each chapter there is a bibliography drawn from a wide range of materials and a series of questions designed to test and expand on the subject matter of preceding pages. It is important that students are encouraged to pursue further reading from these references. The choice of questions aims to keep links between the various topics in the book firmly in the forefront of the student's mind so that a co-ordinated view of contract will eventually emerge.

CONCLUDING REMARKS

Lawyers specialising in this field of law will spend a considerable amount of time considering whether there is a binding agreement, the scope of the agreement, the significance of breach and the remedies available. There are, however, other important issues which emerge and are covered in this book. For example, should the parties to a long-term commercial relationship be bound by the terms of a contract made many years ago when market conditions were radically different? How relevant are the old rules on agreement and promises to modern standard-form contracts prepared by an economically stronger party and presented to a weaker on a 'take-it-or-leave-it' basis? Does it make a difference if the economically powerful party is a competitive private sector enterprise, such as a motor vehicle manufacturer, or the monopoly provider of a service? How relevant are the traditional rules of contract law to the contracts entered into by government departments such as the Ministry of Defence or the Department of Health? If the vast majority of contractual disputes are not decided by the courts who should decide or settle them, and how? These are important questions to be considered by today's students and tomorrow's practitioners. All these issues are related, and it is social, economic and political changes that have thrown them up. Mass production, globalisation, standardisation, imperfect competition, increased governmental regulation have all created strains upon modern/contract law and the need for a broader view of it, if it is to remain legitimate in the eyes of those who use it.

REFERENCES AND FURTHER READING

Atiyah, P (1989) *An Introduction to the Law of Contract*, 4th edn, 'Part 1: The development of the modern law of contract', Clarendon Press, Oxford. For a much fuller account of the history of modern contract law, see Atiyah's seminal book, *The Rise and Fall of the Freedom of Contract* (1985), Oxford University Press, Oxford, or Simpson, A (1987) *A History of the Common Law of Contract and the Rise of the Action of Assumpsit*, Clarendon Press, Oxford.

Collins, H (2002) *Regulating Contracts*, Oxford University Press, Oxford.

Wightman, J (1996) *Contract – A Critical Commentary*, Pluto Press, London.

CHAPTER 2

THE SAD TALE OF ANGIE AND GEORGIE

INTRODUCTION

In this chapter you are presented with an integrated case study, based on real-life situations, which you will be asked to refer back to throughout the book. Short problem questions of one or two paragraphs are regularly used in university law schools to encourage students to take the concepts and rules they have learnt about and apply them to new fact patterns. One of the main aims of such exercises is to encourage you to apply the abstract to the specific and to test the limits of a doctrine or judgment by reference to unfamiliar facts. This is because the disputes that contracting parties bring before the court will each have unique elements. What we ask students to do in applying doctrine to new cases is to establish whether the fact pattern before them is sufficient to bring it within a particular doctrine or judicial line of reasoning. Exam papers up and down the country are full of problem questions which attempt to stretch the application of the contractual canon to its limits.

In a book that aims to study contract law in perspective, it is difficult to justify presenting students with small discrete fact patterns which are concerned with just one doctrine. In real life, lawyers are presented with long stories by their clients and part of their task is to sift through these accounts of the harm that has been done to people and determine what is legally relevant or irrelevant. Moreover, a particular set of facts may raise questions about a number of different doctrines which could be argued in the alternative if the case were ever to reach a court. Finally, you will soon realise that most disputes about contract never get to court. This may be because of extra-legal considerations to do with the relationship between the contracting parties, because there is insufficient evidence to support a claimant's case, or because they do not have the financial resources necessary to pursue litigation. These factors will influence the lawyer and client considerably when they are deciding what to do. In addition to the usual array of facts which can be matched to a range of doctrines in the case that follows, there are evidential problems, financial constraints and emotional entanglements which should all have a part to play in the advice that is given to the parties. Read the case study through and respond to the questions at the end before turning to any of the other chapters in the book.

LOVE AT FIRST SIGHT

Angie and Georgie are lovers and have been together for 10 years. They met in the early 1990s when they were both working in the international marketing department of the head office of Emmotts, a national supermarket chain. Georgie is a rather serious type while Angie is very lively and gregarious. Despite these differences they were immediately attracted to each other and found that they had a lot of things in common. Most notably both of them had become disenchanted working for a large impersonal organisation whose only interest was making more profit every year.

Angie and Georgie dated for three months after which they decided that they wanted to be together for the rest of their lives. They were both opposed to marriage but at a candlelit dinner, witnessed by their friend Kirsteen (a buyer for Emmotts) and their parents, they vowed to love, honour and respect each other whatever happened, and to support each other financially and emotionally in sickness and in health. Georgie later embroidered the vows in a tapestry which they hung in the entrance hall of their studio flat for everyone to see. In 1992, Angie and Georgie adopted Zen and five years later, in 1997, they adopted Dylan.

A NEW BEGINNING

A year after meeting they decided to give up their jobs as marketing executives. They sold their flat in London, moved to St Ives and set up a smallholding health food store called Earth2Earth! which specialised in growing and selling a wide range of organic root crops at low cost. They bought a rare but reliable vintage Dormobile at an auction for use as a mobile shop in remote villages and making deliveries. Fortunately, the Dormobile was also big enough for them to live in while they looked for more permanent accommodation. Angie used some of her savings to purchase a computer and printed out some handbills and posters (see end of chapter) which she left around St Ives.

After looking around at a number of different premises, they rented a shop with some land in the main thoroughfare in St Ives from a retiring electrician and part-time musician called Mister C who was going to live next door, rent free, with his sister Missy J. The premises consisted of a shop downstairs, a storeroom in the field behind and a self-contained flat above the shop. They decided to employ a delivery assistant and were delighted when Chelsea, Mister C's granddaughter, applied for the job. Because of their political ideals, Angie and Georgie paid her a wage that was much higher than the average for the area.

A local cartel of organic farmers, known locally as Orange Peril, agreed to supply Angie and Georgie with their top of the range root crops at a very competitive price. They did so on the basis that Angie and Georgie did not sell their vegetables to anyone outside St Ives or in competition with the other stores in the area supplied by Orange Peril. Angie and Georgie were delighted to become involved with an established group and were particularly pleased when they were able to negotiate a further discount because they did not require Orange Peril plc to clean the vegetables before delivering them. This meant that they could fulfil their mission of selling the stock on at a low price and promote the crops as being 'straight from the earth' on their publicity materials.

Their new venture was not well received by local farmers producing non-organic crops. One local farmer called Max was particularly opposed to the scheme. Like others in the area, he ran his own farm shop and was worried that the low prices at which Angie and Georgie intended to sell their stock would mean that he would lose a lot of custom to Earth2Earth!

THE BUSINESS THRIVES

Despite the hostility from local farmers, their business thrived and they soon had a healthy turnover and modest profit. Much of this was due to Missy J who quickly became a great supporter of their enterprise. She spread the word in St Ives amongst her pensioner friends at the local reggae club that the store sold and delivered cheap good-quality food. Angie and Georgie were overjoyed when, as a result of the publicity, *Organic Weekly* ran a very complimentary feature on them. This led to them securing a contract with the Monkish Soup Company to supply them with washed and sliced organic carrots for their 'Winter Warmer Root Soup'. In order to fulfil the contract, they made an agreement with a local student called Marcus that he would deliver the carrots to the Monkish Soup Company three times a week on his way to attending classes at the Chelsea College of Art. In exchange he was paid £400 a week, plus any petrol expenses. On the strength of Monkish Soup Company's assurances that they were likely to place regular weekly orders Angie and Georgie hired an expensive carrot cleaning and slicing machine for £7,000 from the Wacky Machine Company, which speeded up the process of delivering the order. In addition, they converted the storeroom into an office and work area dedicated to this project, and took on more casual staff. Although no paperwork was produced, the agreement ran successfully for 7 years.

During that time they build up a particularly good relationship with Ned, the buyer for Monkish, and came to trust him completely. Ned came to visit them at the beginning of every season and talked through the orders for the months ahead. He talked about joint business plans with them and often made useful suggestions as to how they might increase their profit. Two years ago he told them that Monkish were expanding their business into pesto sauce, and Angie and Georgie started to grow basil under Ned's guidance with a view to supplying Monkish with ingredients for pesto sauce in the future.

On Missy J's recommendation, Dipti, an eccentric amateur cook who lives in the local manor house, started to place orders for carrots, potatoes and other provisions with Earth2Earth! Because of her mobility problems, she also placed a monthly order in advance by email and had her vegetables delivered by Chelsea. In time, Angie and Georgie became very fond of Dipti and often invited her around for a meal. When they discovered that Dipti was almost bankrupt and had recently had her telephone disconnected because she couldn't pay the bill, they suggested that she no longer had to pay for her weekly order. Dipti was overjoyed but said that she could not take charity. She accepted their offer but only if they would agree to her giving them a dish of her home-made Hepworth risotto every week. In reality the risotto was not to Angie and Georgie's taste, and they often threw it away.

THINGS START TO GO WRONG

One sunny September morning at 7am, some weeks later, Dipti phoned Chelsea to say that she was having a special dinner party that evening for some representatives of a national grocery store chain who were interested in buying her secret recipe for Hepworth risotto. Dipti asked whether she could add artichokes to the order she was due to have delivered that morning. Chelsea said that posed no problem and took down the list of additional items on one of Earth2Earth!'s order forms. Unfortunately, Chelsea became distracted while on the phone. She had just had an argument with Marcus, whom she had started dating, and Dylan was pulling at her trousers. She handed him a raw carrot to chew on which he proceeded to jam in the water tank of the carrot cleaning machine. Instead of writing down 'artichokes' Chelsea wrote down 'lots of cokes'.

The next morning Dipti phoned at 7am in a rage. She claimed that the batch of carrots delivered to her the previous day were infected with 'Spotty Greenfingeritis', an unsightly fungal disease, and that her guests had been vomiting all night. Distraught by the whole experience and shaken by the fear that the supermarket representatives would now shun her, Dipti was unable to progress with her new plan to market and sell her risotto to supermarket chains for three weeks.

ATTEMPTS TO GET THEMSELVES OUT OF THE MESS

Angie and Georgie phoned up Orange Peril plc to complain about the infected carrots. The company confirmed that there had been an outbreak of this rare disease across the nation and that the British government had just put a complete ban on the production of carrots for the foreseeable future. In an attempt to avert any further problems, Angie contacted the Monkish Soup Company to warn them that they would be unable to deliver any carrots for a while. They were put through to the company's legal director, Ms Meanlean, who was sympathetic to their problems but pointed out that Monkish was also in financial difficulties. The company's market share was falling and the director of the company was likely to want to sue if Angie and Georgie delivered no carrots. She told them that their Winter Warmer Root Soup was outselling all their other soups and that it was vital to the success of the venture that they get a regular supply of clean organic carrots.

Distraught that the situation could ruin their business, Angie and Georgie contacted Kirsteen and begged her to help them find another supplier from the continent where the carrots did not seem to be affected. Kirsteen suggested that they meet her at the Place de Gourmet, a well-known vegetable market on the North Bank of the Seine. Angie could not secure a booking for the Channel Tunnel but Chelsea managed to find a website that sold cheap ferry tickets and purchased one for Angie and the Dormobile with her credit card. Angie set off, leaving Georgie to look after Dylan, Zen and the shop. But when she got to the ferry port she discovered that the next three ferries had been cancelled because of bad weather, a strike and a shortage of fuel. Angie wanted to complain but had no documentation about the ferry company, her ticket details or the customer service department.

Eventually, she got to Paris and met Kirsteen. They went around the Place de Gourmet where there were hundreds of exhibits and stalls but very little produce left. Kirsteen seemed to be familiar with the people there and introduced Angie to Claude, an established farmer from Normandy. Angie made it clear that she was only interested in good-quality organic carrots and that anything purchased would have to comply with their charter of standards. Claude was adamant that his carrots were far superior to anything Angie could buy in England and claimed that no other carrots in France sold so quickly.

Claude showed Angie some baskets of carrots which were more expensive than those supplied by Orange Peril and would reduce their profits considerably. However, they looked very big and healthy and were a lovely bright orange. Angie talked the deal over with Kirsteen, and they agreed that Angie really had no choice but to buy them as the market was closing and they had to get back to England that night. Angie bought enough of the carrots to satisfy their orders, signed the documents that Claude pushed her way and dragged Kirsteen away from the paperwork so that they would not miss the last ferry home. Claude told he would deliver the carrots to her within 12 hours.

On the way back Angie made clear to Kirsteen how grateful she was to her for helping out at such short notice. She asked her how much commission she owed Kirsteen for helping to arrange the sale. At first Kirsteen said she would take nothing, as Angie and Georgie had been really helpful to her when she was a trainee at Emmotts. But Angie persisted and in the end they decided that Earth2Earth! would pay Kirsteen £500 in £50 instalments. Angie dropped Kirsteen off at her home and drove back to St Ives with a lighter heart. However, her good mood did not last long. When she returned home she found that Claude had called to say that the carrots had been loaded in their truck but would not arrive in St Ives for another two days as the truck was travelling via Turin to deliver an order to a large supermarket chain. When the carrots did arrive most of them had rotted and the remainder could not be sent to Monkish as the carrot washer and slicer would not work. In a fury, Georgie was quick to point out that they were also tasteless and too large to be organic carrots. The final straw came when they found that Claude had also delivered a consignment of turnips that they had not ordered and had charged them for delivering all the produce.

Angie and Georgie sat up long into the night deciding what to do. In the end Georgie declared, 'There is only one thing we can do. Sell the carrots as though these are organic. If we don't sell these then we will go bust – the Monkish Soup Company deal is just too big to lose'. Despite her objections that selling the carrots on as organic might be dishonest, Angie eventually agreed to Georgie's plan as the only one which allowed them to continue the business. With sad hearts, they loaded up the delivery boxes for the next day and went to bed.

THINGS GET REALLY SERIOUS

While Angie had been away, Chelsea had been trying to placate Dipti, but to no avail. She had sent her a box of chocolates but, not only did Dipti send them back, she also drove down to the offices of the *St Ives Times* in her Jaguar to complain about Earth2Earth! Unfortunately for Angie and Georgie, the paper was owned by Max and he encouraged the editor to write a damning feature article about the business. As a result of the article, fewer and fewer people shopped at Earth2Earth! and the business was soon facing financial ruin.

Angie and Georgie fell behind with the rent. They were also being pressed for payment by Orange Peril plc who had recently started legal proceedings against them for their failure to pay for the damaged vegetables. Orange Peril plc claimed that there was no way they could have discovered about the Greenfingeritis and that it was up to Angie and Georgie to check deliveries. Angie and Georgie confided in Mister C and he agreed that, while he was able to live rent free at Missy J's, he was happy to reduce their rent by 25 per cent. However, they still did not have enough money to pay off their bills or to buy in new stock.

When Chelsea heard of the problems they were facing from her grandfather, she was concerned that she would lose her job. She offered to have her wage reduced on the basis that it had always been much higher than was sensible for a new business and she was keen to keep her job as Marcus, with whom she was once more on speaking terms, lived next door. Chelsea also knew that many of the local farmers would refuse to employ her now that she had worked at Earth2Earth! and she was concerned that she would not find alternative employment. Angie and Georgie accepted the offer rather than sack Chelsea, as she was a good worker. They were also aware that she had already brought in a number of new customers from surrounding towns because of her lively personality and knowledge of local surfing conditions. When Chelsea told Marcus what she had done, he was furious as they had been using Chelsea's salary to subsidise his expensive trips to London. Marcus asserted that he could only continue to deliver produce for Angie and Georgie if they paid him more for his trouble.

GEORGIE AND ANGIE SEEK HELP

However, financial ruin still loomed and, one day, while Angie was out, Georgie decided to approach St Ives Bank for a loan so that they could buy some new kinds of stock and relaunch the business. The bank was managed by Max's son Nigel who said the bank would only lend Georgie the money if the loan was secured by a charge on the vintage Dormobile and they started making more effort to sell their produce at farmers' markets around the county and in the North of Brittany. Later that same day, when Angie got home, Georgie explained what had happened at the bank. Angie said she was reluctant to sink more money into the business but, secretly, she was increasingly losing confidence in Georgie's ability to make sound business decisions. She tried to persuade Georgie to at least approach some other larger banks. But Georgie would not hear of it and became furious when Angie would not immediately agree to the loan. Georgie claimed that the bank would never repossess the Dormobile and that, if Angie did not give in, she could pack her bags and go.

They went to the bank and Nigel asked to see Angie alone. The bank had prepared the necessary documents which included a requirement that the charge over the Dormobile be signed by Angie and Georgie. Nigel advised Angie to take her time before she signed but also pointed out that, if she did not sign by the close of business that day, there was likely to be some delay in processing the claim as the bank was closed for a week. The document Angie was given to sign suggested that independent advice should be sought, but Angie was too upset to read it properly or think straight and signed it through a blur of tears.

Angie and Georgie decided that their next goal should be to get Monkish Soup Company to drop their claim against Earth2Earth! With this in mind, Georgie made an appointment with Ms Meanlean for the next day, hoping to persuade her to negotiate a settlement or agree to refer the dispute to mediation. Georgie set off in the Dormobile and arrived at the offices of Monkish Soup Company with time to spare. However, there were no free parking spaces to be found in the surrounding streets and Georgie was eventually forced to go into a nearby multi-storey car park which was known to be expensive. Georgie went through the automatic barrier and parked the Dormobile in the underground section of the car park. It was rather dark but Georgie managed to locate and purchase a ticket from the 'pay and display' machine on that level. Narrowly avoiding a signpost positioned close to a barrier, Georgie put £5 in the machine as requested and received a long yellow ticket covered with lots of unsightly coloured writing. Georgie put the ticket behind the sun visor, anticipating that it would be necessary to show it to an attendant on the way out.

William, a security guard, had recently started work at the car park and was in charge of collecting the supermarket trolleys which customers tended to leave scattered about in there. He was rather ambitious about the number of trolleys he could control at any one time and as he attempted to return the trolleys to the area reserved for them, he lost control of them. They sped off down the dark car park which was built on a slight slope. As Georgie was locking the Dormobile the trolleys slid towards her at a high speed. Georgie did not have enough time to get out of the way and suffered substantial injuries before the trolleys moved on to damage the side panel of the Dormobile. Georgie was rushed off to hospital but telephoned Ms Meanlean from the Accident and Emergency Department to explain what had happened. The lawyer dismissed Georgie out of hand, offered to see Earth2Earth! in court and informed her that henceforth, they would be buying their stock from another shop in the next town!

Monkish feel they have been placing too much trust in one supplier of carrots. They give George one month's notice that they are terminating their contract and make clear that they have decided to put future orders out to tender. Georgie asks if they will be invited to make a bid and is told they can make a bid if they want to. However, at a recent board meeting, it was decided that, as Angie and Georgie had let them down, Monkish would not consider dealing with them again.

THE END OF A BEAUTIFUL RELATIONSHIP AND START OF ANOTHER ...

The same week, Mister C reluctantly told Angie that he did not think the rental agreement was working out. He complained he was kept awake by Dylan and Zen who played on their Gameboys all night, and felt that at his age he deserved some peace and quiet. He suggested that they move out to live in the Dormobile in the garden at the back of the shop until they could find somewhere more suitable to live.

Unable to bear the tension and misery any longer, Angie now declares that she has had enough and is leaving with the children. She tells Georgie that she and Ned have fallen in love and they would like to use the knowledge of basil they have gained and set up a smallholding. She wants to sell up her share in Earth2Earth! and sever her links with Georgie who no longer makes her happy. The financial situation has become so grave that Angie and Georgie come to you for advice. They bring along the documents (on the following page) which may be relevant.

Handbill and Poster

Earth2Earth! – Charter of Standards

You Should Know What You Are Buying

We either grow or purchase our produce from *Orange Peril plc*, an internationally renowned organic food grower. *Orange Peril plc* has won the *Soil Association Company of the Year Award* for the last five years and has been described by *Organics Weekly* as being 'almost single-handedly responsible for a revolution in the market place'.

All our vegetables are grown on extensive farmland in rural Cornwall. The vegetables are grown free from chemicals and pesticides in the way that Nature intended and are free from blemishes. *Orange Peril plc* has been an active opponent to GM crops and has successfully fought off attempts by the government to pilot GM crops within a 10 mile radius of their farm.

Our produce comes straight from the earth! Please don't worry if there is soil on our vegetables. You may not think that it makes them as attractive as pre-packed products from supermarkets but we believe that it keeps them fresh. It also means that we can sell them to you at a much cheaper price because we do not have to pay someone to clean them. The dirt will be brushed off our produce when they are weighed so that you are paying for tasty organic produce and not mud!

Our Pledge To You

An important part of the *Earth2Earth!* philosophy is that our customers deserve reasonably priced good quality vegetables. It is also important to us that the service is brought to you with a smile. We promise to be polite and good natured towards our customers at all times. In the unlikely event that we ever fail in this then do feel free to come and tell us. We will give a free basket of fruit to any customer who feels that we have been less than polite to them.

At *Earth2Earth!* we only sell you what you want. We do not engage in aggressive marketing of our products. Neither do we add produce to your orders which you have not requested.

All contracts made by *Earth2Earth!* are subject to the following terms and conditions:

All deliveries are free within a 10 mile radius of the store. Property in goods supplied shall pass on their acceptance by the customer. Goods found to be inferior in quality, defective or not in accordance with the order cannot be changed after the order has been accepted. The right is reserved to cancel the whole or part of an order within a week before the delivery date. An invoice will be rendered for each order. The invoice will be sent immediately after the delivery is made. *Earth2Earth!* cannot accept any responsibility for damages or losses of any description whatsoever. No goods will be supplied, or services rendered, without an official order. No alteration is to be made to an order without confirmation in writing. An order may be cancelled or suspended in the event of strikes, lock-outs, accidents, actions of the Queen's enemies or acts of God. *Earth2Earth!* shall be entitled, without prejudice to its other rights and remedies, either to terminate, wholly or in part, any or every contract between itself and the customer or to suspend further deliveries under any such contract if a debt remains unpaid or the customer becomes insolvent. Any contract arising from this quotation shall in all respects be construed and operate as an English contract and in conformity with English law and the English court shall have jurisdiction.

Gaumont Associates purchase and delivery contract

THE ONE PART: The entity known as Gaumont Associates hereinafter called the *Vendor* and of the other part the entity known as Angie in the City of St Ives Republic of Cornwall hereinafter called the *Purchaser*. Both parties recognising their respective capacities enter into the present contract on the terms and conditions following:

Clause one:

The Vendor hereby sells and the Purchaser hereby purchases/reimburses the Vendor for the following:

(1) ...3... tons of fresh:

Carrots	[X]
Turnips	[X]
Broccoli	[ ]
Onions	[ ]
Kale	[ ]
Tomatoes	[ ]

in compliance with the French Farmers' Association code of practice, copies of which are available on request.

(2) Six wooden containers used to transport the produce.
(3) All cargo costs necessary to get the produce to its destination to include shipping, petrol for land transportation and insurance.

Clause two:

The Purchaser agrees that any contract formed by the Vendor's acceptance of this offer shall be governed by their terms and conditions of sale and that this order form shall represent the agreed contract between the Purchaser and the Vendor. The Purchaser certifies that the details and description of the produce given in clause one above are true and accurate in all respects.

Clause three:

The Purchaser undertakes to pay to the Vendor in Euros in Paris the total price of the products mentioned in clause one of this Contract. In times of commercial pressure the Vendor shall reserve the right to vary the terms of payment to reflect their additional costs.

Clause four:

The Vendor undertakes to notify the Purchaser within forty-eight hours (48 hours) following the departure of each vessel of the following: number of boxes shipped and volume of each of the same.

Clause five:

The Vendor warrants the Purchaser against any defect which might arise in the vegetables the subject matter of this contract on the following conditions:

(a) For the term of three hours from delivery.

(b) Should any defect develop during the guarantee period and the defect be due to faulty handling the produce will be replaced free of charge. This guarantee is in lieu of, and expressly excludes, all liability to compensate for loss or damage, howsoever caused.

(c) The alleged defect must be verified by the Vendor within a day subsequent to the date of receipt of the written notice which shall be given by the Purchaser.

(d) The replacement of the defective produce may be effected by the Vendor from their farms failing which they shall obtain the produce from other suppliers within a period of 14 days reckoned as from the date of receipt of claim by the Vendor.

(e) The replacement of faulty produce may be effected direct by the Vendor or it may at its option compensate the Purchaser for the expenses which the latter may incur.

(f) This warranty is restricted to the replacement of produce which become defective during the period established in paragraph (a) above due to defects of manufacture or the use of unsuitable materials but not due to improper storage.

This warranty will not come into operation unless the Schedule to this document is completed and signed by the Purchaser. No work will be carried out under the terms of this warranty until this document completed and signed as aforesaid is presented in advance to our service reception.

The rights under this document or the warranty above referred to are not transferable without our written consent.

This warranty shall be of no effect if the produce has at any time been used after the date of sale for the purposes other than those specified in pre-contractual negotiations.

Clause six:

If subsequent to the signature of this contract contingencies should arise such as fire, floods, droughts, disasters, rain, wind, hailstorms, earthquakes, war, military operations of any class, blockade or of any other class outside the control of the parties which totally or partially prevent the performance thereof by the parties, the period of time stipulated for performance of the contractual obligations shall be deemed to be extended for a period of time equivalent to the duration of such contingencies. In the event of these contingencies lasting more than six months, each of the contracting parties is entitled to terminate the contract notifying the other party in writing. In this event neither of the parties shall be entitled to be compensated for any loss which might exist.

The party prevented from performing its contractual obligations on account of any of the contingencies above mentioned shall immediately notify the other party in writing of the existence and duration of same.

The existence of such contingency and its duration in the country of the Vendor or the Purchaser must be proved by a certificate issued by the Chamber of Commerce of the country of the Vendor or the Purchaser respectively.

Clause seven:

The contracting parties agree to perform this contract in good faith. Any difference which might arise as a result of this contract shall be settled by means of amicable negotiations. If such negotiations should fail and it should not be possible to reach understanding the parties shall submit the matter in dispute to an arbitration tribunal whose decision shall be final. The arbitration tribunal shall be set up in the City of Paris and shall consist of a representative of each of the parties and a presiding arbitrator appointed by both parties by mutual agreement. The award of the arbitration tribunal shall settle the amount of the arbitration expenses and the party which is to pay the same. An award adopted by a majority of votes shall be final and binding on both parties.

Clause eight:

The Vendor contracts as a principal and not as an agent of the growers of the produce and has no authority to make any representation or otherwise act on behalf of the growers of the produce.

The produce is not sold subject to any Warranty or other benefit whatsoever unless expressly agreed in writing between the parties.

PURCHASER'S DECLARATION

I/We agree that I/We have not been induced to make this offer by any representation as to the quality, fitness for any purpose, performance, or otherwise of the Goods and subject to the Vendor's acceptance of this offer. I/We agree to be bound by the terms and conditions hereof in all respects including the conditions of sale printed overleaf. In making this offer

I/We have not relied on the skill, judgment or opinion of the Vendor, his
servants or his agents in relation to the Goods.

Angie Kellaher.............   Date.........................

> *Subject to the proviso that 10% of the*
> *payment price will be knocked off for*
> *each hour that delivery is delayed!*

Kirsty Hellman
on behalf of Earth2Earth!

VENDOR'S ACCEPTANCE

I/We accept and confirm this offer subject to its terms and conditions.

Claude de Valera ....Date..................

(Signature of Director or other authorised person for and on behalf of the
Vendor.)

Wacky machine company – Rental agreement for super slicer carrot washer and cutter

IMPORTANT – YOU SHOULD READ THIS CAREFULLY.

Orders placed with the Company will only be accepted on the following terms and conditions. No variation or modification of or substitution for any such terms and conditions shall be binding unless expressly agreed by the Company in writing. No buyer's conditions of order or purchase and no other conditions, particulars, standards, specifications, statements or other matters whether printed, written or verbal shall form part of or be deemed to be incorporated into any contract with the Company unless specifically referred to in the Company's acceptance:

1   TERM OF HIRE

We shall supply the super slicer carrot washer and cutter and you shall rent the Equipment for the minimum period of 10 years and after that until terminated.

2   OUR RESPONSIBILITIES/RIGHTS/LIABILITIES

(a) We shall not be responsible for any direct or indirect or consequential injury, damage or loss to any person or any property arising out of the installation, possession, use or condition of the Equipment. We shall only be responsible for personal injury caused directly by Our negligence.

(b) We shall in no circumstances be responsible for loss of business or profit arising from a breakdown of the Equipment.

(c) (c) We shall not be responsible for any breach of copyright resulting from the use of Equipment rented under this Agreement.

3   YOUR RESPONSIBILITIES/RIGHTS/LIABILITIES

(a) You shall indemnify Us against all liability arising out of the possession or use of the Equipment except liability for personal injury caused directly by Our negligence.

(b) From the date of delivery of the Equipment to You the Equipment shall be at Your risk and You shall insure the same with the Insurers in respect of Equipment Failure on the terms of Group Policy a summary of which is set out in the Insurance Certificate available for perusal at our premises.

4   PROPERTY INSURED

The Insurers insure the Equipment which you have hired under the Agreement, while you maintain it at the Premises.

5   BENEFIT

The Insurers will indemnify you against the cost of Failure. The cover is limited to the lowest of the current market value of the Equipment, or its replacement cost, or £2,000. The Insurance can either meet the cost of repairs which have already been carried out or they can send in repairers at their own expense.

Repairs can only be carried out by Authorised Repairers. Such payments will be made to the Rental Company for the benefit of the insured customer.

6   EXCLUSIONS

Failure does not include failures caused by such things as defects in the electrical supply, misuse, neglect, wilful act, theft or accidental damage, or any other extraneous cause, or interference by any third party or use of the Equipment anywhere except at the Premises or for any unauthorised use. The benefit is limited to that described above, and will not cover any other loss (such as consequential loss, damage to other property, or death or bodily injury).

7   HOW TO CLAIM

Claims should be made by telephone to the Service centre shown in your Welcome Pack, or to your local Rental Company shop within a reasonable time of the Failure. Failure to make a claim within a reasonable time will invalidate any claim.

? QUESTIONS

(1) Before you learn any more about the law of contract and wealth of cases which you are likely to have to read, we would like you to make a list of what you consider would be a fair solution to the problems faced by the various parties in 'The Sad Tale of Angie and Georgie'. Once you have completed the list, keep it somewhere safe and use it as a resource as you progress through the book in order to gauge the ways in which the law of contract complies with your ideas about common-sense fairness.

(2) Is there any additional information you would like to have about the story before you progress? If so, make a list of the additional information you would like to gather before advising the parties. Give reasons why you think it is important to have this information.

(3) If you could go back in time, how would you alter what the parties do in order to minimise the number of disputes which arise?

(4) How many agreements can you identify which you think should be enforceable at law?

PART TWO:

BIG IDEAS IN THE LAW OF CONTRACT

CHAPTER 3

THE RISE AND FALL OF FREEDOM OF CONTRACT

INTRODUCTION

The law of contract cannot be fully understood without reference to the history of ideas which underpin it. It will become apparent in the course of this book that this branch of the law has undergone several important transformations in the last few decades. Reading cases and statutes will lead to familiarisation with the detail of such changes, but it is unlikely to allow you to gain a full appreciation of how it was possible for them to come about and the wider political context which made transformation acceptable to influential stakeholders. In a book of this kind, it is almost impossible to do justice to the rich spectrum of ideas which have been reflected in debates between academics, politicians and the wider community of users of contract law. Instead, the aim of this chapter and the next is to sketch out some key ideas which have influenced the ways in which we look at contracts. Of particular relevance here is the question of the extent to which the state, in the guise of the legislature and the judiciary, should interfere with contracts made by consenting parties in order to redress imbalances of power between them.

Even the briefest perusal of the newspapers will demonstrate that the issues which lie at the heart of this debate reflect a much wider controversy about the role of the modern state. The issue remains a contentious one which has troubled successive governments and debate has become particularly intense since the setting up of the welfare state. The political imperatives of the Conservative party under Margaret Thatcher and their emphasis on the 'rolling back of the state', debate about the 'third way', the growth of the regulatory state and visions of socialism in post-communist states, all hinge on the same critical issue of what constitute the appropriate boundaries between public and private or individual autonomy and central regulation. When you come to argue your first case in front of the country's premier Court of Appeal, a sound knowledge of the intricacies of former precedents and 'black letter' law will serve you well. But it is unlikely that your arguments will stimulate the judges you stand before unless you can provide justification for why the law should make a departure from what has gone before. The aim of the remainder of this chapter is to start you on a journey in which you reflect on these more abstract ideas about contractual relationships.

LEGAL AND OTHER VIEWS OF CONTRACT

The early legal history of contract is extensive, complex and not entirely free from controversy. Medieval law was primarily concerned with crime and land. From an early stage it recognised formal agreements which were written and 'understood' but slowly began to recognise claims arising out of informal, oral transactions as well. Of particular significance is the common law's recognition by the sixteenth century of claims involving four key elements. These were: reliance by the claimant on an undertaking given by the defendant; faulty performance, or non-performance of the undertaking by the defendant; loss to the claimant; and compensation in the form of damages. Later, the language of the courts began to link the idea of undertaking with that of promise. At that time the moral force of, and duty to keep, promises was very strong.

Nevertheless, the law stopped short of declaring that all promises were binding. Starting from an inquiry into the reasons why a promise was given, the doctrine of consideration came to set limits to promissory liability. It eventually did so by requiring that some form of *exchange* took place. This allowed contracts to be distinguished from gifts or gratuitous promises made out of kindness rather than as part of a deal. The types of bargain recognised by the doctrine of consideration included the exchange of money for a service or the exchange of one possession for another. But it was also accepted that promises could be exchanged to form binding contracts as long as there was a connection between them. So if Ethelred offered to pay Edwina three cows for a stable of manure and she accepted, then it can be seen that their promises to give up the cows and transfer manure are related to each other and form a bargain. Edwina's promise would only have been made if Ethelred had made his. Thus, even before the onset of the industrial and commercial revolutions, contract law had developed considerably. It contained basic, interconnecting concepts such as undertaking, promise, expectations, bargain in the sense of commercial exchange, reliance, loss and compensation.

By the nineteenth century, the concept of contract came to be discussed more broadly by philosophers, political scientists, economists and sociologists, and became an important topic of debate. Contract came to be seen as the key to wealth and happiness in the emerging market society. 'Freedom of contract' became a prime ethical, political, economic and legal goal. Brownsword (2006) describes the model as involving freedom for everyone to make an agreement on whatever terms they chose to; and sanctity of contract or the expectation that the courts will enforce the terms that the parties have freely made. Justice was said to require that each individual be at liberty to make free use of their natural powers in bargains, exchanges and promises as long as they did not interfere with the rights of others. Not only were such ideas considered a laudable goal in their own right but were also seen as the key to the economic success of society. One of the most important aspects of this debate was that the individual was considered to be best placed to know what their needs were and should be allowed to make whatever contracts on whatever terms they thought appropriate.

Giving people the utmost liberty to contract was seen as both morally appropriate but as also having a clear economic rationale. Adam Smith's work proved to be particularly influential in the context of discussions about the latter. In the *Wealth of Nations*, published in 1776, Smith analysed exchange in terms of people's 'natural propensity' to 'truck, barter and exchange'. In his view it was this inclination which naturally gave rise to contract, trade and the division of labour. His wide-ranging arguments sought to show how the individual's self-interested pursuit of optimum gain and happiness was both regulated by, and harnessed to, the general good, by the economist's law of demand and supply. His thesis was that by trading with others individuals not only got what they wanted but gave others what they desired. The magical ingredient converting individual acquisitiveness into universal good was labelled the 'invisible hand' by Smith. In his view, the individual neither intends to promote the public interest, nor knows how much they are promoting it. Instead, they intend only their own gain.

As a result of these theories, Smith advocated minimum regulation of the economy, and therefore of contracts, by the state. However, he did see it as a prime function of the law to uphold and enforce contracts made by freely consenting adults. He stressed that promises were not binding as a consequence of some inherent quality but rather because of the expectations they created in the market and which should not be disappointed. So, for instance, a builder might make a contract with a railway owner to build a row of houses for his employees close to the train station. Unable to do all the work himself, the builder enters into a contract of employment with a bricklayer and a carpenter. They in turn make contracts to buy bricks and timber. Unable to supply the carpenter instantly with the particular type of wood they need, the timber orders some from a forrester in Scotland. It very soon becomes clear that each contract is part of a network of commercial relationships which rely on each other. When the courts intervene to protect contracts, they lend a certain amount of certainty to an otherwise unpredictable market. In *The Concept of Law* (1961), Hart argued that

> where altruism is not unlimited, a standing procedure providing for such self-binding operations is required in order to create a minimum form of confidence in the future behaviour of others, and to ensure the predictability necessary for cooperation.

A number of commentators have shown an interest in why the individual came to play such an important role in the philosophical works of this era. Maine (Cocks, 2004) attempted to explain the reasons for this shift in his work on the movement of progressive societies from status to contract. In this he distinguished two theoretical 'ideal' types of society. The first was essentially a pre-industrial society in which power and relationships were based on the status you 'enjoyed'. These included kinship, marriage, neighbourhood and other close, continuing relationships. In such societies individuals were limited in what they could chose to do by the role they played. So, for instance, a tenant farmer might have unavoidable obligations to the local Lord imposed on him. The second type of society identified by Maine was one in which the individual becomes the central figure and their associations are predominantly motivated by reason and economic gain rather than association. Drawing on these ideas, Tönnies (2003) talked of a similar drift from social union to an essential 'separation' of individuals in an industrial society. For him, the latter was merely an artificial construction of an aggregate of human beings in which rationality and calculation were the lynchpins.

The proliferation of the rational, impersonal relationship in the economic models of the eighteenth and nineteenth century was also examined by Weber (1992) who also drew a distinction between what he called 'status' and 'purposive' contracts. The first 'more primitive' type involved the creation of continuing 'total' social and legal relationships, such as those between husband and wife, or landowner and serf. By way of contrast, the archetypal purposive contract was 'the money contract'. In his terms this was specific, quantitatively delimited, qualityless, abstract, economically conditioned and usually achieved some specific, generally economic, performance or result. In his view, what distinguishes such contractual relationships from status relationships is the fact that the reciprocal rights and obligations are limited to those specified in the contract. The purposive market exchange contract created only a tenuous and temporary association while the exchange takes place. Because these impersonal associations were incapable of inspiring the high trust of the kind seen in status contracts, Weber (1992) argued that it was necessary to establish a legal machinery, which, while not raising levels of trust, did at least provide a greater required measure of economic certainty.

THE RELATIONSHIP BETWEEN THE COURTS AND THE MARKET

The perceived role of the courts in this scheme of things can be summed up by reference to the words of Sir George Jessel:

> ... if there is one thing which more than another public policy requires it is that [people] of full age and competent understanding shall have the utmost liberty of contracting, and that their contracts when entered into freely and voluntarily shall be held sacred and shall be enforced by Courts of Justice. Therefore you have this paramount public policy to consider – that you are not lightly to interfere with this freedom of contract.

It is significant that, in the early part of the nineteenth century, the judiciary shifted its thinking towards recognition of both executed *and* executory contracts. In contrast to the executed contract in which exchange is immediate, executory contracts involve the exchange of promises about future conduct. The importance of the courts' recognition of executory contracts was that it allowed the business community to plan ahead. So, for example, if Sunil knows that he can rely on the courts to enforce Linda's promise to pay him £20,000 for 500 mobile phones from last year's stock, he can enter into negotiations with manufacturers of this year's latest mobile phones to supply him with 200 phones for his showroom, confident that he will have funds to pay for the consignment. Moreover, now that the manufacturer has a firm order, it can enter into discussions with different suppliers about the purchase of parts. And so the contract chain goes on without any material object having yet changed hands. In this example, the parties are able to enjoy the confidence and predictability that Hart (1961) talks about. With clear recognition that promises bind future performance, contract showed obvious potential to aid complex planning and risk allocation.

Two further developments in contract law, following fuller recognition of the executory contract, must be mentioned. It has long been accepted by the judiciary that an action for breach of an executory contract can be brought if one of the promisors fails to do what they promised to do. In other words, a party liable on an executory contract is liable not for what they have done but for what they have *not* yet done. As Professor Atiyah's (1979) has explained each contractor must be liable because of his intention, his will, his promise. At the same time, in the early nineteenth century, wide acceptance of the idea of liability based on promises allowed a general theory of contract law to emerge which distinguished it from other areas of law. Academics and judges began to use the idea of promise and freely given consent as the basis of contract law, and contract was no longer merely regarded as an adjunct of the law of property.

The vision of contractual relations which emerged at this time has come to be known as the 'classical' model and we shall use this shorthand throughout the book for the theory of obligations explained above. The approach was clearly designed to serve a free market or *laissez-faire* economy and to act as a framework within which the free play of competitive forces could operate. As we proceed to examine substantive elements of contract law in this book, we will time and again be reminded of the legacy of nineteenth-century thinking and its continuing impact on the law today. For this reason the key features of the 'classical' model as it emerged from around 1800 onwards are summarised in Box 3.1.

THE CHANGING NATURE OF CONTRACT

Approaches to contracts have changed significantly since the heyday of the classical period. But change has taken the form of adjustments to the 'classical' model rather than a grand scale reformulation of the law. The main thrust of modern critiques of contract law is that a new model which moves more firmly away from the classical paradigm is now required. These are themes to which we shall return in the next chapter. In the remainder of this one, we describe how the classical model has adjusted to the changed circumstances of the modern world.

As we have seen, enthusiasm for freedom of contract went hand-in-hand with support for the operation of a free market. But assumptions underpinning the free market approach could be seen to be erroneous since sellers and buyers are rarely on an equal footing. This means that contracts simply reflect

> **Box 3.1:   Presumptions of the classical model**
>
> ○ Contracting parties were possessed of equal bargaining power.
> ○ Contracting parties were self-motivated and self-assertive.
> ○ A party was bound not so much because they had made a promise as because they had made a *bargain.*
> ○ Agreement was based on consent and free choice and it is for the parties rather than the courts to determine what is fair.
> ○ Contractual obligations were self-imposed and imbalances of power largely irrelevant.
> ○ Lack of true consent would very rarely justify the setting aside of a contract on the grounds of such things as fraud, misrepresentation or fundamental mistake.
> ○ Each party must perform, or pay damages for their failure to perform.

power, or lack of it. Responding to the challenge raised by such arguments, Weber (1992) cut straight through the simplistic abstractions of earlier legal and economic thinking on the subject of freedom of contract. In his view, markets for goods and services might be more plentiful and factors of production more mobile than in pre-industrial societies, but this did not in itself result in more 'real' freedom. He argued that the exact extent to which the total amount of 'freedom' within a given legal community is actually increased depends entirely on the economic order and more specifically on property distribution.

Weber's argument was that, as they developed, free markets threw up new economic groups with powerful market interests based on capital and entrepreneurship. As was becoming clear to most people, it was the power relations in society, rather than economic and legal abstractions, which determined the operation of markets and the degree of real freedom in those markets. To his mind contractual 'freedom' provided the opportunity to use property ownership in the market without legal restraints as a means for the achievement of power over others. Weber illustrated his analysis by means of the contract of employment in which the employer was commonly the more powerful party and could offer jobs on a 'take it or leave it' basis. Given the more pressing economic needs of the worker, it was possible for employers to impose their terms on employees. Weber (1992) is not only pointing to the difference between formal and real freedom, but indicating how formal freedom protects and exacerbates inequality.

Durkheim (1964) was also keen to unravel the implications of the prevalent individualist, self-interested view of contract and the idea that contract could be regarded as a microcosm of society or a model for rational human relations. He argued that, within the contractual bond, the element of self-interest inevitably created an inherent contradiction. In his view, while contracting parties needed each other, each sought to obtain what they needed at the lowest price, and to acquire the most rights possible in return for the fewest obligations. In contrast to many of his contemporaries, he was concerned to undermine the prevailing vision of contract as an essentially individualistic and utilitarian act rather than a social one. He suggested that unregulated self-interest would not enable the mechanism of contract to serve as a model for what he termed 'organic solidarity' in society. He would not accept that a society splintered by increasing division of labour could achieve 'solidarity' through the pursuit of economic self-interest within a loose framework of *laissez-faire*. He argued instead that, in economic exchange, the different agents remain remote from each other. In his view, interest is the least constant of all things in the world. Whilst today it might be in my interest to unite with you, tomorrow the same reason may make me your enemy.

It was necessary, in Durkheim's opinion, to place contract in a context wider than that of party autonomy and individual will. For him, the true focal point was not individuals but society, which should provide a framework of norms and laws able to promote social justice. Most significantly, in his view, social regulation of contract required clear recognition of unequal bargaining power. He turned to the example of the employee, and asked what the poor worker could do against the rich and powerful employer, and suggested that there was a palpable and cruel irony in assimilating these two forces which are so manifestly unequal. For this reason, he asserted that society and the law must no longer passively uphold unjust contracts which are antisocial as the agreement of parties cannot render just a clause which in itself is unjust.

POWER IN THE MODERN MARKETPLACE

A series of transformations in British society has served to reinforce the arguments made by scholars such as Weber and Durkheim. These include an increasing concentration of power in the marketplace, the growth of the welfare state and changes in judicial attitudes. These have fuelled a transformation of the law of contract and, in the remainder of this section, we shall consider each in turn.

The concentration of power in the market

Commentators have observed that competitive capitalism inevitably tended towards monopoly. These developments clearly dilute key concepts such as choice and consent in contract and undermine the importance of pre-contractual negotiations. The legal result of this has been the mass-produced standard form of contract presented on 'take-it-or-leave-it' terms by those who are powerful in the market. The allocation of resources in the British economy no longer centres on the free market contracts of 'small enterprisers' but on the operations of massive multinational corporate groups and governmental agencies. A variety of factors have contributed to this movement in Britain. Some, such as cartelisation schemes designed to combat the worst effects of economic depression, the nationalisation of basic industries and the creation of a 'public sector' of the economy have come about as a direct result of government policies. Others, such as the growth of trade associations, encouragement of mergers in the private sector, the development of mass production and the tendency for large companies to take over small ones have been fuelled by the business community.

Contract specialists frequently draw attention to the need to regulate business activity where an organisation has become so powerful that it can dictate terms to anyone with whom it contracts. It is sometimes easy to forget that government contracts made on behalf of us all with public money also pose a significant threat to those concerned about inequality of bargaining power. The twentieth century witnessed a dramatic increase in the state's involvement in contract as a party with the setting up of the welfare state. The most obvious development was that the state has emerged as a *provider* of services such as health-care, social security, education, motorways and defence. This means that they are required to increase contractual activity because of the need to buy in construction and engineering works, technical services and hardware and vast quantities of other supplies and materials from independent contractors. It is in this area of public sector activity that contract has been the subject of major transformation. One of the legal corollaries of this development was a vast increase of government *procurement* contracts where government departments or other public authorities are on one side and a provate party is on the other. In this context, rules of contract that draw on the notion of discrete and private exchanges between parties of roughly the same bargaining strength begin to look obsolete.

In principle, the general law of contract applies to government procurement contracts. There is no special branch of 'government contract law' in this country, no legislative code as for consumer credit or fair trading, and administrative law is largely irrelevant in this context. In fact, the complaint has been made that *no* adequate law has been evolved on public contracts. Any question of the 'adequacy' of the private law rules of contract is also largely redundant. This is a field dominated by standard form contractual documents, prepared on behalf of the government authority involved and rarely negotiated. Disputes that arise are hidden from the public gaze as they are very rarely settled in the courts. It would seem then that the government contract is an instrument of a power relationship which only vaguely resembles the consensual agreement extolled by Maine and Adam Smith. In Turpin's (1979) view:

> the classical law of contract, which was formulated by 19th-century judges was 'a law of the market' .... This law in general did not, and does not, make provision for the peculiar circumstances of government procurement, the unique relationship between the government and its principal contractors, or the specific issues of the public interest that arise in government contracting. p. 251

Government procurement contracts are, in broad terms, an expression of economic and social policies, and the contractor is the instrument whereby services and functions are executed. However, government expenditure of taxpayers' money on goods and services raises questions of public accountability. Although the relationship between the government and its major suppliers used to be described as a partnership with 'fair and reasonable prices' at its base, the current economic climate and concern about the government being ill-served by the private sector have led to changes. In particular, the rules of the European Union have led to more competitive tendering and a more 'free-market' approach to procurement. Hard bargaining, best value for money and the attainment of contract targets are now the order of the day.

Where standard form contracts are the outcome of co-operative planning on the part of all interests, fairness and impartiality are more likely to dominate the transactions based on them. But, in practice, the presence of government power and resources will tend to tilt the balance of bargaining power. As Turpin (1989) suggests:

> the general law of contract has only a subsidiary or contingent application to government contracts .... Although an awareness of the rules of the law of contract influences in these ways the departments engaged in the contracting process, government procurement is a notable instance of those sectors in which, in the words of a distinguished scholar [Julius Stone], 'the coercions of law are ... only in the background'. (p. 165)

It is clear, even from this brief survey, that government-procurement contacts are a rather special area, having only vague links with the general principles of contract law. From procurement policy to 'administrative' remedies, the contracting process is directed from somewhere along the corridors of power. In the absence of litigation or forms of public hearing other than occasional references in *Hansard*, fears of misuse of the system remain.

The regulatory state

Concerns about the concentration of commercial power in the hands of relatively few corporations have led the government to set up a number of regulatory bodies to ensure that consumers are protected in the marketplace, at least as far as basic utilities are concerned. The Competition Commission, set up in 1999 to replace the Monopolies and Mergers Commission, was established to ensure that healthy competition took place between companies. Box 3.2 lists a number of other regulatory organisations with responsibility to oversee activity in the commercial sector. It is important to note that concern about competition must go beyond our own jurisdiction. Increasing worries about the effects of globalisation of markets have largely focused on the ability of a relatively small number of global business interests to dominate markets across the globe. Some of these are thought to have economic power that is at least equivalent to some modern states.

The proliferation of publicly funded regulatory bodies makes clear that the state has also become a regulator

---

Box 3.2: Examples of UK regulators

- Office of Fair Trading (OFT):
  http://www.oft.gov.uk/default.htm
- Office of Communications (OFCOM):
  http://www.ofcom.org.uk
- Financial Services Authority:
  http://www.fsa.gov.uk
- Securities and Futures' Authority:
  http://www.fsa.gov.uk/Pages/accessibility/
  index.shtml
- Takeover panel:
  http://www.thetakeoverpanel.org.uk
- Civil Aviation Authority (CAA):
  http://www.caa.co.uk
- Office of Rail Regulation:
  http://www.rail-reg.gov.uk
- Office of Gas and Electricity Markets
  (OFGEM): http://www.ofgem.gov.uk/
  ofgem/index.jsp
- Office for the Regulation of Electricity
  and Gas (OFREG): http://ofreg.nics.gov.uk
- Office of Water Services (OFWAT):
  http://www.ofwat.gov.uk/

of contracts. Many of the interests of consumers as regards prices, terms and quality of supply are provided for by statute-based regulatory agencies and not by the law of contract. For example, the Financial Services Authority was set up by the government to regulate most financial services markets, exchanges and firms. It sets the standards that they must meet and can take action against firms if they fail to meet the required standards. A key focus of its work is to help retail consumers achieve a fair deal. Whether or not these arrangements satisfy the need to balance value for money with the public interest continues to be hotly contested in the political area. Collins (2002) has argued that:

> The real substance of the issue of the scope of contracts in this context should turn on whether the statutes regulating public utilities provide adequate alternative means of redress for consumers, so that the exclusion of contractual rights is the price paid for the advantages of the statutory scheme for complaints.

Regulation has also increased through the proliferation of statutorily imposed standards across society. The use of contract as an instrument of governmental social and economic policy in this way has led to many contracts becoming institution- alised. This development can be seen in consumer-protection policy, in landlord- and-tenant legislation and in measures to be found in statutes concerning sexual discrimination, disability discrimination and racial discrimination. So for instance, it is

unlawful for an employer to discrim- inate against someone in the terms of your employment or the conditions you work under because of their age, gender, race, disability, religion and belief or sexual orientation. In this context, terms and conditions cover aspects of the employment contract such as hours of work, dress codes, the physical conditions of the workplace, holidays and flexi-time. Box 3.3 lists the key legislation in this field.

Box 3.3: Legislation governing the contract of employment

- Equal Pay Act 1970
- Sex Discrimination Act 1975
- Race Relations Act 1976
- Disability Discrimination Act 1995
- Human Rights Act 1998
- Race Relations (Amendment) Act 2000
- Civil Partnership Act 2004
- Disability Discrimination Act 2005
- Equality Act 2006

Changes in judicial approaches

It will become clear throughout this book that changes in political ideology, in social and economic conditions and, bit by bit, in the law itself, have moved the judicial focus away from freedom and sanctity of contract, voluntary agreement and the 'classical' model generally. This has involved more than a change in judicial approaches, it has involved a change in ideas about the appropriate role of the judiciary. There has been a discernible shift away from strict rules towards less certain notions of 'fairness', 'reasonableness' and 'judicial discretion'.

Of particular value in understanding these fundamental issues is the analysis of judicial decision-making put forward by Adams and Brownsword (2007) in their book *Understanding Contract Law*. They argue that the common law increasingly displays signs of the *tensions* created by two *competing* judicial philosophies. These are a formalist approach, which focuses on rules, and a *realist*, result-orientated approach. Out of a number of possible stances along the continuum between these two positions, a judge may be seen as a strict adherent to the 'paper rules' (a textural formalist) at the expense of justice or commercial convenience. Alternatively, he or she may be a 'strong realist', even an iconoclast, like Lord Denning, for whom precedent is no bar to achieving the right result. As you read the chapters that follow, it would be useful for you to keep these different approaches in mind as you will see some excellent examples of both.

Adams and Brownsword (2007) argue that these different approaches to legal method actually reflect the broader political ideologies discussed above. The market philosophy sees the function of the law of contract as the facilitation of competitive exchange, which demands clear contractual ground rules, transactional security and the accommodation of commercial practice. At its most extreme, market individualism encompasses the notion of 'freedom of contract' and 'sanctity of contract'. This accords the parties the maximum licence in setting their own terms, and the ability to hold parties to their freely made bargains however bad a bargain it happens to be. They compare this to a trend in judicial reasoning towards consumer-welfarism, which stands for:

> reasonableness and fairness in contracting. More concretely, this is reflected in a policy of consumer protection and a pot-pourri of specific principles. For example, consumer-welfarism holds that contracting parties should not mislead one another, that they should act in good faith, that a strong party should not exploit the weakness of another's bargaining position, that no party should profit from his own wrong or be unjustly enriched, that remedies should be proportionate to the breach, that contracting parties who are at fault should not be able to dodge their responsibilities, and so on. Crucially, consumer-welfarism subscribes to the paternalistic principle that contractors who enter into bad bargains may be relieved from their obligations where justice so requires. (p. 39)

It should be readily apparent that, in line with political and economic developments, 'consumer-welfarism' has been a key driving force behind contract decision-making over the last 50 years or so. The trend has been such that some commentators have argued that the protection offered to some categories of contractor, most notably 'consumers' is such that the legislature and judiciary have recreated the status contract.

CONCLUDING REMARKS

When one attempts to put the twentieth century's 'transformation' of contract into overall perspective, it is possible to discern two outstanding and related features. First, as regards the institution of contract itself, account must be taken of the new widespread use of the standard, non-negotiable form of contract and the vastly increased involvement of the state as a regulator, supplier and purchaser. Second, as regards the changing nature of the law itself, the essential point is that what has occurred is not so much a transformation but a bifurcation of contract law brought about in large part by the competing ideologies identified by Adams and Brownsword (2007) as 'market individualism' and 'consumer welfarism'. Throughout our examination of the case law, we will meet shifts of approach by the courts away from traditional 'classical' analysis to a range of different approaches to the issue in question. The tension that this creates may be expressed in a variety of ways and is not easily alleviated. For example, should the courts adopt a 'hands-off' approach or adopt a paternalistic interventionalist role. Is the key objective freedom and facilitation of exchange for the parties, or one of fairness? Are the requirements of contract-makers best served by legal certainty or does justice requires flexibility in the law? Perhaps it may be said, as Atiyah (1979) argues, that contract theory is in a mess and has in its modern formulation to serve too many different masters.

REFERENCES AND FURTHER READING

Adams, J and Brownsword, R (2007) *Understanding Contract Law*, 5th edn, Sweet & Maxwell, London.
Atiyah, P (1979) *The Rise and Fall of Freedom of Contract*, Part III, particularly Chapters 14–16, 21 and 22, Clarendon Press, Oxford.
Brownsword, R (2006) *Contract Law: Themes for the Twenty-first Century*, Oxford University Press, Oxford.
Campbell, D and Vincent-Jones, P (eds) (1996) *Contract and Economic Organisation*, Dartmouth, Aldershot.
Cocks, R (2004) *Sir Henry Maine*, Cambridge University Press, Cambridge.
Collins (2002) *Regulating Contracts*, Oxford University press, Oxford.
Daintith, T 'Regulation by contract: the new prerogative' (1979) 34 *Current Legal Problems* 41.
Durkheim, E (1964) *The Division of Labour in Society*, Palgrave Macmillan, London.
Equality and Human Rights Commission: http://www.equalityhumanrights.com/en/Pages/default.aspx
Friedmann, W (1972) *Law in a Changing Society*, 2nd edn, Chapter 4 'The changing function of contract', Stevens and Son, London.
Gilmore, G (1974) *The Death of Contract*, Ohio State University Press, Columbus.
Harden, I (1992) *The Contracting State*, Open University Press, Milton Keynes.
Hart, H.L.A (1961) *The Concept of Law*, Clarendon Press, Oxford.
Kessler, F (1943) 'Contracts of adhesion – some thoughts about freedom of contract' 43 *Columbia Law Review* 629.
Renner, K and Kahn-Freund, translated by Schwarzschild, A., Institutions of Private Law and Their Social Functions, Routledge, London Rev ed 1976.
Smith, A. (1776, reprinted 1993) *Wealth of Nations,* Hackett Publishing Co.
Tönnies, F (2003) *Community and Society*, Dover Publications Inc.
Turpin, C (1979) 'Government contracts: a study of methods of contracting' 31 MLR 241.
Turpin, C (1989) *Government Procurement and Contracts*, Longman, Harlow.
Weber, M (1992) *Economy and Society*, University of California Press, California.

? QUESTIONS

(1) 'The economic correlate of common law contract is a free enterprise society'. Put forward detailed arguments in support of this proposition.

(2) Discuss the following view of contract:

'During the process of production, the owner assumes a mask, increasingly severe, sinister, and in the end almost despotic. Now, as he leaves the intimidating and gloomy factory with his wares, his features unwrinkle, they become bland, modest and agreeable. The man who stands in the market with his goods, though the same person, now wears

Continued

a disguise that changes his appearance beyond recognition, that of the "guardian of commodities". Every recollection of that lower sphere of production ... of despotism ... has vanished from the thoughts of the man, and the appearance of the commodity reveals no traces of it. The capitalist has now become ... an equal among equals. He has dealings with his own kind only'. (Renner, *The Institutions of Private Law and their Social Functions*)

(3) To what extent does the classical contract model help you to identify what constitutes legitimate contractual arrangement in 'The Sad Tale of Angie and Georgie'

(4) What are the benefits of applying an exchange model to distinguish contracts from gifts and promises in that case study?

CHAPTER 4

FROM FORMALISM TO REALISM: CONTEMPORARY CRITIQUES OF CONTRACT LAW

INTRODUCTION

In the last chapter we visited classical contract theory and considered the various challenges to it, with particular emphasis on those posed by the regulation state and welfarism. The response of many members of the judiciary and the legislature has been to try to adjust the classical model so that it better suits the goals of social policy and the marketplace of today. So, for instance, the judiciary has seen fit to provide greater protection for certain categories of people, most notably consumer, in order to mitigate the inequalities of the market place and social life. Later chapters in this book, such as those on implied terms, consideration and unfair terms, will sketch out some of the detail of how some sense of balance has been achieved during this 'neo-classical' period. What has emerged is a mixture of approaches in which market individualism still competes for attention with the more modern notion of consumer welfarism. However, the classical, albeit in a modified form, continues to have much influence on how lawyers approach contracts. In the minds of many contemporary academics in the field, this is an unsatisfactory development. A number have suggested that we have only tinkered with the classical model when what is needed is a rethinking of the principles which should underpin this field of law. A growing number of scholars have argued that the very relevance and legitimacy of the assumptions underpinning the classical model are in crisis.

In this chapter we seek to look at some contemporary critiques of contract which encourage us to look at contractual relationships in different ways. The strength of these various theories, and the reason why they have so much resonance in a book of this kind, is their attention to how contract is used and operates in everyday life. Commentators have expressed concern that the study and practice of law may become too narrowly based and tend to divorce itself from the general culture of which we are all a part.

Rather than seeing the function of law as being to *declare* how contracts ought to be, many of the approaches we will examine are based on the premise that law should *reflect* what constitutes ethical and workable commercial practice. The shift is described here as being from formalism to realism. The new breed of authors whose work is considered owe much to a socio-legal or realist tradition of scholarship, which takes as its starting point the need to understand how the law is received by the community it seeks to regulate.

SOCIO-LEGAL APPROACHES TO CONTRACT LAW

The socio-legal movement in law was in large part a reaction against traditional approaches to studying law, which tended to focus on the importance of the rules at the expense of studying their impact. Legal formalism, with its emphasis on how things *ought* to be, tended to encourage the spurious idea that law is in some way autonomous, an end in itself, rather than a means to social order. By way of contrast, socio-legal scholars have sought to put law firmly in its social, political and economic contexts. They look for relationships between law, legal systems and the wider society; and ask questions about the functions and effects of legal rules.

Socio-legal scholars have argued that there should be a connection between law and the standards of everyday life if law is to retain its legitimacy. According to this school of thought, the standards by which individuals and groups *actually* govern their relations consist only partly of the law to be found in statutes and judicial decisions. In other words, the centre of gravity lies not in legislation nor in judicial decision, but in society itself. It is argued that 'living law', or the rules and norms that people in the commercial sector use to govern their contracts, may be more advanced than doctrine developed by the courts because of an ability to develop quickly in response to problems in the marketplace. In her study of the cotton industry, Bernstein (2001) has argued convincingly that a 'private legal system' operates to create and maintain successful co-operative contracting relationships. She has argued:

> The stability of this and other cooperative-based commercial systems may also be due, in whole or in part, to the fact that social norms of honour, particularly when reinforced through group activity and a basic human desire to think of one's self as *trustworthy*, are more powerful motivators of transactional behaviour than economic models of behaviour typically assume. (p. 1774)

The development of standards within industries has also been encouraged by lack of access to the courts, as contract litigation is commonly regarded as a last resort. Moreover, profits earned from relationships maintained through goodwill and the compromise of differences often outweigh damages awarded against a company that now trades elsewhere. It could be argued then, that the business community has, for reasons of perceived convenience, efficiency and cost, been virtually impelled to develop its own customs, practices and techniques designed to avoid or mitigate business or 'legal' risk and loss.

The judiciary has not been insensitive to the need for the law to remain relevant to practice. For example, in the seventeenth century, in order to remedy weaknesses in the common law of the time, the judges began to incorporate into it what was known as the 'law merchant'. This was a body of relatively sophisticated rules and techniques developed for use in agreements between merchants, or in particular trades or centres of business. But the question of whether it is the law that should be sensitive to practice, or everyday practice of contracts that should be mindful of formal law, remains controversial. It is an issue that poses serious questions about the role of law and the judiciary, since for some there seems to be a growing remoteness from commercial realities on the part of the law.

It would seem that, to a large extent, business has withdrawn from contract law because of its expense, the time it takes to litigate and the irrelevance of formal to everyday notions of obligation. This is particularly the case as far as dispute resolution is concerned. The business community has come to place much greater reliance on bilateral negotiation, commercial mediation and arbitration in preference to the courts, which in turn means that the raw material from which judicial precedents are set is depleted. Some observers have gone further and suggested that the classical model would no longer be recognised in the modern world of commercial contracts. These arguments suggest that we should go beyond the material contained in most textbooks on the subject because of their propensity to focus only on the issue of what the formal law is. In short, we need to move from a position in which law is taken to be synonymous with commerce to a position where the most logical question to pose is of whether commercial exchange needs law.

NON-CONTRACTUAL RELATIONS IN BUSINESS

In the latter half of the last century, a number of important empirical studies of the use of contract law on a day-to-day basis were undertaken which provided fertile ground for reconsideration of the relevance of classical and neo-classical models. These studies are important because they have prompted the emergence of new theories about the role of contract that help us to visualise alternatives to the traditional models. The most obvious starting point for a discussion of the lived world of contract is the work of Stewart Macaulay who was the first legal researcher to explore in a systematic way the use that the business community made of contracts. He started with the assumption that contracts had the *potential* to serve two key functions. The first of these is the rational planning of transactions with careful provision for as many future contingencies as can be foreseen. The second is the existence, or use of, legal sanctions to induce performance or compensate for non-performance. In his seminal work, Macaulay (1963) saw planning as involving such things as the definition of performances, the effect of defective performances and the legally binding nature, or otherwise, of the agreement. His expectations about the role that contract might play in exchanges would have been familiar to classical scholars who focused considerable attention on planning and dispute resolution. What proved innovative about his work was the response of manufacturers and lawyers to his questions about the actual use to which the contract was put.

Somewhat surprisingly, Macaulay (1963) found that business people were not very concerned about planning their transactions in detail in advance. In a later study, Beale and Dugdale (1975) found that business people in the engineering industry considered it expensive to plan in detail. This was especially the case where a dispute or loss seemed unlikely. Lengthy negotiations resulting in detailed planned contractual documents took place only where high-risk, complex, expensive items, such as aircraft, were involved. Indeed, Macaulay (1963) found that detailed negotiations at the beginning of a relationship have even been found to be a sign of *mis*trust. It would seem that it is good relations and profit margins rather than legal rights and duties which are uppermost in the minds of commercial contractors when they make contracts. In Macaulay's 1963 study, most respondents discussed what constituted performance for the purposes of the contract and the effect of certain things happening during performance. But less than half negotiated the consequences of non-performance and even less gave thought to the type of legal sanctions that would apply in such situations.

Macaulay (1963) found evidence of two widely accepted norms of business practice which bound the parties and business community in ways not anticipated by the classical model with its heavy emphasis on individualism and self-interest. First, an adherence to the principle that commitments should be honoured in almost all situations and a strong feeling that one should not 'welsh' on a deal. Second, that one ought to produce a good product and stand behind it. Neither of these motivations was as altruistic as might at first appear to be the case. Firmly behind these norms was a sure knowledge of the commercial value of trouble-free, continuing relationships with good customers.

It is clear from the burgeoning empirical literature on the day-to-day use of contract that, contrary to the classical model's assumption about the importance of certainty, flexibility is highly valued within the business community. Performance of contractual obligations often takes a significant amount of time. So, for instance, the supply of aircraft parts to the Royal Air Force might involve a contractual relationship spanning years. Similarly, an architect might be employed to design a building and supervise its construction over a three-year period or longer. During this time, ideas, technology, world politics and fashions are likely to alter. Changes in market conditions and costs mean that adjustments to contracts are common, expected and necessary. The country's entry into war at short notice might mean, for instance, that more aircraft parts need to be produced or that the price of imported components increases rapidly. Similarly, the design of a civic theatre may have to be reconsidered when the builders find a site of archaeological interest when digging the foundations.

Empirical studies have discovered a number of instances in which one party sought an adjustment once an agreement had been made. In law, such unilateral proposals to vary an existing agreement require a new agreement to be negotiated and a new type of exchange to take place to seal the bargain. But in the business world, such adjustments, and even withdrawals from the contract, were in many instances allowed by the other party 'without dispute' or renegotiation. Cancellation was not always cause for an action for breach but, like bad debts, a recognised risk that could be budgeted for. One lawyer in Macaulay's study (1963) commented that there is a widespread attitude within the business community that one can back out of any deal within vague limits. Campbell and Harris (1993) have argued that, when the parties realise that there is a lack of fit between the real deal and the contract, they expect, and are commonly able to renegotiate on an extra-legal negotiating basis.

Even when such adjustments to the working agreement do not occur, there are limits to what those drafting a formal paper deal can predict or have time to express in words. This means that, when a judge or lawyer looks for the plain meaning of the original contract, it is often the case that it does not reflect what the parties want to achieve. As a result, it has been argued that traditional forms of analysing contracts are inadequate because they fail to understand the importance of ongoing alterations to long-term commercial contracts and the *implicit dimensions* of contracts. That is not to say that traditional doctrines have ignored the need for flexibility. It will be seen from the chapters that follow that even the most traditional of lawyers anticipate the need for such things as variation of contracts and interpretation of agreements in the context of a previous course of dealing or trade custom. But the emphasis of the classical model is on treating contracts as disembedded associations between individuals motivated only by financial gain in the short or medium term. For some, this is an inadequate response to contractual realities in the marketplace. Campbell and Collins (2003) have argued that judicial reasoning has developed only a weak capacity to incorporate these dimensions into its analysis of contract. In their words:

> If the law seeks to protect and enforce contractual agreements, the recognition that it has a partial and incomplete understanding of those agreements suggest that it fails in many instances to achieve its goals by enforcing not the agreement of the parties in all its relevant dimensions but a truncated perception of that agreement…misunderstandings of this practice create the risk that legal regulation will either fail adequately to support the practice when required or misdirect its controls so that they are ineffective.

A succession of empirical studies have found that the use of litigation in the business community is rare and many research participants have argued that they would *actively avoid* introducing lawyers into a dispute because they did not understand the give and take of business. In fact, it seems that the parties to contracts frequently disregard the contract or legal sanctions available in negotiating a dispute. Lewis (1982) has suggested that this is because legal remedies are seen as inflexible, destructive, impractical, unfair, not reflecting commercial practice and difficult to enforce. As Macaulay (2003) has argued more recently:

> Business people do know that there are such things as actions for breach of contract. They also know that their reputation with their trading partner is valuable, and they do not knowingly do things that would damage it without a good reason. Most of the time, I would guess, avoiding breach of contract litigation is not something that business people spend much time thinking about. Insofar as this is true, the style of contract analysis used by judges will not matter much to people who are not law professors.

Socio-legal researchers have also discovered that it is not just that law is marginalised but that other normative frameworks are used to replace it. Studies suggest that widespread use is made of non-legal sanctions such as complaints, replacement procedures, negotiated settlements and blacklisting and that the effectiveness of these measures renders recourse to the courts unnecessary. Underpinning these various informal sanctions is an economic need to stay on good terms with those parties with whom business people were likely to want to contract with again. This finding alone provides a stark contrast to the classical model of contract which envisages a 'discrete' one-off exchange between strangers.

However, the failure of legal doctrine to reflect how contracts work in an everyday context and the fact that the courts may rarely be used by some sectors of the business community should not necessarily lead us to the conclusion that the law completely lacks legitimacy. It is possible that law plays a more indirect role in the contractual sphere than has been suggested so far. Other authors have argued that, while business people honour informal norms and sanctions while a contractual relationship is progressing well, when it breaks up they may well want recourse to the sort of 'end-game' rules that appear in formal written agreements. Moreover, although they may not use the courts, that is not to say that formal doctrine, favourable precedents and the threat of legal enforcement of contractual obligations are not used as bargaining tools in the process of negotiating an out-of-court settlement or compliance with a demand. In this way, it may be that formal doctrine continues to have a radiating effect or symbolic power not anticipated by some empirical studies. Even where disputes do not arise, the law may play some part in fostering confidence. If litigation is not thought about on a day-to-day basis, it may nonetheless constitute a vague symbolic threat which serves to encourage reliability. The question which remains is whether we want the law of contract to be more than this.

FEMINIST CRITIQUES OF CONTRACT

The argument that the beliefs which underpin social relations are co-operative rather than constantly antagonistic is one that has been taken up in feminist critiques of the law of contract. The identification of a correlation between masculine ways of reasoning and the ethos and philosophy of classical legal doctrine has been central to feminist engagements with the law. It is argued that the values with which the classical model of contract is associated are essentially masculine values.

There is a clear resonance between the concerns of feminists and those of the empiricists discussed above. Feminist writers have suggested that, whilst feminine subjects prefer to focus on context, relationships and discretion in resolving disputes, masculine subjects prefer to work with pre-determined and logical rules which, although inflexible, produce certainty. Empirical work in the field suggests that feminine subjects typically see moral dilemmas in the context of long-term goals. Their worlds are worlds of connection and networks in which an awareness of the links between people give rise to a recognition of responsibility for one another. Most significant for present purposes is the way in which this approach can be seen as opposed to an individualistic model of the type favoured by classical theorists.

It is arguable that there is no branch of the law in which the hostile egoism of possessive individualism is more clearly reflected than in classical contract and neo-classical models which take people away from the pre-existing web of community emphasised by socio-legal scholars. It has been suggested that doctrinal writers and judges alike have tended historically to legislate against the emotive and relational dimensions of contracts and that in its most extreme form the legal subject of contractual exchange has been viewed as a mere expression of economic relationships or callous cash nexus divorced from any form of lasting connection. According to this way of thinking, exchanges are the only way in which individuals come to recognise the needs of others. Applying this reasoning to the contractual doctrine of frustration, the late Mary Jo Frug (1992) saw as masculine a position which stressed the plausibility of only one outcome in a model of contract predicated on discrete and abstract relationships. In her view, this led somewhat inevitably to a literal interpretation of the contract and an inappropriate emphasis on the value of certainty. By way of contrast, she characterised as feminine a position as one that was grounded in a pluralistic, context-sensitive model of contract relationships which offered a multiplicity of objectives was centred on good faith and forbearance.

It follows that, for the feminist critic, the classical and neo-classical models have become associated with masculine values such as performance, control, security of transaction and standardisation for its survival. By way of contrast, feminist scholars have argued that contractual doctrine removes disputes from their everyday existence by narrowing the issues for discussion into distinctive and limited legal categories which stifle the setting in which the dispute occurs. Not only do classical and formalistic approaches to the subject concentrate on specific events and moments in time, they purport to rely on linear modes of reasoning. In this way, it has been argued that accounts of disputed events which are entirely adequate by the standards of common-sense morality prove to be legally inadequate because of judicial assumptions about how a story should be told, and how and when blame should be assessed. The emphasis placed by the judiciary on abstract principles and linear accounts also reflects the tendency of the common law to seek universal and guiding principle to frame all decisions. Such generalisations assume universal truths and a neutral or objective way of seeing things which tend to suppress alternative ways of framing accounts or grievances. Viewed in this way, it is clear that the classical model is ill-equipped to create a space in which the sort of context discussed in empirical studies and by feminists can be heard and understood.

RELATIONAL CONTRACT THEORY

It is in the work of relational contracts theorists that the most successful attempt has been made to use the concerns raised by empiricists and feminists about context and substantive norms of justice. The work of Ian Macneil (2001) has been particularly influential in building an alternative theory of contract which is as compelling as the classical model. One of the most interesting aspects of his work is his contention that, in looking for the terms of the contract, we should start with the context *before* moving on to the express provisions. Four core propositions inform the relational approach to contract:

- Every transaction is embedded in a complex web of relations.

- Understanding any transaction requires an appreciation of anything which is significant to the transaction regardless of whether it is something which is relevant to formal legal rules about contracts.

- Effective analysis of any transaction requires a recognition of all relationships and sequences which impinge on performance.

- This contextual analysis produces a more sensitive approach to the contractual relationship than an approach which privileges the formal agreement.

Macneil (1980) draws an important distinction between two types of contract. The *discrete* or 'spot' contract is one where the parties come together for a one-off transaction. This happens, for instance, when a passing tourist buys a packet of chewing gum from a stranger in a newsagents. This type of contract is one in which the goods and money are exchanged immediately and the parties do not anticipate dealing with each other again. At the opposite end of the spectrum is the *relational* contract, which forms part of a long-term relationship between the parties whose business interests become more integrated as a result. In this sort of contract, flexibility, trust, co-operation and harmonious settlements of disputes are likely to be privileged. It is for these reasons that relational contracts have been likened to marriages and discrete exchanges likened to one-night stands.

A closer reading of Macneil's work demonstrates that he does place value on some of the tenets underpinning the classical model but only insofar as they relate to the atypical case of the discrete contract. Moreover, he has argued that even the most discrete of exchanges between strangers has some relational elements. The most casual and brief of contracts, such as the purchase of a daily paper, involves a complex network of suppliers of paper, journalists and transport. Moreover, the parties may share common expectations of what is entailed in the exchange, which are based on common practice.

Macneil's work has not been universally understood in the UK. A particular misconception is that his approach is prescriptive: that the standards he talks about are those which he thinks should frame contractual relations. In fact McNeil has frequently asserted that values such as co-operation are those which the business community already use. But as Wightman (1996) eloquently reminds us:

> Although such terms as trust and co-operation are used here, it is important to see that there is no suggestion that relational contracting is just a mush of altruism, where self-interest has disappeared. The issue is not the existence of self-interest, but the form of its expression. Take, for example, the relationship between a main contractor and various subcontractors on a major construction project such as a large bridge. It will be in the self-interest of all the firms for the project to be completed successfully, but this will not happen if every technical breach is pounced on as an excuse for terminating and claiming damages.

Macneil has argued that all contracts, whether discrete or relational, rely on shared understandings about the particular meanings to be attributed to contracts and contractual behaviour. For him the failure of the classical model is its inability and unwillingness to recognise the importance of context, humanitarian factors and implicit understandings in contract. In his view, this renders it obsolete in practical terms because of the ways in which it distorts understanding of the marketplace. It would seem then that the importance of relational contract theory relies not only in its revelations about the components of contracts which are vital to an understanding of them but in its revelations that these are the very elements that are marginalised by classical theorists.

CONCLUDING REMARKS

There is no doubt at all as to the importance of empirical work on contracts for anyone interested in the relationship between business transactions and contract law. These studies indicate that business policy and practice often operate to marginalise the formal law of contract in everyday business transactions. To the extent that business transactions operate 'outside' contract, this amounts to a rejection by the business community of legal doctrine. Does this matter? According to Macaulay's (1963) evidence, it would seem that it does not, unless you are a lawyer who is losing fees. None of the business people that Macaulay (1963) interviewed appeared to be losing sleep over their non-contractual relations. But, another view is that it would be dangerous to 'write off' contract as a business device on the strength of the empirical studies conducted. Rather, it could be argued that greater efforts should be made to make the law relevant to the business community. After all, the basic function of contract has long been identified as facilitating business exchanges.

What becomes clear from the analysis contained in this chapter is that the theories underpinning the law of contract are in a state of flux. Criticisms of the classical model focus on its emphasis on procedural justice at the expense of substantive justice, its privileging of rules over understanding and context, and its inability of reflect the day-to-day world of contracts. We saw in the last chapter that welfarist interventions on behalf of consumers have mitigated the more extreme injustices of a model based on the assumption that the parties to a contract exercise free will. But conceptually, these interventions remain exemptions to general rules rather than a general platform from which to launch a more general discussion about the importance of looking at inequality or context in all contracts. It becomes clear that the pragmatism of the common law confers status on certain types of contracting parties but fails to address the issue of whether there is such a thing as a general law of contract in English law. In the chapters that follow, we will see these issues being raised again and again. But what remains important for present purposes is whether and how relational contract theory can deliver its promise of a more responsive law of contract which is relevant.

REFERENCES AND FURTHER READING

Beale, H and Dugdale, T 'Contracts between businessmen: planning and the use of contractual remedies' (1975) 2 *British Journal of Law and Society* 45.

Bernstein, L 'Opting out of the legal system: extralegal contractual relations in the diamond industry' (1992) 21 (1) *Journal of Legal Studies* 115.

Bernstein, L 'Private commercial law in the cotton industry: creating cooperation through rules, norms, and institutions' (2001) 99 *Michigan Law Review* 1724.

Brownsword, R (2006) *Contract Law: Themes for the Twenty-first Century*, 2nd edn, Oxford University Press, Oxford.

Campbell, D (2001) *The Relational Theory of Contract: Selected Works of Ian Macneil*, London, Sweet and Maxwell.

Campbell, D and Collins, H (2003) 'Discovering the implicit dimensions of contracts' in Campbell, D, Collins, H and Wightman, J (eds) *Implicit Dimensions of Contract: Discrete, Relational and Network Contracts*, Hart Publishing, Oxford.

Campbell, D and Harris, D 'Flexibility in long-term contractual relationships' (1993) *Journal of Law and Society* 166.

Collins, H (2002) *Regulating Contracts*, Oxford University Press, Oxford.

Deakin, S, Lane, C and Wilkinson, F ' "Trust" or law? Toward an integrated theory of contractual relations between firms' (1994) 21 *Journal of Law and Society* 329.

Devlin, P 'The relation between commercial law and commercial practice' (1951) 14 (3) *Modern Law Review* 249.

Frug, Mary Jo 'Re-reading contracts: A feminist analysis of a contracts casebook', (1985) 34 *Am UL Rev* 1065.

Lewis, R 'Contracts between businessmen: reform of the law of firm offers and an empirical study of tendering practices in the building industry' (1982) 9 (2) *Journal of Law & Society* 153.

Macaulay, S 'Non-contractual relations in business – a preliminary study' (1963) 28 *American Sociological Review* 55.

Macaulay, S 'Elegant models, empirical pictures, and the complexities of contract' (1977) 11 *Law and Society Review* 507.

Macaulay, S 'Relational contracts floating on a sea of custom? Thoughts about the ideas of Ian Macneil and Lisa Bernstein' in Symposium in Honour of Ian Macneil, (2002) 94 (3) *Northwestern University Law Review* 775.

Macaulay, S (2003) 'The real and paper deal: empirical pictures of relationships, complexity and the urge for transparent simple rules' in Campbell, D, Collins, H and Wightman, J (eds) *Implicit Dimensions of Contract: Discrete, Relational and Network Contracts*, Hart Publishing, Oxford.

Mulcahy, L and Wheeler, S (2004) (eds) *Feminist Perspectives on Contract*, Cavendish Press, London.

Vincent-Jones, P 'Contract and business transactions: a socio-legal analysis' (1989) 16 *Journal of Law and Society* 166.

Wightman, J (1996) *Contract – A Critical Commentary*, Pluto Press, London.

? *QUESTIONS*

(1) Read over the story of Angie and Georgie and note down all the agreements made in the story which you think *ought* to be enforced by the courts, regardless of whether they would be. Look back at your notes. Can you identify common characteristics which each of the agreements you have identified share? What are these?

(2) How important do you think context is to Angie and Georgie in determining whether or not to sue for breach of these agreements? Would you advise them to try and sue? What would they achieve? Give reasons for your response.

(3) Imagine that you have been asked to prepare a 10-minute presentation for a radio programme in which you need to convey the distinction between relational and classical contract theory. Sketch out what you would say and then add a section that makes the case for the importance of the distinction.

PART THREE:

MAKING A DEAL

CHAPTER 5

APPROACHES TO FINDING AGREEMENT AND PRE-CONTRACTUAL NEGOTIATIONS

INTRODUCTION

The rules relating to the formation of contracts are designed to establish the moment a contract comes into existence so that the parties are clear about the exact time and place that their obligations to each other begin. This is clearly important if people are to be able to rely on agreements and plan other deals on the back of them. If a contractual relationship breaks down and one of the parties seeks to be compensated, it is also critical to be able to trace back when the parties first became beholden to each other. In considering whether a contract has been formed, English law looks for *agreement* between the parties. The typical contract is conceived of as a two-sided bargain voluntarily and deliberately entered into by two people. This chapter focuses on agreement and is concerned with the following questions. First, how do lawyers analyse the process by which the parties to a contract reach agreement? Second, how does business practice relate to the legal analysis of agreement?

Most lawyers would say that the answer to the first question is well settled by the leading cases, which provide a rational and structured account of the negotiation and agreement process. However, others whose views were rehearsed in the last chapter, would say that the 'rules' of offer and acceptance, on which the legal concept of agreement rests, are unsatisfactory. This is because it has been argued that they are largely irrelevant to the conduct of business today. Moreover, they are often awkward tools which are only rarely used by the courts in the settlement of disputes. Who is right?

DEFINITIONS, FORM AND OBJECTIVITY

In the search for agreement, the courts have for some time looked for an 'offer' and an 'acceptance'. *Offers* have traditionally been defined by the courts as expressions of a willingness to enter into a legally binding contract on certain terms. The expression may manifest itself in words or in conduct. A contract formed during the purchase of a daily newspaper may, for instance, be completed without the buyer or seller saying anything to each other. However, they must do something which indicates expressly or by implication that the offer is to become binding on the person making it (the offeror) as soon as it has been accepted by the offeree. An *acceptance* is a final and unqualified expression of assent to the terms of an offer. So, if Sally emails Carl to say 'Would you like to buy a consignment of 20 of the latest skateboards for £2,000? I can deliver next Thursday', and Carl emails back the response 'Great. I promise to send you a cheque for £2,000 and will stay in on Thursday', there is an agreement which would be recognised by English law. It can be seen from this simple example that acceptance turns an offer into agreement. Figure 5.1 shows this transaction in pictorial form.

Traditionally, the courts have *not* sought to protect the expectations of parties as they negotiate with each other during the pre-contractual stage. This distinction

Figure 5.1:   Elements of a contract

| negotiations leading to a firm offer | **acceptance** → | binding contract |

pre-contractual stage   contractual stage

has a logical basis. It is not until a contract is formed that the law of contract has a role in governing the relationship. It is also the case that English law recognises contracts in which the exchange agreed upon is completed at the same time as the acceptance matches the offer (executed contracts). It also recognises exchanges of promises about future conduct (executory contracts). By way of example, the law would recognise as a contract the purchase of a newspaper in which money and a newspaper exchanged hands as the purchaser indicated the price they were prepared to pay and the shopkeeper made clear that the paper could be taken away. It would also recognise as a contract an agreement in which the shopkeeper agreed to deliver a daily newspaper to the customer's address every day and the customer agreed to settle their bill every month. In both cases, a contract is made as soon as the agreement is reached. If the shopkeeper fails to deliver the paper or the customer refuses to pay their bill, then there is a breach of contract.

It often comes as a surprise to students to discover that only in certain cases does the law require contracts to be in writing. Carl and Sally's agreement discussed earlier in this chapter would have been just as valid if they had communicated by telephone or had the conversation face to face over coffee. Although written contracts are common, the fact that transactions are frequently conducted on the basis of standard forms of printed contract is a matter of business expediency and is not a *legal* requirement. A contract may be in writing. It may be signed by the parties, but it could also be concluded verbally, by conduct, or some mixture of all three. What marks out a written contract and makes it attractive is that having something in writing is often the best evidence of the terms agreed by the parties. For this reason the Consumer Credit Act 1974 requires that hire purchase and other credit transactions are in writing and signed by the parties as a consumer protection measure.

When looking for agreement, the courts are not concerned with what the parties were thinking or really intended to do. The tests imposed by the courts are *objective*. This means that, for practical reasons, the courts infer intention from what the parties do and say rather than from what they are actually thinking. If the parties have, to all outward appearances, agreed to the same terms on the same subject matter, generally neither could deny that they intended to agree. So, in the email transaction between Carl and Sally discussed above, the court would not be concerned with Carl's objection that he never really intended to buy Sally's skateboards but was just exploring possibilities. They would focus instead on what the reasonable person would assume to have been his intention on reading the email exchange. The subjective *consensus ad idem* theory, popular in the nineteenth century, which required that there could be no contract without a genuine 'meeting of the minds' has largely passed from the law, although we shall see that it continues to have some influence in cases where mistakes are made in the pre-contractual negotiations. But, whatever the test in looking for agreement, it commonly involves *construing* the language used by the parties in order to establish whether the parties have, from an objective viewpoint, reached agreement.

In reality, finding an offer and acceptance may not always be as straightforward as the examples involving Carl and Sally suggest. Often this is because negotiations leading to a contract may be prolonged and involve a series of statements made by the parties as they move slowly towards agreement. For instance, before sending the email in which he accepts Sally's offer, Carl may have asked for further information about the specifications of the skateboards or their colour. By the same token Sally may have specified convenient collection times and methods of payment which were not acceptable to her. But greater levels of complexity are also introduced when one begins to study the *context* in which commercial transactions take place.

WHAT ARE THE COURTS LOOKING FOR?

The exact moments when offer and acceptance occurs are not always clear, as the parties often proceed towards contractual responsibility in a haphazard fashion. You probably know enough about the operation of contract law by now to be able to predict that the notions of offer, counter offer, invitation to treat and acceptance are elusive. When people carry out lengthy negotiations it may be hard to say exactly when an offer has been made and accepted. Neither the courts nor business people find it easy to determine exactly when an agreement has been concluded.

As the arguments in subsequent chapters unravel, it will become apparent that inter-business contracts often fail to fit neatly into the 'doctrinal handcuffs' of rigidly interpreted rules. As the work of Macaulay (1963) discussed in the last chapter has shown, business people are much less strict than lawyers as regards contractual certainty. They often feel that insistence on adherence to contractual 'detail' is bad for continuing business relations and may amount to a poor strategy to tie oneself to very detailed terms at the time of agreement when the future is uncertain. While acceptance must be unconditional, contractors often prefer to punctuate the agreement with a variety of adjustment devices which allow for flexibility as market conditions change and performance proceeds. Renegotiation and price variation clauses are two examples of such devices.

Despite the needs of business, a close study of doctrine reveals that the frameworks for analysis handed down to generations of students has involved the creation of a formal and relatively inflexible set of rules which prescribe exactly what has to be done before a contract comes into place. You will undoubtedly learn a lot about these 'rules' of offer and acceptance during your course. Exam papers across the country will be full of problem questions in which emails are sent and not delivered, letters lost and answerphone messages unheard. It will become clear to you that the English courts have developed highly distinctive methods for analysing the point at which a contract comes into being, and that this rests on the identification of particular sequential stages in the course of negotiations. Over time these have become rather formulaic and divorced from the original notion of true agreement. It will be seen from the cases discussed in this chapter that this approach can often produce unsatisfactory results. The most obvious example of this is when the parties clearly intend to do business with each other, have reached an understanding and have begun to perform their part of the bargain without satisfying all the rules. Although the courts have found ways to enforce many of these agreements, they have done so at the expense of coherence. This in turn has led to much debate about the modern-day relevance of this formalistic approach.

CRITICS OF THE FORMALIST APPROACH

Critics of this formalist approach assert that the offer–acceptance model presents an unrealistic, rigid and oversimplified view of business agreements. They argue that undue emphasis is placed on the idea of binding promises, certainty, or on the notion of offer and unqualified acceptance. The critics complain that the degree of certainty required by the law undermines the need for a degree of flexibility in business. The American commentator Mooney (1966) is scornful of the traditional textbook analysis:

> We learned that there are certain expressions of mutual assent to which the law appends an obligation arising from the express or plainly implied 'promises' of the parties. The legal obligation is strictly limited to the promises. These promises are discovered in *the* unvarying method by which human beings contract with each other, namely by means of 'offers' embodying 'promises' directed by 'offerors' of particular 'offerees' who 'accept' by manifesting assent either by tendering a promise or an act…. Case variations were hung on the construct like ornaments on a Christmas tree, glittering but essentially useless. (p. 215)

It is also worth noting that numerous editions of Cheshire and Fifoot's *Law of Contract* issued this warning regarding offer and acceptance:

> It must again be emphasised that the phrase 'offer and acceptance', though hallowed by a century and a half of judicial usage, is not to be applied as a talisman, revealing, by a species of esoteric art, the presence of a contract. It would be ludicrous to suppose that businessmen couch their communications in the form of a catechism…. The rules which the judges have elaborated from the premise of offer and acceptance are neither the rigid deductions of logic nor the inspiration of natural justice. They are only presumptions, drawn from experience, to be applied in so far as they serve the ultimate object of establishing the phenomena of agreement. (Furmston, 2006 p. 47)

In the everyday world of business, promises seldom occur in the manner suggested by a number of textbooks, which focus on rules. Overemphasis on promises reflects simplistic 'party autonomy' and 'as you promise so you shall be bound' views of contract and fails to pay attention to the realities of business negotiations, the safeguard and contingency 'buffers' which the parties themselves build into agreements and the mass of contract terms now emanating from statutory provisions.

Although 'doctrinal rules' relating to agreement are based to a great extent on the relatively simple contractual situations of a century or more ago, it could be argued that they are not as immobile or 'black letter' as some would suggest. From a generally stated 'base line', some have argued that they shade off towards a more realistic middle ground which is more in keeping with the complexity and approximate certainty of business life today. Collins (2003), for instance, suggests that many of the leading cases can be much better understood if seen as attempts to determine the exact point at which it is *reasonable for a party to rely* on what the other has said rather than a detailed analysis of when their deeds and words mirror each other exactly. We shall return to the idea of reasonable reliance as a basis on which to impose obligations in Chapter 7. For present purposes, suffice it to say that this alternative construction may get no closer to determining whether there has been a genuine agreement, but it does produce results which are more flexible and attuned to business culture and practice. In a complicated commercial case heard by the Privy Council, *New Zealand Shipping Co Ltd v Satterthwaite & Co Ltd* (1975), Lord Wilberforce argued in a similar vein:

> It is only the precise analysis of this complex of relations into the classical offer and acceptance, with identifiable consideration, that seems to present difficulty, but this same difficulty exists in many situations of daily life, e.g. sales at auction; supermarket purchases; boarding an omnibus; purchasing a train ticket; tenders for the supply of goods ... these are all examples which show that English law, having committed itself to a rather technical and schematic doctrine, in application takes a practical approach, often at the cost of forcing the facts to fit uneasily into the worked slots of offer, acceptance and consideration. (p. 167)

What was striking about this case was that a majority of their Lordships were willing to engage in an ingenious application of the legal concepts of agreement and consideration in order to achieve 'commercial reality', and that it was the minority that stayed within the bounds of traditional analysis. It would seem that the 'rules' must be used with extreme care in an area where considerations such as the parties' intention, trade custom, special circumstances and policy may all play their part.

CASE STUDIES OF ALTERNATIVE STYLES OF REASONING

Before going on to consider the formal rules relating to the formation of contracts in Chapter 6, it is useful to reflect on the different *approaches* to contract formation which are discernible from the case law. This can be done quite succinctly by analysing the judgments in two similar cases. In the 1970s, the Conservative city council in Manchester had a policy of selling council houses to tenants who wished to buy them. They devised a simple procedure to be followed which the tenants could use without the help of a solicitor. Following an election, the council became Labour-controlled and the new administration discontinued the sales except in cases in which there was already a binding contract in place. Two tenants, who were informed that their sales could not proceed, decided to sue the council, as they believed that a contract for sale had been formed which they should be allowed to enforce.

In *Storer v Manchester City Council* (1974), Mr Storer had applied to buy his council house and the town clerk had forwarded to him an 'Agreement for Sale' detailing the purchase price and mortgage arrangements. Mr Storer had signed and returned the Agreement before the Conservative council's policy had been discontinued by Labour. In their analysis of the case, the Court of Appeal adopted a conventional approach to finding a contract based on a series of concepts dating back to the classical contract period. They looked for a firm offer and a firm acceptance of that offer, and decided that the procedure followed by the parties had reached the stage at which a binding contract had been concluded. Lord Denning stated that:

> [Mr Storer] had done everything which he had to do to bind himself to the purchase of the property. The only thing left blank was the date when the tenancy was to

cease…. The corporation put forward to the tenant a simple form of agreement. The very object was to dispense with legal formalities. One of the formalities – exchange of contracts – was quite unnecessary. The contract was concluded by offer and acceptance. The offer was contained in the letter of 9 March in which the town clerk said: 'I… enclose the Agreement for Sale. If you will sign the Agreement and return it to me I will send the Agreement signed on behalf of the Corporation in exchange.'… The acceptance was made when the tenant did sign it, as he did, and return it, as he did on 20 March. It was then that a contract was concluded. The town clerk was then bound to send back the agreement signed on behalf of the corporation. The agreement was concluded on Mr Storer's acceptance. It was not dependent on the subsequent exchange …. The final point was this. Counsel for the corporation said that the town clerk did not intend to be bound by the letter of 9 March 1971. He intended that the corporation should not be bound except on exchange. There is nothing in this point. In contracts you do not look into the actual intent in a man's mind. You look at what he said and did. A contract is formed when there is, to all outward appearances, a contract. A man cannot get out of a contract by saying: 'I did not intend to contract', if by his words he has done so. His intention is to be found only in the outward expression which his letters convey. If they show a concluded contract that is enough. (pp. 826–8)

In the later case, *Gibson v Manchester City Council* (1979), the facts were more challenging for traditionalists. The purchasing procedure was slightly different and had not advanced as far as in *Storer*. Mr Gibson had applied to the council for details of the price and mortgage terms applicable to the purchase of his council house. The City Treasurer replied that the council 'may be prepared to sell the house to you at £2,725 less 20 per cent = £2,180'. The letter gave details of the mortgage likely to be made available and asked Mr Gibson, if he wished to proceed, to make a formal application. He did this and the council took the house off the list of council-maintained properties and placed it on their house purchase list. Mr Gibson claimed that the City Treasurer's letter amounted to an offer which he had accepted.

The Court of Appeal agreed with Mr Gibson's analysis despite the fact that the transaction did not fall neatly into a conventional analysis of offer and acceptance. Bearing in mind the court's decision in *Storer* and prompted by considerations of fairness, Lord Denning supported the decision as follows:

To my mind it is a mistake to think that all contracts can be analysed into the form of offer and acceptance. I know in some of the textbooks it has been the custom to do so; but as I understand the law, there is no need to look for a strict offer and acceptance. You should look at the correspondence as a whole and at the conduct of the parties and see therefrom whether the parties have come to an agreement on everything that was material. If by their correspondence and their conduct you can see an agreement on all material terms, which was intended thenceforward to be binding, then there is a binding contract in law even though all the formalities have not been gone through. For that proposition I would refer to *Brogden v Metropolitan Railway Co* (1877)…. It seems to me that on the correspondence I have read (and, I may add, on what happened after) the parties had come to an agreement in the matter which they intended to be binding. (p. 586)

What makes his judgment so worthy of note is that Denning is suggesting that there is no need for one component to be identified as an offer and another as acceptance. He argues that we should be looking to the overall transaction rather than becoming bound by formalistic rules which do not capture the *spirit* of the transaction. To use a simple metaphor, Denning is looking for the presence of a cake, whereas those adopting a more formalistic analysis have looked for the ingredients of the cake and whether they have been put together in a 'correct' sequence.

Denning's approach in this case was, however, rejected by the House of Lords who adopted the traditional, formalist position. In Lord Diplock's words:

> My Lords, there may be certain types of contract, though I think they are exceptional, which do not fit easily into the normal analysis of a contract as being constituted by offer and acceptance; but a contract alleged to have been made by an exchange of correspondence between the parties in which the successive communications other than the first are in reply to one another is not one of these. I can see no reason in the instance case for departing from the conventional approach of looking at the handful of documents relied on as constituting the contract sued on and seeing whether on their true construction there is to be found in them a contractual offer by the council to sell the house to Mr Gibson and an acceptance of that offer by Mr Gibson. I venture to think that it was by departing from this conventional approach that the majority of the Court of Appeal was led into error. (p. 974)

As a result, it was decided that no offer to sell had been made by the council. The City Treasurer's letter had stated that the council *may* be prepared to sell and it invited Gibson to make a formal application to buy. It was argued that no clear intention to be bound could be evinced on a true construction of the words used and the letter amounted to no more than an invitation to negotiate further.

CONCLUDING REMARKS

In the chapters that follow, we will begin to take a closer look at the rules of offer and acceptance referred to in this chapter and other tests of enforceability which rely on particular types of behaviour. It may well be of use to return to this chapter when the details of these rules have become more apparent. The purpose of this chapter has been to encourage you to interrogate traditional ways of analysing agreement and, as you read through the cases, to consider whether the formalist approach is serving the needs of the business community and wider society. The interface between theory and practice, the competing needs of certainty and flexibility and concerns about open-ended standards are all issues which will be revisited again and again.

REFERENCES AND FURTHER READING

Beale, H and Dugdale, T 'Contracts between businessmen: planning and the use of contractual remedies' (1975) 2 *British Journal of Law and Society* 45.

Collins, H (2003) *The Law of Contract*, Lexis Nexis Butterworths, London.

Furmston, M (2006) *Cheshire Fifoot and Furmston's Law of Contract*, 15th edn, Oxford University Press, London.

Lewis, C 'The formation and repudiation of contracts by international telex' (1980) LMCLQ 43.

Mooney, E (1966) 'Old kontract principles and Karl's new kode. An essay on the jurisprudence of our new commercial law' (1966) 11(2) *Villanova Law Review*, 213.

Wheeler, S and Shaw, J (1994) *Contract Law: Cases, Materials and Commentary*, Oxford University Press, Oxford.

?

(1) Read through the decisions in *Gibson v Manchester City Council* (1979)
    and draw up a list of reasons why the sale of the council house should
    not have gone through. Now rehearse the opposing arguments. Would
    you apply the same reasoning if the case concerned a deal between the
    council and a local construction company with its own team of lawyers?

(2) Read through the decision of the Court of Appeal in *Baird Textile Holdings
    Ltd v M&S plc (2001)*. Imagine you are a judge in the House of Lords on
    an appeal of the case. How would you decide the case? Give detailed
    reasons for your position.

CHAPTER 6

THE MOMENT OF RESPONSIBILITY: KEY CONCEPTS IN DETERMINING WHETHER AGREEMENT HAS BEEN REACHED

INTRODUCTION

In the last chapter, we looked at the expectation that a contract is only formed when there is a valid offer which is met with an acceptance of that offer. Collins (2003) refers to this marrying of offer and acceptance as the 'moment of responsibility'. The main focus of case law in this area has been on finding a way of determining when it is appropriate to attach legal liability to statements or the conduct of the negotiating parties. It was made clear in the last chapter that the idea that there are rules which allow us to identify an 'offer' and 'acceptance' is an artificial one. Despite the tendency to aspire to clear, if somewhat illogical, rules, in practice it is often difficult for the judiciary to separate the two concepts of offer and acceptance out. Negotiations leading up to a contract are often messier than some textbooks would have us think. In this chapter we will turn to some of the key concepts that have been used by the judiciary in an attempt to organise cases according to a coherent set of principles. In the chapter that follows we will turn to look at some of the difficulties which have arisen in using traditional concepts of offer and acceptance in the complex world of business.

If the courts are disposed towards a formalistic approach, it is important for students to understand the method of analysing negotiations in this way. An examination of the various things that occur in the pre-contractual stage requires an understanding of a range of terms such as invitation to treat, unilateral and bi-lateral offers, counter offers and revocation that have been used to distinguish the various activities which are akin to an offer or acceptance but do not quite fulfil the relevant criteria. It is to these various terms that we now turn. A major issue underpinning many of the judgments we will be considering is the courts' reluctance to bind the parties to a contract at an unexpectedly early stage.

OFFERS, INVITATIONS TO TREAT AND ADVERTISEMENTS

As was made clear in the last chapter, an offer has traditionally been defined by the courts as an expression of a willingness to enter into a binding contract was manifested by words or conduct. In determining whether something constitutes an offer, the courts place considerable emphasis on certainty and completeness. In other words, the offer must be clear enough for the person accepting it to understand the key matters on which the parties are in agreement. These commonly include issues such as price, quantity, the timing and manner of performance. There must also be an indication that the person making the offer intends to be bound as soon as the offer is accepted.

As a general proposition, offers must be distinguished from other statements made at a pre-contractual stage known as 'invitations to treat'. This is an old-fashioned expression which describes attempts by one party to encourage the other to enter into negotiations with them or make them an offer. Most people come across several examples of invitations to treat each day without being aware of this term of art used by lawyers to describe them. Each time you pass a shop which declares that it has the 'lowest prices in town' or an advertising board which declares that a certain airline offers 'lower prices than all its competitors' you are being tempted, or invited, to approach them with a view to buying a product or service from them. But few would expect the claims made to be substantiated. They are part of the 'puff' or sales technique used to encourage customers to enter a shop or access a website. But, as one moves on to look at other inducements and more specific wording, it becomes clear that there are fine lines to be drawn between what should be taken seriously and what should not.

A number of problems have arisen over whether the display of goods in a shop window or on the shelves in a shop with prices attached amounts to an offer. It could easily be argued that the display could amount to an offer if the price is clear and the goods can be clearly seen and inspected. However, as early as the mid-nineteenth century in the case of shop displays, the courts took a different view, which was endorsed in the supermarket case of *Pharmaceutical Society of Great Britain v Boots Cash Chemists (Southern) Ltd* (1953) in which the terms on which a shop was prepared to sell displayed items appeared very clear. In this landmark case in which the focus was on the mechanics of buying and selling in one of the first self-service stores, a Boots customer selected goods from the shelves and presented them at the cash desk where she paid the price. Some of the goods were required by the Pharmacy and Poisons Act 1933 to be sold only under the supervision of a registered pharmacist and a pharmacist was present at the cash desk for this purpose. Boots were alleged to have infringed the Act because the contract had been formed before the woman presented the goods at the cash desk. The Pharmaceutical Society argued that the sale took place when the customer put the goods into her wire basket, so accepting the offer constituted by their display on the shelves. If this were so, certain medicines and poisons were being 'sold' without supervision contrary to the Act. However, the Court of Appeal disagreed and ruled that the sale took place at the cash desk. They argued that display of the goods did not mean that they were on offer. Instead, they argued that an offer to buy was made by the customer at the cash desk subject to supervision and possible refusal. In their view, the display of goods was merely an 'invitation to treat'.

This decision really rests on a policy choice which supported commercial innovation and convenience rather than on orthodox analysis of contract formation. The same issue usually arises in the context of criminal statutes where the *Boots* ruling has led to difficulties; (see, for instance, *Pilgram v Rice-Smith* 1977). In *Fisher v Bell* (1961), a case involving the alleged offence of 'offering for sale' a flick-knife contrary to the Restriction of Offensive Weapons Act 1959, the court was asked to analyse the law in relation to priced goods in a shop window. Although the statute was clearly intended to cover the situation, it was held that the display was merely an invitation and that no offence had been committed because an offer had not been made.

It has been argued that the law would be better served to regard displays or advertisements as offers subject to the condition, sometimes found in advertisements, that stocks remain available, as this position would better reflect the expectations of the public and business community. Parties may of course indicate that their statements do not constitute offers. Estate agents often do this by including a form of words on printed details of properties, such as the statement that: 'These particulars do not form, nor constitute any part of, an offer, or a contract, for sale'. However, the courts are not well disposed to this approach. Even where an advertisement in the 'For Sale' columns of a newspaper contains specific wording, a court would almost certainly, on the basis of the 'limited stocks' argument, regard the advertisement as an invitation to treat. This was 'business sense' according to Lord Parker in *Partridge v Crittenden* (1968), another statutory offence case in which the defendant inserted a notice in a periodical named *Cage and Aviary Birds* stating 'Bramblefinch cocks, bramblefinch hens, 25s each'. If the advertisement had been construed as an offer and demand had exceeded the defendant's supply, he could have faced any number of actions for breach of contract, as well as being guilty of an offence under the Protection of Birds Act 1954.

The issue of identifying whether a statement in an advertisement was *specific enough* to be construed as an offer which was intended to be binding was also addressed by the Court of Appeal in the famous case of *Carlill v Carbolic Smoke Ball Co* (1893). The case concerned a slightly different type of contract from the ones discussed so far, which have revolved around the bilateral negotiations in which two parties swap other of offers and acceptances. In contracts termed 'unilateral', the person making the offer waives the requirement that notification of acceptance be communicated to them. Instead, they can simply require that the contract can be accepted by any person who hears about the offer has doing something in a prescribed way. This means that acceptance can take place without the person making the offer even being aware that a contract has been formed. This may sound illogical but it is important to remember that the requirement of notification of acceptance is there to protect the person making the offer. It is for them to choose whether they wish to waive this right. An example of a contract formed in this way is a poster advertising that there will be a reward of £500 for anyone who returns a missing car to its owner at a specified address. The offer is accepted when a person performs the act of returning the car. A failure to provide the reward to someone who had done all that was requested of them would constitute a breach of contract.

In considering cases involving unilateral offers, the courts have been keen to stress that the offer must be sufficiently certain and much consideration has been given to the issue of what constitutes a valid offer. As a result, these cases are of significance to cases involving both unilateral and bilateral contracts. In the much cited *Carlill* case, the Carbolic Smoke Ball Company produced a medical preparation called the Carbolic Smoke Ball. They inserted an advertisement in the *Pall Mall Gazette* in which they offered to pay £100 to anyone who caught influenza after having used the Smoke Ball in a specified manner and for a specified period of time. They also stated that they had deposited £1,000 with the Alliance Bank as a sign of their good faith in making these payments should anyone fall ill. On the strength of the advertisement, Mrs Carlill bought a smoke ball from a chemist, used it as prescribed, but nevertheless caught influenza. It was held that there was a contract between the parties and that the claimant could recover £100.

Much discussion in the case centred on the specificity of the wording of the advertisement. Bowen LJ stated that the advertisement in question 'was intended to be understood by the public as an offer to be acted upon' and Lindley LJ said: 'Read this how you will … here is a distinct promise, expressed in language which is perfectly unmistakeable, that £100 will be paid by the Carbolic Smoke Ball Co to any person who contracts influenza after having used the ball three times daily, and so on'. In finding that the company's advertisement was to be construed as an offer, the court rejected the claim that it was 'a mere puff' or a vague and non-actionable invitation to treat. The offer therefore constituted an express promise to pay £100 to any party who fulfilled its terms. When Mrs Carlill used the smoke ball as prescribed, she should be regarded as accepting the company's offer. The fact that communication of acceptance was not required was inferred from the wording of the offer and the nature of the transaction. The offer was seen as a serious one, showing an intention to create legal relations and therefore imposing a legally enforceable obligation on the company. Many commentators view the case as one which challenges the traditional conceptualisation of offer but it is clear that policy issues also underlie the court's ruling, decided as it was in an age of 'quack' medical preparations produced by rogues who did not deserve to succeed in the courts.

COUNTER OFFERS

The point has already been made that, in trying to determine whether agreement has been reached, the judiciary place considerable emphasis on certainty and completeness. They look for a firm offer and a firm acceptance of that particular offer. In other words, acceptance is expected to correspond *exactly* to the terms of the offer, like a mirror image. The search for agreement is often complicated by the fact that, in the run up to the 'moment of responsibility', negotiating parties will often become involved in drawn out discussions and exchanges in which each makes requests for further information or clarification. This is made clear in Box 6.1 in which an email exchange between Hannie and Josie relating to the sale of some concert tickets is reproduced.

When trying to detremine whether and when a contract between Josie and Hannie has taken place, it is important to make clear that, if a response to an offer differs from the offeror's terms, it is not taken as being an acceptance. Instead it is labelled a counter offer. These types of offer are viewed as rejections of the original offer and bring them to an end. This means that negotiators can not be selective about the parts of an offer they

> **Box 6.1: Josie and Hannie's negotiations**
>
> **Email 1:** Hi Josie, Just writing to find out whether you are still trying to get rid of those four tickets for the The Klaxons concert next week. Hannie
>
> **Email 2:** Dear Hannie, Yes I am but need a quick deal. I have two left for the Sunday performance at 9pm. I would like to get about £30 for them. Josie
>
> **Email 3:** Hi Josie, Great! Consider it done. Is that £30 per ticket or in total? I am happy to pay £30 per ticket for the chance to see them. The tickets sold out within half an hour of going on sale. Hannie
>
> **Email 4:** Dear Hannie, £30 cash per ticket. I am off to a festival on tomorrow so you would need to drop by and pick them up before then. Please email back immediately. Josie
>
> **Email 5:** Hi Josie, No problem. I will come round now. We don't have any cash on us – will you take a cheque? Hannie
>
> **Email 6:** Dear Hannie, Sorry I don't want a cheque. I have an unauthorised overdraft and the Bank will take the money to pay it off. Any chance you could stop off at a cash point on the way round? I will be in until 9pm.
>
> **Email 7:** Hi Josie. Will do. See you about 8pm. Hannie

choose to accept. Moreover, once an effective acceptance has come about, the person who made the offer can no longer withdraw it because the acceptance binds them to what they have offered and turns the terms of the offer into the terms of a contract. It follows that acceptance does not take place when the person to whom the offer is made rejects the offer, accepts it subject to certain qualifications or claims to be accepting an offer which is different from the one made.

These points are well illustrated in the case of *Hyde v Wrench* (1840) in which Wrench offered to sell his farm to Hyde for £1,000. Hyde said in reply that he would give £950 for it. Wrench turned down this proposal. Later Hyde wrote that he was prepared to pay £1,000 after all. This communication was ignored and Hyde sued to enforce an alleged sale at £1,000. It was held that no contract existed. Hyde had rejected Wrench's original offer by his counter offer of £950 and he was unable to revive it by changing his mind and tendering a purported acceptance. The latter was considered to be nothing more than a new offer which Wrench was entitled to refuse.

The rigid application of this rule can cause difficulties where the intention of the offeree is clear but they introduce an additional element to the negotiations which has the effect of nullifying their 'acceptance'. In *Northland Airliners Ltd v Dennis Ferranti Meters Ltd* (1970), the sellers, a company in North Wales, negotiated with the buyers, a Canadian company, for the sale of an amphibian aircraft. The sellers sent the following telegram: 'Confirming sale to you Grummond Mallard aircraft .... Please remit £5,000'. The buyers replied: 'This is to confirm your cable and my purchase Grummond Mallard aircraft terms set out your cable ... £5,000 sterling forwarded your bank to be held in trust for your account pending delivery .... Please confirm delivery to be made thirty days within this date'. The sellers did not reply but sold the aircraft to a third party at a higher price. The Court of Appeal held that there was no contract between the claimant and defendant. The buyers' reply introduced two new terms, one as to payment and the other as to delivery, and the sellers were not bound to reply to this counter offer. Applying this analysis to the email exchange between Josie and Hannie, one reading would be that a sufficiently clear offer does not appear to emerge until email 4, email 5 constitutes a counter offer, email 6 a reiteration of the original offer and email 7 an acceptance on the exact terms offered.

However, case law suggests that an inquiry as to *whether* the offeror might modify his terms does not necessarily amount to a counter offer. In *Stevenson, Jacques & Co v McLean* (1880), it was held that Stevenson could still accept McLean's offer of a certain quantity of iron 'at 40s nett *cash* per ton', even though he had telegraphed to McLean requesting details of possible credit terms. Bearing in mind that, as was known, Stevenson was buying for resale in an unsettled market, his words were 'nothing specific by way of [counter] offer or rejection, but a mere inquiry which should have been answered'. The case makes clear that the dividing line between a request for additional information and a counter offer is a fine one. Viewed in this way, email 5 in the exchange between Josie and Hannie could be construed as a mere request for additional information rather than a counter offer.

COMMUNICATION OF THE ACCEPTANCE

The general 'rule' is that acceptance does not create a contract until it is communicated to the person making the offer. Mental acceptance or mere acquiescence, without more, is not sufficient. This is the case even where the person making the offer waives the need for communication by indicating that acceptance by silence will suffice;

see *Felthouse v Bindley* (1862). The requirement is that the person accepting the offer must say or do something which indicates to the person making the offer that they accept the terms. It follows that the courts have not been prepared to find acceptance of an offer where there have been faults in the method of communication, which mean that a message has not been received. Examples might include instances when a mobile phone line goes dead and acceptance is not communicated, an acceptance is not heard because of background music in a club or in cases where the fax machine of the person trying to accept the offer breaks down and fails to deliver a message. In each of these situations the application of the general rule would require the courts to find that no contract had been formed.

There are several explanations for this general rule. First, the requirement reflects the fact that the law expects both parties to be clear about the agreement they are entering into before it imposes legal obligations on them. The courts have also been concerned that the parties should know the exact moment that an offer has been accepted. If acceptance was able to occur without the person making the offer being told, then only one party would know that legal obligations had been created. Being clear about the exact moment when they are bound to each other also allows each of the parties to enter into further deals with others on the strength of the first. So, for instance, in the example of Josie and Hannie given above, Josie might agree to buy some CDs from a friend on the basis that Hannie will be honouring her contract for the sale of the concert tickets later that day. Finally, on an evidential note, it could be extremely difficult to prove acceptance if the person accepting the contract was under no obligation to communicate it.

An established exception to the general rule that the offeror must receive notification of an acceptance developed in the guise of the 'postal rule' and has troubled generations of law students. The exception emerged in an era in which the post was a very popular and relatively fast form of communication, but the principal established continues to have some relevance today. The postal rules allows that, where the person accepting the offer sends their acceptance by post, the offer is regarded as accepted as soon as the letter of acceptance is put in a postbox rather than when it is received. The authority for this proposition comes from the judgment in *Adams v Lindsell* (1818). The rule shifts the burden of risk from the person accepting the offer to the person who made the offer, because the latter is bound by a contract before they are aware of the fact of its existence. In considering the rule, it is important to stress that it can easily be avoided. It is always open to the person making the offer to specify how an offer should be accepted, as Josie does in email 4 in the Box 6.1. In coming to their judgment, the court in *Adams* appears to have decided that a person making an offer who is prepared to accept the risks inherent in using the postal system should also bear the risk of an acceptance getting lost or there being a delay. It would seem that the person making an offer would be well advised to *exclude* the postal rule by the terms of their offer and insist that they will only be bound on actual receipt of a posted acceptance. In affirming the rule in *Adams*, Bramwell LJ in the Court of Appeal in *Household Fire Insurance Co v Grant* (1879), advised that the prudent offeror should stipulate that: 'Your answer by post is only to bind if it reaches me'.

More recently, in *Holwell Securities Ltd v Hughes* (1974), an offer to sell a house was made in the form of an option stated 'to be exercisable by *notice* in writing to the Intending Vendor at any time within six months hereof …'. Such a notice, properly addressed, was posted within the time limit allowed but was never delivered. It was held that there was no contract as the terms of the option, on their true construction, required acceptance to be actually communicated. In their judgments, Lord Justices Russell and Lawton placed emphasis on the definition of 'notice' as a means of making something known, and if not known, then it follows that it can not constitute notice. The court went so far as to suppose that there *was no single or universal rule* determining the effect of a posted acceptance, and that the postal rule 'probably does not operate if its application would produce manifest inconvenience and absurdity'. It would seem then that the question is one of interpretation on a particular set of facts, practical considerations and convenience rather than deductions from a general rule.

ELECTRONIC COMMUNICATION

It is clear from the discussion above that for many years the courts were troubled with relatively simple communication problems involving instantaneous oral negotiations or more time-consuming postal communications. As the number of large-scale corporations participating in global markets has increased and the means of communication become ever more speedy, new questions about the point at which a contract has formed have arisen. Since the founding principles relating to receipt of acceptance were discussed in the nineteenth century, new methods of communicating, such as telex, fax, email and other web-based exchanges, have come into being. Unfortunately, the case law in this area lags seriously behind technological developments. Nonetheless, we are able to gain insight into the principles that govern such exchanges in a set of cases decided in the later part of the last century.

In *Entores Ltd v Miles Far East Corporation* (1955), the Court of Appeal was asked to consider the impact of new technologies on formation of contracts. Rather than following the postal rule, they argued that, where such communications were instantaneous acceptance took place when it was received rather than where it was sent. The exception highlighted by Lord Denning was where the person making the offer did not receive the message through no fault of their own. The problems of delayed receipt when using electronic transactions was considered by the Court of Appeal in *The Brimnes* (1975). It was held that communication by telex was effective when it appeared on the recipient's machine, even though the message was not read until the next working day. This was because it had been received during office hours and it was reasonable for the person sending the acceptance to assume that someone would look at it during that time.

However, in the case of *Brinkibon Ltd v Stahag Stahl* (1983), the House of Lords gave a qualified endorsement of *Entores*, warning that its 'rule' could not be applied universally in view of the many variants in the use of telex. The court argued that, although telex was an instantaneous form of communication, receipt was not always instantaneous. For example, a message could be sent out of office hours with the intention that it would be read at a later time or there could be some undiscovered fault with a machine. Rather than impose a fixed rule, the court opined that the position should be resolved by reference to the parties' intentions, sound business practice and by a judgment as to where the risk should lie. It would seem from this that the communication should take effect at the time when the acceptor could reasonably have expected it to be read. By analogy electronic mail, sent to an electronic 'postbox' that will only be checked once or twice a day, could be said to have been 'communicated' once the normal time for checking has passed. A similar approach might need to be used in relation to messages left on a telephone answering system in that they should only be regarded as having been communicated once a reasonable time for the offeror to have heard it the message has elapsed.

If this line is taken, it is clearly to the advantage of the person making the acceptance because it allows an acceptance to be treated as effective when the person who made the offer remains unaware of it because of their failure to check incoming messages within a reasonable time. These problems sit rather uncomfortably with traditional approaches to the identification of agreement. Rather, they provide an example of Collins, 2003 claim that what the courts are often concerned with, and should be concerned with, is not the mechanics of offer and acceptance but a consideration of the point at which it is reasonable for the parties to assume a contract has come into being.

Communicating by email

There is some debate as to whether the established rules governing instantaneous and postal communications are adequate for modern-day use. In particular, there has been some disagreement between scholars as to whether existing categories cover communications by email. As these now outnumber paper communications and are the preferred way for many in business to communicate with clients, the point is worth serious consideration. One of the problems posed by emails is whether receipt occurs when the email is downloaded onto a server, when it appears on the recipient's computer or when the email is actually read by the recipient. Another new issue which arises in this context is that an email address may consist of a name or number followed by the name of the service provider, but not indicate the physical location of the sender or the recipient. This leaves open the associated difficulty of *where* the acceptance becomes binding.

Some have argued that the postal rule should apply to acceptances made by email, as technically they are not transmitted 'instantaneously' and differ from other forms of communication discussed above in that the information is broken down and sent in 'packets' through different routes. On the other hand, emails often go astray. This means that the sender cannot be sure that their message has been transmitted successfully and this renders it unreasonable for them to rely on the communication having been received. Even if the sender asks for a delivery receipt, that receipt simply confirms that the message has been delivered to a mailbox, but not to the offeror. But it has been argued that an email with a delivery receipt is more like recorded delivery post than an instantaneous communication. As a result it could be argued that it should properly be subject to the postal rule.

Others have suggested that the usual receipt rule should apply because the sender is ultimately in a position to know if the email has or has not been sent. It follows from the reasoning in *The Brimnes* that, viewed in this way, the acceptance should become binding when it reaches the offeror's business premises or the place of their internet service provider during normal office hours. Article 11 of the E-Commerce Directive provides some guidance in respect of non-business-to-business contracting by requiring that electronic orders and acknowledgements will be taken to be received when the addressee can access them. This would seem to suggest that the downloading of the message from the server would constitute receipt. However, the directive does not clearly explain the legal position of electronic offer and acceptance, or even define when a contract is concluded. The result is that the law remains uncertain.

Click-wrap contracts

More recently, still new dilemmas about the formation of contract have been posed by the expansion of e-commerce. People have been making contracts through the agency of machines for some time. Every time you put your car through an automatic car wash, you make a contract through the medium of a machine. But using machines takes on new characteristics where the web is concerned. Since the web now hosts the fastest growing marketplace in the world, it is a pressing issue for contract lawyers to ensure that doctrine develops to support such exchanges. For a start, the web allows the making of more specific and customised contracts than is possible with a fizzy drinks machine. It allows you to place an order for a particular book from a host of different agents, with the option of gift wrapping and different methods of delivery. The web also allows people to make contracts across jurisdictions and continents with more ease than was previously possible.

To date, most commentators have attempted to apply traditional reasoning to web-based contracts by looking for invitations to treat offers and acceptances in the same way as lawyers have done for decades. Analogies with exchanges in a real marketplace are often facilitated by the design of websites. Many allow you to 'browse' through their products in the same way you might in a shop, provide you with a 'virtual shopping basket' and, once browsing is complete, instruct you to proceed to a 'virtual checkout'. These 'click-wrap' contracts are negotiated by the seller displaying their terms and conditions, and the buyer clicking on buttons to evidence their satisfaction with the choices made. Goods displayed on the virtual shelves of a website can by analogy be treated as an invitation to treat in the same way as the goods on the shelves in the *Boots* case. Once the purchase indicates what they are interested in buying, the supplier's programme checks the availability of the item. If it is in stock, the purchasers make offers by entering their credit card details and clicking on a button to confirm their choices.

However, while we tend to think of the web as akin to an instantaneous form of communication, it is not akin to the average transaction in a high-street store. This new technology actually gives consumers more time to ponder the terms and conditions prescribed by the seller in the comfort of their own home or office. It also allows closer inspection of detailed terms and conditions than is usually feasible. Many websites do not allow a buyer to proceed to the stage where they can order a product or service unless the purchaser indicates that they have pulled up, looked at and understood the company's terms of business. Some also allow the buyer to proceed along the 'negotiation' process in a number of clear-cut stages in which they are given several opportunities to reconsider their position and choices. Concern that these characteristics render the transaction somewhat different from those cases discussed so far is reflected in the fact that there are a growing number of regulations that focus specifically on electronic contracts.

It has been argued that these transactions are more akin to instantaneous telephone conversations, as it will be immediately obvious to one of the parties if the other becomes disconnected. Accordingly, the sender of a message in a click-wrap contract is in a position to know whether the message has been transmitted successfully almost as soon as it has been sent. This would seem to make the receipt rule more relevant than the postal rule. The Consumer Protection (Distance Selling) Regulations 2000 provide some protection for the consumer by requiring that certain information be provided before the contract is concluded. This includes the identity of the supplier, the price, arrangements for the delivery and supply of goods or services, and information on cancellation rights. This information must be provided to the consumer in another durable medium, which is 'available and accessible' prior to delivery.

CONCLUDING REMARKS

In this chapter we have looked at some of the key concepts underpinning the courts treatment of offer and acceptance. It can be seen from the various cases surveyed that it is far from an easy task to determine when and where a contract has been formed. Recent cases on new forms of communication create new challenges to doctrines which were developed with very different market places in mind. In the chapter that follows, we will turn to look at another set of problems which question the concepts underpinning doctrine and their relevance to the business community.

REFERENCES AND FURTHER READING

Collins, H (2003) *The Law of Contract*, 4th edn, London: LexisNexis Butterworths.
Dickie, J 'When and where are electronic contracts concluded?' (1998) 99 (3) *Northern Ireland Legal Quarterly* 332.
Gardner, S 'Trashing with Trollope: a deconstruction of the postal rules' (1992) 12 *Oxford Journal of Legal Studies* 170.
Murray, A (2000) 'Entering into contracts electronically: the real W.W.W.' in Edwards, L and Waelde, C (eds) *Law and the Internet: A Framework for Electronic Commerce*, 2nd edn, Hart, Oxford.
Simpson, A 'Quackery and contract law: the case of the Carbolic Smoke Ball' (1985) 14 *Journal of Legal Studies* 345.

?   *QUESTIONS*

(1) Do you think that Angie and Georgie's customers should be able to hold them to all the promises made in their Charter of Standards? Give reasons for your answers.

(2) Kilkenny Fares is an airline company and places the following advertisement in a national newspaper: 'Rock bottom prices. Flights from Liverpool to Chicago for £100 return plus taxes. Enough for everyone!' On the morning the advertisement appears Martha-Marie immediately phones the booking line to be told that there are no flights at that price left.

Continued

? *QUESTIONS (Continued)*

Do you think she should be able to take her case to court and demand a ticket at the price advertised? What arguments do you think she could make in her claim? What arguments can you think of which could be used by Kilkenny Fares to refute her claim? Draw up detailed arguments and cite legal authorities to support your argument.

CHAPTER 7

THE MOMENT OF RESPONSIBILITY: LAW AND PRACTICE

INTRODUCTION

In the last chapter, it became evident that the exact moment an offer and an acceptance occur is not always clear, as the parties often proceed slowly towards contractual responsibility. In this chapter we move on to look at the problems caused when negotiating and contracting parties do not behave in the ways that the courts expect them to. It is clear from a range of empirical studies of the use of contract law within the business community that rather than being the exception, non-compliance with the law of contract is the norm. In this chapter, I draw attention to a series of circumstances in which the expectations of the business community and the expectations of lawyers are clearly in opposition. These include problems relating to the 'battle of the forms' lack of certainty, tenders, reasonable reliance and legitimate expectation; and performance during the course of the contract. It could be argued that these various case studies are more than just discrete problems at the margins of the modern development of the law of contract. Rather, they could be seen as central to suggestions that the neo-classical model of contract is lacking in legitimacy amongst the business community. One of the difficulties facing the judiciary is whether it should prescribe what the parties need to do in order for a contract to be enforceable or merely enforce what seems to be standard business practice.

THE BATTLE OF THE FORMS

In their influential study of contracts between businessmen in the engineering industry, Beale and Dugdale (1975) found that the majority of firms used standard forms when negotiating contracts. These tended to have the primary obligations such as price, item, delivery date and terms of payment typed on the front and a number of standard conditions relating to contingencies on the back. Where two businesses were roughly equal in terms of their bargaining power, each party attempted to get its 'back of order' conditions accepted by the other party. The result was a battle as to whose terms and conditions take priority. This provides us with an excellent example of how practice in the business sector differs from the judicial expectations of pre-contractual negotiations. The result in many cases is that no contract exists. Whilst the parties may appear to have agreed, in reality they are 'separated' by the express wording of the documents they exchange.

The facts of *Butler Machine Tool Co Ltd v Ex-Cell-O Corporation Ltd* (1979) illustrate how communications can give rise to such a battle. This was a case in which the Court of Appeal rather unconvincingly used the rules relating to counter offer (see Chapter 6) to solve a complex practical problem. The facts are illustrated in pictorial form in Figure 7.1. In this case, the quotation and acknowledgment prepared by the sellers referred to one set of conditions and the order to another prepared by the buyers. Each contained terms which differed significantly from the other. On whose terms, if anyone's, was the contract made? The court held that the seller's quotation

Figure 7.1:   The battle of the forms

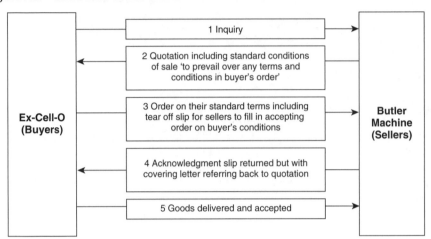

(2) was an offer, the buyer's order (3) a counter offer, and the seller's return of the acknowledgement slip (4) an acceptance of the buyer's counter offer. The contract was therefore made on the buyer's terms. The significance of this finding was that, although the price quoted by Butler was £75,500, their terms contained a 'price-escalation' clause under which Ex-Cell-O was required to pay at prices at the date of *delivery*. The buyer's terms contained no such clause. When Butler tried to invoke the clause, claiming a further £3,000, a dispute arose, resulting in Butler's eventual failure in the Court of Appeal.

It has been argued that, by ignoring the seller's covering letter (4), the Court's rationale is unconvincing. It seems clear that the sellers did intend to re-import their terms and conditions into the bargain. If the letter had been taken to be another counter offer, it could be said that, when the buyers took delivery (5), it constituted acceptance of it by conduct. The result of this alternative analysis would be that the seller's, rather than the buyer's terms would have prevailed. The possibilities are numerous, but what is clear is that there was no agreement of the kind anticipated in classical doctrine. Possibly there was no agreement at all.

The case reveals the limitations of an overly formal approach to contract formation and the difficulties that such an approach has in coming to terms with everyday business practices which do not fall neatly into the classical paradigm. The parties clearly wanted and intended to enter into a commercial relationship with each other, but the notion that they were fully attuned to every detail of their legal commitment is clearly a falsehood. Rather than solving the problem of the battle of the forms, the case could be said to create an additional one by encouraging people in similar situations to keep on sending their own standard forms with each communication in the hope that they would send the 'last shot'. Whilst the majority in the Court of Appeal were persuaded that the transaction could be analysed according to the rules of offer and acceptance, the case provided Lord Denning with another opportunity to argue that traditional analysis of such situations was overly formulaic and out of date. Convinced that the parties had concluded a contract, he argued, in line with his reasoning in *Gibson*, for a more holistic approach to contract formation in which the court played a proactive role in determining the contents of the deal. Where there are differences in the standard conditions of each party that are irreconcilable, then he suggested that the conflicting terms should be scrapped and replaced by a reasonable implication.

The 'hit or miss' nature of the traditional approach to contract formation is borne out in subsequent cases. In *British Road Services v Arthur Crutchley Ltd* (1968), British Road Services (BRS) delivered a large consignment of whisky to Crutchley's warehouse. The driver handed Crutchley a delivery note which incorporated BRS conditions of carriage. The note was stamped by Crutchley, 'Received under Crutchley's conditions'. The court held that this amounted to a counter offer, which BRS accepted when handing over the whisky. The contract was therefore concluded on Crutchley's terms.

It is clear that some of the reasoning in leading cases is different to reconcile. In *Cie de Commerce et Commission SARL v Parkinson Stove Co Ltd* (1953), Parkinson sent an order to Cie for a quantity of steel sheets on a printed form containing the following provision reproduced in Box 7.1. Cie omitted to sign and return the acknowledgement slip attached to the form, but on receipt of the order replied to Parkinson: 'We acknowledge receipt of ... your order No. K. 4851 dated March 5, which we received today

> **Box 7.1: Cie de Commerce**
>
> 'This order constitutes an offer on the part of Parkinson on the terms and conditions and at the prices stated herein and to constitute a binding contract on Parkinson, said offer must be accepted by execution of the acknowledgement in the form attached by Cie, it being expressly understood that no other form of acceptance, verbal or written, will be valid or binding on Parkinson.'

and for which we thank you'. Subsequent correspondence left no doubt that the parties regarded themselves as bound, but when Parkinson cancelled the order and Cie sued for breach, Parkinson claimed that there was no concluded contract because of Cie's failure to return the acknowledgement slip. In the alternative, they argued that Cie's letter of acknowledgement could not be construed as a sufficient acceptance of Parkinson's offer. Neither argument found favour at first instance, but the Court of Appeal held that there was no concluded contract and, accordingly, that Cie were not entitled to damages. It was felt that Cie's letter of acknowledgement, which did not strictly adhere to the terms of the offer, did not amount to an acceptance of the order. However, it has been noted that it is difficult to envisage how they could have more clearly indicated their acceptance of the order, short of returning the acknowledgement slip itself.

The eventual decision is scarcely an illustration of what Pilcher J, in the court of first instance, referred to as the tendency of the courts 'always [to] lean towards giving legal effect to documents which the parties themselves regard as constituting a binding contract in law'.

PERFORMANCE DURING FORMATION OF THE CONTRACT

Similar sorts of dilemmas arise in cases where the parties start to do what they have undertaken to do before a contract has been formed. The general rule is that, once performance starts, then a contract should be recognised. The problem is in determining the terms on which an agreement has been reached. It is important to stress from the start that it is far from uncommon practice for the parties to start performance early. Indeed, this often makes good business sense. Pressures of time, the need to meet targets, efficient use of labour and fear of market fluctuations all mean that this could be seen as sound commercial practice rather than lack of patience. Moreover, empirical studies of business practice suggest that a number of informal practices often exist within industries to protect those who start to perform without the safety net of a valid contract. These include loss of respect and a diminishing of trust in those who 'welsh' on a deal. Despite this, the problem remains a live issue for the judiciary. On the one hand, they are eager for the law to reflect efficient commercial practices, on the other, a number clearly feel constrained by the expectation that they should look for a particular sequence of events which anticipates that formation of the contract will be complete before performance begins.

Difficulties over performance prior to completion of negotiations occur in a number of settings, but debate around 'letters of intent' provides a good example of a practice which has caused problems for neo-classical models of analysis. A letter of intent, sometimes called 'an instruction to proceed', states that the sender *intends* to enter into a contract with the addressee. This is a common device in the construction industry where business people regularly rely on such letters. On their true interpretation, letters of intent probably create no contractual obligation which would be recognised in English law. But where they include an instruction to proceed with performance and *such performance has begun*, the courts have been prepared to allow that, when the contract is eventually agreed, it will have retrospective effect.

This practice was extensively discussed in the case of *Trollope and Colls Ltd v Atomic Power Construction Ltd* (1962). The facts were that in February 1959 Atomic Power received a tender for civil engineering work in the construction of a nuclear power station from Trollope and Colls. The tender was for a lump-sum price and incorporated conditions authorising variations in the form, quality or quantity of work. It provided that such variations were to be taken into account in ascertaining the contract price. The tender further incorporated a fluctuation clause relating to labour and material costs. Considerable changes were made after the date of tender, necessitating amendment of drawings, specification and quantities. Trollope and Colls were notified of these changes and in June 1959 they were asked to start work by a 'letter of intent' from Atomic Power which stated: 'We have to inform you that it is our intention to enter into a contract with you for [the works]. As soon as matters outstanding between us are settled we will enter into a contract agreement with you, and in the meantime please accept this letter as an instruction to proceed with the work necessary to permit you to meet the agreed programme'. Work began and on 11 April 1960, by which time all outstanding matters had been agreed but no contract had been signed, a dispute arose over the basis on which Trollope and Colls should be paid for the work they undertook before 11 April.

Trollope and Colls contended that they should be paid on a *quantum meruit* basis for the work carried out before that date. *Quantum meruit* is a quasi-contractual remedy which allows payment to be made for the value of the work done where there is no formal contract. Atomic Power argued that the tender as adjusted outlined how payment should be assessed. It was held that the parties having acted in the course of negotiations on the understanding that, if and when a contract were made, it would govern what was being done meanwhile, the contract which came into existence on

11 April 1960 governed the rights of the parties as to *prior* work. This approach was said to be justified on either of two grounds. First, a stipulation necessary for the business efficacy of the contract, that the variations clauses should apply retrospectively could be implied. Second, that the tender constituted an offer that contemplated variation of the work. Acceptance of that offer was taken to be an acceptance of the offer which embraced the changes requested and that these had been agreed in anticipation of the ultimate acceptance. Megaw J concluded that there is 'no principle of English law which provides that a contract cannot in any circumstances have retrospective effect'.

A similar situation arose in the case of *Trentham Ltd v Archital Luxfer Ltd* (1993) but, in this dispute, complete performance took place before a contract had been formed. Here, Trentham were engaged by a client to design and build industrial units. Trentham entered into negotiations with Archital Luxfer to supply and install aluminium windows. This work was completed and paid for, but Trentham sued Archital Luxor for alleged defects in the windows, after they were sued by their client for delays and defects. Archital denied the existence of any contract. Whilst no written contract had come into existence, Trentham claimed that a binding contract was nevertheless formed on the basis of written exchanges, oral discussions and the performance of the transaction by both parties.

According to Steyn's leading judgment in the Court of Appeal, this was a contract which could not 'be precisely analysed in terms of offer and acceptance'. He based this decision on the following points. First, he argued that English law adopts an *objective* approach to contract formation in which 'the governing criterion is in the reasonable expectations of [in this case] ... sensible business people'. Relying on *Gibson*, he further argued that, although the coincidence of offer and acceptance is the normal mechanism of contract formation, 'it is not necessarily so in the case of a contract alleged to have come into existence during and as a result of performance'. Following the line of reasoning in *Trollope*, he suggested that, if a contract only comes into existence during and as a result of performance of the transaction, it will frequently be possible to hold that the contract impliedly and retrospectively covers pre-contractual performance.

The ability of the neo-classical model to provide a remedy in such cases has been challenged even further in a set of cases in which performance occurred but negotiations did *not* result in a contract. The fact that a contract has not been finalised clearly hampers the court in applying contractual remedies. However, the courts have shown themselves willing to entertain restitutionary or 'quasi-contract' claims based on the notion of unjust enrichment in these situations. The idea is that natural justice and equity require those who have received a benefit to pay for the value of the work on the *quantum meruit* basis discussed above; see *Peter Lind & Co Ltd v Mersey Docks and Harbour Board* (1972).

This solution to the absence of a contract and contractual remedies arose in *British Steel Corporation v Cleveland Bridge and Engineering Co Ltd* (1984). In that case, Cleveland entered into negotiations with British Steel for the supply of a number of steel nodes and issued a letter of intent to British Steel requesting them to start work pending the preparation and issuing of the official form of sub-contract. British Steel declined to contract on Cleveland's terms as they had their own standard forms of contract and were concerned about the question of liability for loss caused by late delivery. Complicated negotiations continued but no agreement was reached. All of the nodes were eventually delivered late but none of them were paid for. British Steel sued for the reasonable value of the nodes on a *quantum meruit* basis because no contract had been concluded. It was held by Robert Goff J that the parties had not reached agreement and no contractual relationship had come into existence. Thus the letter of intent could not be used to identify terms as to payment and performance. British Steel recovered £230,000 on its *quantum meruit* claim but Cleveland's counterclaim for £870,000 failed, there being no binding terms regarding delivery or payments for late delivery for the claim to be measured against. The remedy offered in this case could be seen to cause problems for the integrity of contractual doctrine since it undermines the purpose of making certain contracts unenforceable. It would seem that responding to business reality can create a dangerous 'no man's land' between practice and the conventional view of contract formation.

CERTAINTY

Even when a valid contract has come about as a result of compliance with the rules discussed above, an agreement may fail to be enforced by the courts because of its vagueness or incompleteness. This raises related concerns to those considered in preceding sections about the extent to which standard business practice is and should be reflected in the development of doctrine. Once again, it is important to stress that it may be quite sensible in a commercial context for the parties to be flexible about certain terms. So, for instance, in a long-term contract the parties will not want to set a fixed price for goods supplied on a

---

Box 7.2: Sale of Goods Act 1979

Section 8

(1) The price in a contract of sale may be fixed by the contract, or may be left to be fixed in a manner agreed by the contract, or may be determined in the course of dealing between the parties.

(2) Where the price is not agreed as mentioned in subsection (1) above the buyer must pay a reasonable price.

(3) What is a reasonable price is a question of fact dependent on the circumstances of each particular case.

---

regular basis as there may be considerable fluctuation in market conditions. A price which seems reasonable and fair in 2008 will not necessarily be so in 2018. A contract which does not specify price or standards is not necessarily vague or incomplete, as there may be clear indications of what constitutes the 'going rate' and acceptable policy within particular industries. The courts and legislature have not been immune to such needs. The Sale of Goods Act 1979 currently makes provision for a price to be agreed after the contract has been formed (see Box 7.2). Even so, problems have arisen where the parties are not silent on the matter of price but vague. The issue of uncertainty and incompleteness goes to the heart of some of the criticisms which have been directed at the classical contract model. It will be remembered from Chapter 4 that, in his call for a different set of principles to underpin the modern law of contract, Ian MacNeil has placed considerable emphasis on the need for flexibility rather than certainty.

The issue of vagueness or incompleteness arose in the case of *Hillas & Co Ltd v Arcos Ltd* (1932) in which the court was prepared to temper over-reliance on formality in order to place an agreement into its business context. The facts of the case were that Arcos (sellers) and Hillas (buyers) entered into and performed a contract for the supply of Russian timber for the year 1930. Hillas took up an option for Arcos to supply further timber 'of fair specification' for delivery during 1931. But Arcos was unable to supply this timber because they had sold it to a third party. When sued for breach, they argued that the 1931 agreement was void for uncertainty. The House of Lords disagreed. They argued that, on the basis of an analysis of the Russian timber trade in which both of the parties were involved, a detailed analysis of the concluded 1930 contract and expert evidence on the nature of that trade, the words 'of fair specification' *could* be construed with sufficient precision to establish a binding agreement between the parties for 1931 supplies. In his consideration of the relevant principles to apply to the case, Lord Wright reflected on how the tension between the need for certainty in the law and flexibility in the business community could be accommodated. He argued that:

> Business men often record the most important agreements in crude and summary fashion; modes of expression sufficient and clear to them in the course of their business may appear to those unfamiliar with the business far from complete or precise. It is accordingly the duty of the court to construe such documents fairly and broadly, without being too astute or subtle in finding defects; but [that] does not mean that the court is to make a contract for the parties, or to go outside the words they have used, except in so far as there are appropriate implications of law, as for instance, the implication of what is just and reasonable to be ascertained by the court as a matter of machinery where the contractual intention is clear, but the contract is silent on some detail. Thus in contracts for future performance over a period, the parties may neither be able nor desire to specify many matters of detail, but leave them to be adjusted in the working out of the contract …. As obvious illustrations I may refer to such matters as prices or times of delivery in contracts for the sale of goods. (p. 367)

Where the dividing line between certainty and uncertainty, enforceability and unenforceability is drawn may well depend therefore on the court's willingness to accommodate business practice. Decided cases demonstrate some difference in approach between different members of the judiciary. A conservative court would no doubt reject the argument that the judiciary should strive to settle an important matter that the parties had chosen to leave unsettled in their original agreement. Their approach would be to insist that a good contract must be a concluded bargain which settles everything that needs to be settled and leaves nothing to be determined by *further* agreement. This was the line adopted in *May and Butcher Ltd v The King* (1934). In this case the parties entered into a contract under which the Government's Disposals Board agreed to sell old tentage to May and Butcher over a certain period of time. The contract required that the price was to be 'agreed from time to time' and disputes submitted to arbitration when a disagreement about the price arose. May and Butcher claimed that a reasonable price should be determined by the court or that a price should be fixed under the arbitration clause. But it was the Disposable Board's contention that there was no contract. Their view was upheld by the House of Lords. Although the Sale of Goods Act 1893 provided for a 'reasonable price' to be calculated where the contract was silent on the point, it was held that, in this case, the contract was not silent because there was a vague provision for the parties to agree on price which did not specify a procedure through which a price could be agreed. In Lord Dunedin's view, this failure led inevitably to the conclusion that there was no valid contract. Arbitration was also excluded as a way to resolve the issue since a failure to agree was taken to be different from a dispute.

The Court of Appeal went the other way in *Foley v Classique Coaches Ltd* (1934), a decision which reflects Lord Wright's words in *Hillas*. Here, the contract between the parties provided that Classique Coaches Ltd should buy petrol exclusively from Foley 'at a price to be agreed by the parties from time to time'. There was also an arbitration clause in the contract which the court took to apply to any failure to agree as to price. After three years Classique Coaches Ltd came to the conclusion that they could get cheaper petrol elsewhere and sought to repudiate the contract on the basis that it was incomplete. Foley brought an action, claiming a declaration that the agreement was binding, damages for breach and an injunction restraining Classique from buying petrol other than from them. The court found in Foley's favour, being impressed by the fact that the parties had for three years clearly believed that they had a contract and they had provided machinery for dealing with any failure to agree as to the price. It was held that the petrol should be supplied at a reasonable price.

Similar issues emerged in two cases involving leases. In *King's Motors (Oxford) Ltd v Lax* (1969), it was decided that an option in a lease for a further period of years 'at such rental as may be agreed on between the parties', was, in the absence of an arbitration clause, void for uncertainty. This allowed the landlords to terminate the lease even though the option had been duly exercised. Uncertainties of this kind may prove to be a loophole through which an unwilling party can escape from an agreement. However, in *Sudbrook Trading Estate Ltd v Eggleton* (1983), a lease gave the tenant an option to purchase the premises 'at such price as may be agreed on by two valuers, one to be nominated' by each party. When the landlord refused to appoint a valuer, the House of Lords held that the option in effect provided a formula enabling *a reasonable* price to be fixed. Since the ancillary machinery for determining that price had broken down, the court felt able to substitute its own machinery. It was stressed that, with a partly performed agreement, 'the court would strain to supply the want of certainty'; see also *Didymi Corporation v Atlantic Lines and Navigation Co Inc* (1988).

One of the most interesting certainty issues to have attracted academic commentary over the last decade is that of the incomplete agreements in *Baird Textile Holdings Ltd v Marks and Spencer plc* (2001). Baird had been one of the principal suppliers of garments to Marks and Spencer for 30 years. The Court of Appeal accepted that the commercial relationship between the two parties was close and both parties worked for many years on the assumption that the relationship was a long-term and co-operative one. Baird alleged that the senior executives of the two firms had regular consultations on strategy, sales, design technology and logistics. Baird even appointed managers selected by Marks and Spencer to monitor performance. They worked to seasonable timetables laid down by the high-street store and accepted their standards as to place of production and approval of sub-contractors.

Despite the proximity of the relationship, Marks and Spencer deliberately abstained from concluding any express contract which laid out their respective rights and obligations. This was because they felt they could achieve much greater flexibility by avoiding a contract. When Marks and Spencer terminated the contract without warning, Baird had to lay off 4,000 staff and claimed losses of £54 million. One of the issues before the Court of Appeal was whether a long-term contract requiring substantial notice to be terminated could be *implied* in this case, or whether the relationship amounted to a series of short-term seasonal contracts. It was recognised that, for an agreement to come into existence, there must be both an agreement on essentials with sufficient certainty to be enforceable and an intention to create legal relations. Baird's contention was that there was sufficient certainty about the terms of an implied contract. In particular, they asserted that in exchange for agreeing to:

(a) supply garments year by year on a seasonal basis;

(b) allow Marks and Spencer to be closely involved in the design and manufacture of the garments;

(c) establish and maintain a work force and capacity to meet demand and be responsive;

(d) not act in a way contrary to Marks and Spencer's interest;

(e) deal with Marks and Spencer in good faith;

(f) That the relationship would continue long term, Marks and Spencer would acquire garments at reasonable quantities and prices, and would only terminate after reasonable notice.

Clearly there was a long-term commercial relationship but did this constitute a long-term contractual relationship? The Court of Appeal thought not. Whilst Marks and Spencer's refusal to conclude an express contract was not determinative of the issue, the courts were not prepared to imply a long-term contract on the terms suggested. They reasoned that Marks and Spencer's obligations were insufficiently certain and there were no objective criteria by which the court could assess what was a reasonable quantity or price. In the words of Mance LJ:

> [E]conomic conditions and intentions may all change, and businessmen must be taken to be aware that, without specific contractual protection, their business may suffer in consequence. I do not think that the law should be ready to seek to fetter business relationships, even – and perhaps especially – those as long and close as the present, with its own view of what might represent appropriate business conduct, when the parties have not chosen, or have not been willing or able, to do so in any identifiable legal fashion or terms themselves. (para. 76)

Significantly, reference was made in the case to academic discussion with regard to 'relational contracts' (see Chapter 4) and the legal implications to which they give rise. But the court considered that even in relational contracts the requirement of certainty still applied. Whether or not this is a fair interpretation of the basic tenets of relational contract theory, the facts of this case make clear the extent of the rifts that can occur between doctrine and commercial realities. A number of very important issues are at stake in this case which provides us with a potent reminder that respect for party autonomy remains a fundamental principle underpinning the modern law of contract. As Collins (2003) reminds us, it is not enough to call for greater recognition of how commercial relationships are conducted in practice. We must also understand the political context in which such judgements are made. In his words:

> The normative complexity of legal doctrine invokes a broad-ranging ideological dispute conducted for the most part by an intellectual elite, which responds only indirectly to the changing currents and social forces in society. A better understanding of any transformation in the law of contract would have to analyse how alterations in economic institutions, variations in political theory, new emphases of public policy, and fresh rationalisations of the coherence of legal doctrine all combine to create a new character for the legal regulations of transactions. (p. 200)

COMFORT LETTERS

Similar tensions have arisen in the area of 'comfort letters'. These are representations by one party which reassure the other about their commitment to the contract or ability to carry it out. The purpose of such letters is to increase confidence in pre-contractual negotiations but the question has arisen of whether they carry sufficient intention to be bound to form part of the contract. The cases involving 'comfort letters' suggest that the doctrine may be becoming overly subtle in this area. So, for instance, in *Kleinwort Benson Ltd v Malaysia Mining Corporation* (1989), Malaysia Mining set up a wholly owned subsidiary, Metals Ltd, to trade in tin on the London Metals Exchange. Malaysia Mining also sought a loan of £5 million from Kleinwort Benson, a merchant bank, to supplement Metals' existing capital. Before making the loan, Kleinwort Benson asked Malaysia Mining for a guarantee of their subsidiary's indebtedness to them. A guarantee is a binding promise to pay another's debts if they fail to pay. Malaysia Mining declined to do this but said that the loan would be covered by their 'comfort letter'. Kleinwort Benson replied that this would be 'no problem' but that the rate of interest charged would be slightly higher. Malaysia Mining's comfort letter stated that: 'It is our policy to ensure that the business of Metals Ltd is at all times in a position to meet its liabilities to you'. Malaysia Mining also said they would not reduce their current financial interest in Metals Ltd until the loan had been repaid. In 1985 the world tin market collapsed and Metals Ltd went into liquidation with the loan (now £10 million) unpaid. Kleinwort Benson sued Malaysia Mining for the full amount on the basis of the comfort letter, which they maintained had contractual effect.

The test applied at first instance was whether or not there was an intention to create legal relations. However, on appeal, the Court of Appeal held that the correct test to determine the status of a comfort letter was to ask whether a promise was being made. It was argued that the letter amounted to a policy statement only and did not form the basis of a contract. Ralph Gibson LJ considered that a 'true' construction of the relevant parts of the comfort letter made clear that Malaysia Mining were accepting 'a moral responsibility only' to pay its subsidiary's debts. His reasoning implies that appropriate wording could establish a promissory obligation which would appear to make the comfort letter a guarantee or the equivalent. The facts of this case do not sit easily with the presumption that business agreements are binding and raises interesting questions about the significance of reliance on the promise. If the Court of Appeal had 'found' a promise to pay, as the court of first instance did, it would at least have avoided criticism to the effect that its decision was commercially unrealistic. As Brown has commented:

> There should be no room in the proper flow of commerce for some purgatory where statements made by business people, after hard bargaining and made to induce another business person to enter into a business transaction would, without any express statement to that effect, reside in a twilight zone of merely honourable engagement. The whole thrust of the law today is to attempt to give proper effect to commercial transactions. It is for this reason that uncertainty, a concept so much loved by lawyers, has fallen into disfavour as a tool for striking down commercial bargains.

It is worthy of note that other jurisdictions have not been so cautious about imposing liability in such situations. In *Banque Brussels Lambert v Australian National Industries Ltd* (1989), the wording of the comfort letter was such as to enable the Australian court to find a promissory obligation and a breach of contract and the New South Wales court opined that comfort letters were little different from letters of guarantee.

'LOCK-OUT' AGREEMENTS

In recent years, a new species of agreements liable to be set aside because of uncertainty have emerged in the form of agreements to negotiate. In *Walford v Miles* (1992), Walford brought an action for breach of an oral 'lock-out' agreement in which Miles promised not to negotiate with or consider offers from other people during the pre-contractual stage. In exchange for this undertaking, Walford supplied a letter of creditworthiness from their bank. However, the 'lock-out' agreement contained no time limit and their Lordships considered that Miles had in no legal sense locked himself into negotiations with Walford. Arguments claiming that the agreement contained an implied term that Miles would continue to negotiate in good faith with Walford for a reasonable period of time failed to impress the House of Lords, which considered the agreement to be too uncertain. In Lord Ackner's view: 'the concept of a duty to carry on negotiations in good faith is inherently repugnant to the adversarial position of the parties when involved in negotiations', a view which is clearly out of line with the thinking of the relational contract theorists discussed in Chapter 4. It may be doubted that Lord Ackner's analysis was entirely appropriate to describe the relationship between these parties which envisaged close co-operation between them. Miles had agreed, for instance, to continue working in the business as Walford lacked expertise in the field.

The decision has not met with unanimous approval. Adams and Brownsword (1991) see it as based on 'a formalist concern for certainty of terms in conjunction with a robust market-individualism'. However, the case has subsequently been applied by the Court of Appeal in *Pitt v PHH Asset Management Ltd* (1993) with a different outcome. In this case, Pitt was twice 'gazumped' when PHH withdrew from an agreement for the sale of a property 'subject to contract'. In each case, PHH received a higher offer from a third party. Nevertheless, PHH later agreed to sell to Pitt and they promised not to consider any further offers in return for Pitt's promise to exchange contracts *within two weeks* of receipt of the draft contract. It was held that this was a binding 'lock-out' agreement which PHH, who had again withdrawn, had broken. The key factor which distinguished this agreement from the one in *Walford v Miles* was the specified time limit which provided the requisite degree of certainty. Otherwise it would appear that certainty will only be found, and reliance protected, where performance has already taken place, as in such cases as *Hillas, Foley* and *Trentham*.

TENDERS, REASONABLE RELIANCE OR LEGITIMATE EXPECTATION

An additional issue which sits outside traditional analysis of the formation of contract is the position of tenders in the pre-contractual process. Contracts governing important, high-cost business projects, such as major construction or engineering works, or the supply of military or other equipment, are usually negotiated on a competitive tender basis. This means that interested parties are invited to bid for the contract work. The request for tenders may be communicated by an advertisement or invited from a group of favoured companies. According to traditional rules of analysis, this would normally be seen as an invitation to treat. A contractor who chooses to submit a tender in the form of a quotation would thereby be making an offer, which might be accepted or not. Unless the initial invitation stated that the contract would be awarded to the lowest bidder, *any* tender may be chosen on the basis of business considerations. For example, in March 1995 the UK Government decided to buy a mixed fleet of 35 helicopters from a consortium at a cost of £1.2 billion rather than accept a £300 million lower bid from a US company. This option was taken against financial advice from the Ministry of Defence but was justified on the ground that it safeguarded 5,000 British jobs.

However, if a request for a tender clearly indicates that a certain type of bid such as the highest or lowest will be successful, it is viewed as an offer capable of acceptance by the person who puts in the tender which satisfies the condition. This is because of the extra level of specificity. This issue arose in *Harvela Investments Ltd v Royal Trust Co of Canada Ltd* (1986) in which sellers of shares invited tenders from two parties and bound themselves to accept the higher bid. The bid that was accepted mentioned a fixed sum, which was slightly lower than the other bid but in the alternative offered 100,000 Canadian dollars in excess of any other offer. It was held that the invitation to bid was a unilateral offer to be bound by whichever bid was the higher. This was because it requested the performance of an act (the submission of the higher bid) which, once performed, converted the offer into a bilateral contract of sale to the higher bidder. As the bid which had been 'accepted' did not conform to the seller's own instructions, it was invalid. By accepting that bid, the sellers were breaking their own rules.

The issue of whether the pre-contractual tendering process warranted special protection was considered in *Blackpool and Fylde Aero Club v Blackpool Borough Council* (1990). In that case the council invited tenders for a concession to operate pleasure flights from Blackpool airport to be submitted by noon on a given day. The Aero Club, which had operated the flights prior to the licence coming up for renewal, submitted a tender in time. But owing to an error on the part of a council employee, it was marked as having been received late and was consequently not considered. The concession was awarded to another bidder. The club's claim that the council was in breach of a contract which bound them to consider all valid bids was upheld.

What was the contract that the club claimed had been breached? Earlier in this chapter we argued that the period during which negotiations take place is one in which the law of contract has traditionally given no protection to the parties. What is significant about this case is the way in which the court sought to protect the pre-contractual period by using the terminology of contract. It did this by arguing that, in addition to the contract to provide pleasure flights, there was a second contract governing the conduct of the tendering process, the terms of which were laid down by the council and which protected all those putting forward a tender. As Bingham LJ observed:

> Where, as here, tenders are solicited from selected parties all of them known to the invitor, and where a local authority's invitation prescribes a clear, orderly and familiar procedure ... the invitee is in my judgment protected at least to this extent: if he submits a conforming tender before the deadline he is entitled, not as a matter of mere expectation but of contractual right, to be sure that his tender will after the deadline be opened and considered in conjunction with all other conforming tenders. (p. 30)

The court did not go as far as to claim that this contract was like the other contracts we will consider in this book. Rather, it suggested that it was a *collateral* contract, that is to say an additional contract which was subordinate to the main contract. There is another reason why this case is relevant to a book which seeks to place contract law in perspective. Bingham LJ also argued that to have come to an alternative conclusion would have allowed an unacceptable discrepancy between the law of contract and the confident assumptions of the commercial parties involved that their tenders would be considered as long as they complied with the conditions laid down by the council; see also *Heathcote Ball and Co v Paul Barry* (2000).

CONCLUDING REMARKS

In the *Gibson* case discussed in Chapter 5, Lord Diplock argued that the law relating to the mechanics of contractual agreement is 'well settled, indeed elementary'. He recognised that there may be certain types of contract which do not fit easily into the normal analysis of a contract as being constituted by offer and acceptance. But he considered these to be exceptional. In the last three chapters it has been argued that these well-polished 'rules' are not always capable of satisfactorily meeting the demands made upon them by the business world. The difficulties which arise when the judiciary focuses on contracts as discrete exchanges, or on the detail of what has been written down, are evident. By way of contrast, Macneil's vision of the relational approach to contract is to start with the relationship and then move on to the contract (see Chapter 4). The change in emphasis may seem to be a subtle one but the implications for the methods used by the judiciary when trying to identify agreement are considerable. When context comes before rule, a very different vision of the role of the judiciary and law of contract could be promoted.

In this chapter we have identified some of the problems which arise in the run up to making a contract. We have also begun to unravel some of the tensions which have arisen when law on the books is compared with the everyday realities of commercial practice. The cases we have looked at are far from unusual. As long ago as 1975, Beale and Dugdale found in their study of contracts between business people in the engineering industry that contracts formed as a result of detailed negotiation were comparatively rare, especially where the parties were known to each other. What these data and the cases reveal are the tensions which become apparent when common understandings of obligation and judicial reasoning are at odds. In the interests of pragmatism, we have seen from the cases in this chapter that the judiciary have found ways of getting around these limitations. But this has been at the expense of principles, and there is a danger that the exceptions and reasoning involved begin to make a mockery of the philosophy underpinning the doctrines. This suggestion should be borne in mind as we progress in the next chapter to look at the notion of acceptance.

REFERENCES AND FURTHER READING

Adams, J 'The battle of the forms' (1983) JBL 297.

Adams, J and Brownsword, R 'More in expectation than hope: the Blackpool Airport case' (1991) 54 MLR 281.

Ball, S 'Work carried out in pursuance of letters of intent – contract or restitution' (1983) 99 LQR 572.

Beale, H and Dugdale, A 'Contracts between businessmen' (1975) 2 *British Journal of Law and Society* 45.

Brown, I 'The letter of comfort – placebo or promise?' (1990) JBL 281.

Clarke, J 'Enforceable obligations in comfort letters in Australia' (2004) 4 *JIBFL* 136.

Collins, H (2003) *The Law of Contract*, 4th edn, LexisNexis Butterworths, London.

Cumberbatch, J 'In freedom's cause: the contract to negotiate' (1992) 12 *Oxford Journal of Legal Studies* 586.

Howarth, 'Contract, reliance and business transactions' (1981) JBL 122.

Lewis, R 'Contracts between businessmen: reform of the law of firm offers and an empirical study of tendering practices in the building industry' (1982) 12 *British Journal of Law and Society* 153.

Mckendrick, E 'The battle of the forms and the law of restitution' (1988) 8 *Oxford Journal of Legal Studies* 197.

Rawlings, R 'The battle of the forms' (1979) 42 MLR 715.

? QUESTIONS

(1) Is it appropriate for tendering problems identified in this chapter to be remedied through use of quasi-contract rather than mainstream doctrine? Give detailed reasons for your response.

(2) Imagine that you have just started in a new job as a legal officer in the Department of Trade and Industry. Your line manager tells you that she is under a lot of pressure from the business sector to introduce regulations about tendering practices following the decision in *Trollope*. She asks you to draft some regulations to help her clear up 'this terrible mess'. Do you think regulations would be a good idea? What principles do you think should underpin such regulations?

(3) In 'The Sad Tale of Angie and Georgie' there are a number of agreements. Can you identify a specific point when agreement between Angie and Georgie and the following come into being:

(a) Mister C;

(b) Chelsea;

(c) Orange Peril;

(d) Wacky Machine Company and Ned;

(e) Dipti;

(f) Marcus;

(g) Monkish Soup Company;

(h) Claude;

(i) Kirsteen;

(j) St Ives Bank;

(k) Multi-storey car park?

What are the terms of the various agreements? Can you give any examples from the case study where the timing of an agreement was critical to the identification of terms included in it?

Continued

? *QUESTIONS (Continued)*

(1) 'In stressing objective certainty and completeness the requirements of traditional contract have perpetuated the idea of a contract as a rationally complete and discrete transaction' but 'most contracts are part of a wider relationship composed of previous dealings, other contracts or shared business standards, which are ignored by this objective, individualised approach' (Ball, 1983). Appraise this statement critically.

(6) If you could change one aspect of the law relating to acceptance, what would it be? Give reasons for your response.

CHAPTER 8

CONSIDERATION AND ESTOPPEL

INTRODUCTION

In this chapter, we look at another key component which the judiciary look for in contracts – consideration. The doctrine is fundamental to the classical model, which expects every contract to involve an *exchange* which comes about as a result of striking a bargain. It is the mechanism through which the judiciary have sought to distinguish between gifts and legally enforceable exchanges. A lot of what has been written about the doctrine of consideration makes it seem as though it is a very complex notion. In fact the key concept behind it is very simple. If you want to enforce a contract, you must give something to the other party and receive something in return.

It is important to understand from the start that evidence of consideration may be needed more than once in the life of a commercial relationship. Whenever the parties need to vary the terms of the original agreement, they will need to provide fresh consideration as, in the eyes of traditionalists, this is a fresh deal. It will be seen that it is this condition which has caused the most tension between the requirements of doctrine and the needs and practices of the business community. We learnt when looking at the work of Macaulay and others in Chapter 4 that business people are not as concerned with formalities as lawyers. The commercial pressures or tight deadlines which they work with on a daily basis mean that they are often prepared to accept changes to contractual arrangements without even considering what they need to do to make the variation legally binding.

Attempts have been made to circumvent the rigour of the consideration doctrine by the development of the equitable doctrine of promissory estoppel. One of the most significant characteristics of the doctrine is the fact that it shifts the conceptual focus away from the notion of exchange to that of reliance. Where the latter is concerned, the emphasis is on whether a party has acted reasonably when relying on an undertaking relating to variation of the contractual terms rather than looking for a fresh exchange. The notion of reliance has been much discussed in academic circles as an alternative to understanding contractual obligations as exchanges. Estoppel is one of the areas in which this thinking has found its way into doctrine. As a result the comparison of these two models is a major focus of this chapter and a theme which we carry over to the next, when we look at the problems of misrepresentation in pre-contractual negotiations.

CONTRACT AS BARGAIN AND EXCHANGE

We shall start with an exploration of the fact that traditionally the common law concept of contract has been founded on the concept of exchange and bargain. What this means is that, for a contract to be enforceable, each of the parties to it must give something and receive something. Every time you buy a newspaper you give money in exchange for it but the thing you exchange does not have to be a material object. I get paid a monthly salary in exchange for the services I provide as a lecturer. Those of you who have taken out student loans have been given money in exchange for a promise to pay it back. It might also be the case that a person promises *not* to do something (forbearance) by way of providing consideration. This would be the case, for instance, if I agreed not to bring a lawsuit to recover a sum of money owed to me if the debtor agreed to pay by instalments over a 12-month period together with interest. The principle underlying all the examples given so far is that both the parties to a contract have to achieve something as a result of the exchange. Lack of exchange renders informal, gratuitous promises or gifts unenforceable at law because they lack the required *reciprocity*.

A promise to do something in the future can also amount to consideration. The ability to enforce a contract which relies on an exchange of promises about things yet to be performed marked an important stepping stone in the law of contract. Critically, it allows for forward planning in the commercial sector. Consider the example of the building of Wembley stadium. The contracts between Wembley National Stadium Limited and the construction company Multiplex were legally enforceable *before* construction actually started. The contract was formed on the basis that Multiplex *promised* to construct the stadium and Wembley National Stadium Limited *promised* to pay them for the work. At this stage the contract is said to be *executory*. Actual performance of the act (or the forbearance) embodied in such a promise amounts to *executed* consideration. In other words the contract is executed when the promise is performed. In the case of a unilateral contract, it is executed when a promise is exchanged for a completed act.

Contract law textbooks reveal centuries of 'leading' cases on consideration, which deal with a variety of legal propositions and exceptions regarding the nature of this contractual requirement. However, for an introductory study of the law as it operates *today*, it is doubtful if full attention needs be given to the extensive and complicated accumulation of 'old' case law on consideration. Points from such cases do still arise but more often than not, modern cases tend to demonstrate moves in judicial thinking *away from* strict theories. Lord Denning (1979) expressed the view that the effect of the doctrine of promissory estoppel since 1947:

> has been to do away with the doctrine of consideration in all but a handful of cases. During the 16 years while I have been Master of the Rolls I do not recall any case in which it has arisen or been discussed.

Taking these statements as our cue, we will confine ourselves to an examination of consideration's main features and then proceed to a closer look at promissory estoppel and other moves away from traditional models.

ECONOMIC VALUE

The consideration supplied by the parties must be something of value in the eyes of the law to make it binding. Generally speaking, value has been taken by the courts to mean *economic* value. The economic value of consideration is usually obvious and this is probably the main reason why few consideration disputes reach the courts. Services and goods are generally exchanged for the going market rate. However, it is important to recognise that the courts are willing to acknowledge nominal economic consideration such as peppercorn rent. This is because the notion of freedom of contract which dominates the classical model of contract is based on the principle that it is not the job of the courts to police whether a contract is a *good* bargain. They are only there to ensure that there is some bargain. In other words, party autonomy trumps judicial meddling. It has been long argued that the parties should be free to set their own price or promise in accordance with the value they personally attach to the exchange. This position demonstrates a clear logic. If contract reflects a bargain which has been struck, then it is for the parties to do the bargaining and determine what suits them best. It is for this reason that the agreement between Angie, Georgie and Polly to pay the latter double the market rate in wages would be enforceable in the courts. According to judicial authority, the adequacy of the consideration is for the parties to consider at the time of making the agreement, not for the court when it is sought to be enforced.

Whilst this general approach to bargains continues to frame the case law, nowadays, the courts are more sensitive to the ways in which imbalances of bargaining strength and the use of excessive commercial pressure or undue influence can undermine the notion of free exchange. The result is that, in some cases, a grossly inadequate consideration may militate against a court's sense of fair bargain. In *Lloyd's Bank Ltd v Bundy* (1975), although Lord Denning stated that 'no bargain will be upset which is the result of the ordinary interplay of forces', the court struck down a contract of guarantee by which the defendant, an elderly farmer not well versed in business affairs, mortgaged his house as security for the debts of his son's business. This was done at a time when the company was already in dire financial straits, and not long before its eventual collapse. It was felt that, in the circumstances, the consideration moving from the bank was grossly inadequate and, at the late stage at which the guarantee was given, all that the company gained was a short respite from impending doom. The legislature has also played an increasingly active role in the regulation of exchange in certain contexts, such as carriage of goods by sea, rents and interest rates.

BARGAIN AND THE TIMING OF CONSIDERATION

The classical view of contract expects consideration to be exchanged as part of a bargaining process. Thus it is said that something wholly performed *before* an agreement is reached cannot amount to consideration. Instead, it is known as *past* consideration. The idea rests on the idea that, if something has been voluntarily given before the bargaining begins, then this should be treated as a voluntary gift or service. For example, if I give you some legal advice in connection with problems you are having with your landlord and two weeks later you agree to pay me for it, this does not amount to an exchange which would be recognised as a contract. My voluntary contribution occurred before the subject of money was discussed. Put simply its bargaining value was used up or spent in advance. The service was offered at a time when we had no expectation of exchange or bargain.

However, in a business context, it may be argued that, if the service was requested, it might have been understood by the parties that payment would be forthcoming. In these circumstances the courts have been prepared to allow that a later express promise to pay merely confirms and quantifies an earlier implied promise on your part: see *Re Casey's Patents* (1892). However, this alternative reading of such situations has proved controversial and is seen by some as undermining the whole notion of *contemporaneous* bargain on which traditional reasoning is based.

The sort of problems which might arise in connection with this rule in the commercial sector are illustrated in *Pao On v Lau Yiu Long* (1980). In this case, the defendants made a contract with the claimants. They sold shares to the claimant who in exchange promised not to put them on the market for at least 12 months. The defendants, who retained a large block of shares in the same company, had required this, as they did not wish to see the value of their holding depressed by a sudden sale of the claimant's shares. The defendants later promised to indemnify the claimant against any loss he might incur if the shares fell in value during the year. The Privy Council was willing to marry together the claimant's promise not to sell, albeit given as part of the original contract of sale, and the defendants' subsequent promise to indemnify. It has been said that the claimant was 'only getting what he was really, morally and commercially, entitled to'. The case also supports the growing idea that, in appropriate circumstances, the court should have regard to a *continuing commercial relationship* between parties rather than concentrating on 'discrete' transactions or arrangements within that relationship, a proposition which sits comfortably with the arguments of relational contract theorists.

CONSIDERATION AND EXISTING CONTRACTUAL DUTIES

It follows from what has been said about past consideration that a party can not offer up as consideration something that they have a pre-existing duty to do. If a duty already exists, then this 'consideration', like past consideration, has already been used and spent. The position can be outlined by using an example from the case study in Chapter 2. Chelsea agreed to carry out certain obligations as a shop assistant for Angie and Georgie at a fixed weekly wage for a five-year period. As a result of severe financial pressures on their business, Angie and Georgie find they are unable to pay Chelsea at the agreed rate. Rather than terminating her employment, they agree to pay Chelsea a lower wage for the same work. Because she enjoys her work and would find it difficult to find another job locally, Chelsea agrees to the change. Is the variation of the contract binding in law? The traditional viewpoint would be that it is not. Each new or varied contract requires fresh consideration, and Chelsea has already agreed to offer up her services in exchange for an agreed wage and for a fixed term. It might be useful to think of the issue in two stages. There is an original contractual agreement followed by a variation of it. According to traditional reasoning, the variation can only stand if Chelsea agrees to do *more* for Angie and Georgie in exchange for their new promise. This would be a new agreement with additional consideration for the second contract.

The problem the courts are faced with is that the parties to a contract often change the terms of performance without any reference to the formal requirements of this doctrine. In the majority of cases this happens because of a change in circumstances or market conditions. These cases serve to remind us that it is extremely difficult for the parties to an ongoing commercial relationship to predict what will happen in the future at the time of making their contract. Many have claimed that the English law of contract with its emphasis on exchange and the 'moment of responsibility' has paid insufficient attention to the need for flexibility in ongoing commercial relationships. Despite these concerns a strict line on this issue has been taken in much of the case law. So for instance, in *Stilk v Myrick* (1809), a crew had been engaged to sail a vessel from London to the Baltic and back at the rate of £5 a month. Following the desertion of two of the 11 crew members, the captain promised to share the deserters' wages among the remaining crew if they would work the ship back to London. But when the ship returned its owners refused to honour the captain's promise. It was held that the seamen's claim for the extra pay failed for lack of consideration. The crew were already bound by their contract to meet the normal emergencies of the voyage and were doing no more than their duty in sailing the ship back. Similar facts arose in *Hartley v Ponsonby* (1857), except that in this case 17 out of 36 crew deserted and the voyage became very hazardous. The extra danger in this case was used to justify a different decision from that in *Stilk v Myrick* (1809). It was held that, because of the new danger, the remaining crew had been discharged from their original contract and were free therefore to enter a new one at higher wages which reflected the extra risk.

A number of subsequent cases have re-opened the debate about past consideration and questioned the basis on which this aspect of the doctrine is based. In the 1950s Lord Denning made a radical departure from the traditional stance. He felt able to find that such a promise was good consideration in two cases where a party merely promised to perform an existing legal duty in return for a promise. In *Ward v Byham* (1956), a case involving a pre-existing statutory duty, he argued: 'I have always thought that a promise to perform an existing duty, or the performance of it, should be regarded as good consideration, because it is a benefit to the person to whom it is given' (p. 320). And in *Williams v Williams* (1957) which involved a matrimonial dispute he opined:

> Now I agree that, in promising to maintain herself while she was in desertion, the wife was only promising to do that which she was already bound to do. Nevertheless, a promise to perform an existing duty is, I think, sufficient consideration to support a promise, so long as there is nothing in the transaction which is contrary to the public interest. (p. 307)

The cases shift the focus from strict formulae of fresh bargain and new exchange to a more pragmatic discussion of whether there is any *practical benefit* to the person to whom the promise is given, regardless of whether the consideration has already been 'used'. The only limitation imposed by Denning was that there should be no public policy reasons for not enforcing the promise.

These points re-emerge in the more recent case of *Williams v Roffey Bros and Nicholls (Contractors) Ltd* (1991) which has excited considerable interest in the issue. In that case, Roffey, as main contractors entered into a contract with a housing association for the refurbishment of a block of flats. Roffey sub-contracted the carpentry work to Williams for £20,000. Part way through the work, Williams was in financial difficulties because he had tendered too low and had failed to supervise his workmen properly. There was a distinct possibility that Williams would not complete on time or would stop work altogether. Facing a penalty clause in the main contract for late completion, Roffey agreed to pay Williams a further £10,300 at a rate of £575 per flat completed in order to get the job completed. The carpentry work on eight more flats was finished but, with only a further £1,500 having been paid by Roffey, Williams stopped work and sued for damages in respect of the eight completions. In line with the judgement in *Stilk v Myrick* (1809), Roffey argued that Williams had provided no consideration to support their promise of additional payment and Williams was merely doing what he was already obliged to do.

The Court of Appeal held that Roffey *was* bound by their promise. Approving the decision in *Stilk v Myrick*, they nonetheless argued that the present case could be distinguished because something new was being offered up. In the view of Glidewell LJ, as long as the promisee obtains a practical benefit under the revised agreement and there is no economic duress or fraud, then the promise to do what Williams was already bound to do can constitute good consideration. In his view, there were a number of reasons why the benefits obtained and detriment avoided by the main contractors offered a new element. Firstly, they ensured that the claimant continued work and did not stop in breach of the sub-contract. Secondly, it allowed the main contractor to avoid the penalty for delay in the main contract. Finally, it allowed them to avoid the trouble and expense of engaging other people to complete the carpentry work.

The decisions demonstrate a willingness on the part of the judiciary to enforce arrangements which reflect good business sense in changing market conditions. The main contractor, when giving his promise of additional payment, is making the best of a bad job, and the variation in the arrangements is of benefit to him. In his estimation it is less disadvantageous to pay the sub-contractor more than to run the very real risk of having to pay his client even more under the terms of the penalty clause in the main contract. On this basis, the court leaves the parties to their rearrangement. The case also takes account of the long-term commercial inevitability of the renegotiation of terms during the performance of the contract. Treating each variation of terms as a new contract requiring fresh consideration may be a logical approach to contracts where an ongoing relationship of dependence does not exist. But, as *Williams v Roffey* shows, an overly formalistic approach to the issue in all contracts can create an absurd situation in which the law undermines perfectly fair and logical alterations which benefit both parties. This view of the case can be seen, in more technical language, in the words of Russell LJ: 'Consideration there must be but in my judgment the courts nowadays should be more ready to find its existence so as to reflect the intention of the parties to the contract where the bargaining powers are not unequal' (p. 18). This view is far from being new. Over 60 years ago, the American realists insisted that a true understanding of business law's purpose assumes an understanding of the facts of business life.

The reasoning in *Williams v Roffey* has not gone uncriticised (see for instance *South Caribbean Trading Co v Trafigura Beheer*, 2005) but it has been instrumental in spurning some interesting debates about the legitimacy of doctrines which fail to reflect the realities of the commercial sector in which such variations, negotiated in the absence of duress or undue pressure are common.

STRETCHING CONSIDERATION TO ITS LIMITS

Our discussion of consideration has centred on the idea that enforceable contracts have to be paid for with consideration. In *Williams v Roffey*, the expectation amongst formalists that valid consideration should always reflect something new were stretched to their limits. However, it was clear that modification of the contract enabled Roffey to obtain some fresh benefits. Although the sub-contractor merely promised to continue his original obligations, the practical benefit to Roffey was sufficient to make the new deal binding. In this section, we consider the slightly more complicated position if the variation of the contract involves one party *giving up* some of their rights in a situation in which the other party provides no further consideration to support the promise.

As we have seen above, the general rule is that failure to provide new consideration in attempts to vary a contract are fatal to the enforceability of subsequent arrangements. This position as regards a *reduction* in what is being exchanged was established as early as *Pinnel's Case* (1602) in which it was stated that payment of a lesser sum in satisfaction of a greater amount owed did not satisfy the law of contract. The rule in *Pinnel's Case* was affirmed by the House of Lords in *Foakes v Beer* (1881–85). In that case, Foakes owed £2,000 to Beer who sued and obtained judgment from a court that Foakes should pay her. Foakes needed time to pay and it was eventually agreed that Beer would take no further proceedings in return for an immediate payment of £500 plus specified instalments until the whole judgment was satisfied. After the £2,000 was paid, Beer claimed £360 interest on the judgment debt. The court upheld her claim. Foakes's payment of the lesser (capital) sum did not discharge the greater (capital plus interest) debt. The court determined that Beer could recover the full amount, even if she had promised to forego interest as Foakes had provided no consideration for that promise. The 'remorseless logic' of the common law demonstrated here is that new agreements in which one party promises or assures the other party that she will accept *less than* is due to her under the contract are *not* supported by fresh consideration and are not enforceable.

Despite its logic, this particular application of the common law rule has never been free from criticism, not least because it does not always make sense in a commercial context. Financial compromise, involving the waiving of part of a debt, may be good business sense especially in times of cash-flow problems. In *Foakes v Beer* (1881–85) itself, Lord Blackburn, reluctantly acquiescing in the majority view, stated that:

> I think it is not the fact that to accept prompt payment of a part only of a liquidated demand can never be more beneficial than to insist on payment of the whole. And if it be not the fact, it cannot be apparent to the judges …. What principally weighs with me … is my conviction that all men of business, whether merchants or tradesmen, do every day recognise and act on the ground that prompt payment of part of their demand may be more beneficial to them than it would be to insist on their rights and enforce payment of the whole. Even where the debtor is perfectly solvent, and sure to pay at last, this often is so. Where the credit of the debtor is doubtful it must be more so. (p. 115)

In any event, the rule in *Pinnel's Case* is now so hemmed in by exceptions that there must be few cases today in which the principle is in fact applicable. At common law the original agreement can be superseded so as to exclude the rule by a *variation* in the debtor's performance. This may include a variation in the method, time or place of payment by the debtor to support the creditor's promise to waive part of the debt. So for instance the debtor may make payment of a smaller sum in a different currency. Provision by the debtor of something different in kind, such as a stocks and shares instead of the agreed £2,000 also falls under this heading. Although case law suggests that the variation must originate with the creditor and be to their advantage, it is clear that, as in *Williams v Roffey*, the common law has shown itself prepared to respect variations of contract where nominal fresh consideration is provided as long as it benefits the creditor.

In 1994 the Court of Appeal decided a case which revived disquiet regarding the mismatch between the rule in *Pinnel's Case* and regular business practice. It also presented an opportunity to bring the prevailing argument in *Williams v Roffey* to bear upon that early seventeenth-century decision. In *Re Selectmove Ltd* (1995), the company owed large sums in unpaid tax and national insurance contributions (NIC) to the Inland Revenue which presented a petition to wind up the company. The company alleged that an agreement had been made by which the Inland Revenue would not take such action on the debt if the company paid future tax and NIC as they fell due and paid off arrears at £1,000 per month. In return for these forbearances, the company were in effect only doing what they were already obliged to do by law. In the event they made late payments of both new demands and instalments of arrears, and the Inland Revenue sued to enforce the original obligation.

The court in *Re Selectmove* was sympathetic to the *Williams v Roffey* argument that a promise to perform an existing obligation may amount to good consideration if there are practical benefits to the promisee. As in *Williams v Roffey*, the rearrangement with the Inland Revenue made good business sense in the circumstances. The company had been kept out of liquidation by paying off its debts in instalments and this was clearly an outcome the Inland Revenue preferred. Despite this, it was held that the agreement was unenforceable for lack of consideration. Whilst the Court of Appeal could have found a benefit to the creditor, it decided that it was bound by the House of Lords' decision in *Foakes v Beer*. Thus the rule remained that in common law part payment of a debt is no consideration unless there is some variation in performance.

The upshot is that *Williams v Roffey* does not apply where the pre-existing obligation is an obligation to pay, as opposed to an obligation to supply goods or services, and the proposed variation is that payment should be reduced. These are the sole circumstances in which *Foakes v Beer* applies. It must be the case that further developments are required to eliminate the 'rough edges' that presently exist in this area of the common law which now appears to lack clear underlying principles.

EXCHANGE OR REASONABLE RELIANCE

The rules in *Pinnel's Case* and *Foakes v Beer* have also been undermined by the development of new equitable doctrine. In 1947, in the now famous *High Trees* case, it was established that in certain circumstances a promise by one of the parties not to enforce their full contractual rights has a *degree* of binding effect in equity even though this renegotiation and variation of the contract is not supported by new consideration. The facts of the case were that in 1937 the Central London Property Trust (CLPT) let a block of flats in London to their subsidiary company HTH for 99 years at a ground rent of £2,500 per annum. In 1940, as a result of bombing raids, many of the flats were empty and CLPT agreed to reduce the rent to £1,250 because the original rent could not be paid by HTH out of the profits they received from rents. HTH provided no consideration to support CLPT's promise to forgo half the ground rent.

By 1945 the flats were again fully let, and the receiver of CLPT wrote to HTH claiming future payment of rent at the full rate and 'arrears' of almost £8,000. A law suit ensued in which a young Denning adjudicated the claim. He accepted the legitimacy of the claim for full rent *from 1945 onwards*. He reasoned that the 1940 agreement had been a temporary arrangement and that the conditions giving rise to it had disappeared. However, Denning added that CLPT could *not* sue for the full rent in the period from 1940 to 1945 because it was inequitable to do so. It was held that, if a claim for arrears were made, HTH would be able to use CLPT's promise as a *defence* to the action.

This new application of an old equitable principle, which became known as promissory estoppel, has since received a considerable amount of attention. The effect of the doctrine is to hold promisors to their word and prevent them from going back on a variation of contract where others have relied on it and it would be unjust or inequitable. However, a number of elements must be present if this doctrine is to be invoked. Firstly, there must be a *pre-existing contractual relationship* giving rise to rights and duties between the parties. Secondly, after the contract has been made, one party must later make a clear *promise* or assertion that they will *not fully enforce their existing rights*. They may do this for a variety of reasons including sound business practice in changing circumstances. Thirdly, it must be intended that the promise be *relied upon* and the promisee must in fact rely upon it. According to Lord Denning, in *Alan & Co Ltd v El Nasr Co* (1972), this does not necessarily mean detrimental reliance. In his view the promisee must only have been led to act differently from how they would otherwise have acted, such as paying the agreed lower rent. The *effect* of promissory estoppel is to *stop* the promisor from retracting the promise and insisting on their strict legal rights under the existing contract.

What distinguishes this equitable doctrine from the rule established in *Williams v Roffey* is that the emphasis is not on finding consideration for the variation. Instead the focus is on reliance. It is also important to note that the doctrine of promissory estoppel largely relates to *temporary suspension* of the original contract. On giving reasonable notice, the promisor is able to insist on a *resumption* of his strict rights. However, this will not always be possible and in such circumstances the variation can become final and irrevocable if positions can not be resumed. Where rights are only suspended, the promisor can sue to enforce his original rights as to *the future*, but cannot recover any balances 'owed' while his forbearance took effect. Moreover, the general view is that the promisee can only use the *promise as a defence* to such an action but *cannot sue* on the promisor's promise to waive his full rights as he provided no consideration for it. In other words, the doctrine can be used as a 'shield and not a sword'. Technically then, it does not create new rights so as to abolish the doctrine of consideration by the 'back-door' but can provide temporary relief from an unworkable contract in certain situations.

As it is an equitable doctrine, one of the requirements for the application of promissory estoppel is that it must be *unjust* for the promisor to go back on the promise they have given. As a result the doctrine is applied at the court's discretion. It was on this ground that Lord Denning based his judgment in *D & C Builders v Rees* (1966). In that case, D & C, a small firm of builders, did work for Rees at a cost of £482. Having pressed for payment for several months, they eventually and reluctantly agreed with Rees's wife, who knew they were in financial difficulties, to accept £300 'in completion of the account'. Mrs Rees told them that if they refused to take the lesser sum, they would get nothing. D & C later sued for the balance of the original debt. The court decided that their promise to accept £300 not supported by consideration from Rees was of a type to raise the estoppel principle but the court decided it was necessary to take account of the nature of the dealings which had taken place between the parties. They found that Mrs Rees had held the claimants to ransom and, as such, her conduct amounted to unfair pressure. The judges concluded that as a result it was inequitable to permit D & C to go back on their promise and recover the whole debt.

The *High Trees* decision has since found acceptance with the House of Lords, subject to some uncertainty about its limits. But there have been judicial differences between

Lord Denning, who sought to further extend the doctrine, and the House of Lords, which has given warnings about the need for 'coherent exposition'. The practical result of the establishment and development of promissory estoppel in the post-war years and the decision in *Williams v Roffey* is that an increasing number of revised agreements are being enforced which reflect fair and commercially viable alterations to agreements. It has become clear that, while traditional doctrines may make philosophical sense, they do no always make sense in a practical context.

PRIVITY OF CONTRACT: CONTRACTS AND THIRD-PARTY BENEFICIARIES

A doctrine which is closely related to consideration is that of 'privity'. Whereas the doctrine of consideration is concerned with establishing the line between enforceable and unenforceable promises, the doctrine of privity determines, among other things, *who* may enforce a contractual promise. In *Dunlop Pneumatic Tyre Co v Selfridge and C Ltd* (1915) the Lord Chancellor, Viscount Haldane, stated that certain principles were fundamental to the English law of contract and that one of these was that only a person who is party to a contract may sue on it. Like other fundamental contractual principles, this one appears to be simple, even obvious, and in the vast majority of cases privity causes no problems. Only the negotiating parties are involved and each agrees to perform stipulated obligations for the benfit of the other. In turn each of those giving consideration may enforce the promise of the other. The problem with the privity rule is that a person may not enforce a contract made for their benefit if they are not a party to the contract.

In *Dunlop v Selfridge* (1915), Dunlop sold tyres to Dew and Co. Part of their agreement was that Dew would not resell the tyres below a certain price. It was also agreed that, if they did resell the tyres, they had to include a similar provision in the contract. Dew resold some of the tyres to Selfridge who agreed to observe the term about the minimum price the tyres were to be sold for, but in the event did not comply with it. As a result Dunlop tried to bring an action against Selfridge to enforce the promise that they had made to Dew. Clearly the doctrine of privity interfered with Dunlop's marketing strategy and in their eyes devalued their product in the marketplace. But Dunlop were unable to enforce their resale price maintenance policy against Selfridge because they were not a party to the contract in which Selfridge made their promise to Dew. It is clear from the judgment that the judges in the Dunlop case were clearly frustrated that Selfridge was able to hide behind the doctrine of consideration so that they did not have to stand by the agreement they had made (see further, *Beswick v Beswick*, 1968).

Another way of looking at this case is on the basis of the related rule that consideration must move from the parties for them to be able to use the contract. Dunlop clearly provided no consideration to support Selfridges promise to Dew. Looked at from this perspective, Lord Dunedin, although agreeing with the decision, felt compelled to state that:

> I confess that this case is to my mind apt to nip any budding affection which one might have had for the doctrine of consideration. For the effect of that doctrine in the present case is to make it possible for a person [Selfridge] to snap his fingers at a bargain

deliberately made, a bargain not in itself unfair, and which the person [Dunlop] seeking to enforce it has a legitimate interest to enforce. (p. 335)

It is possible to go much further with the doctrine of privity. The doctrine, established in the mid-nineteenth century and resting on clear-cut views of agreement (consent) and consideration (bargain), seems eminently logical at first sight. But in the changing circumstances and values of the twentieth century, it produced a wide range of evasions and exceptions.

A key problem with the doctrine is that, in many circumstances, two people may make a contract for the benefit of a third party in which they clearly intend for them to have an entitlement. In the *Beswick v Beswick* (1968), for instance, an uncle assigned his business to his nephew. In return the nephew agreed to pay the uncle a weekly sum of £6, 10s for the remainder of his life and, in the event of the uncle's death, to pay his aunt £5 per week. Although the aunt was able to sue on the contract in her role as administrix, she would not otherwise have been able to enforce the contract because of the privity rule, despite the clear intentions of the parties.

Concern about the impact of the doctrine of privity is longstanding. As a result, a series of exceptions to it have developed which have involved statutory provisions allowing third parties to avoid the doctrine in certain transactions. The law of trusts has also been used to circumvent the rule. Ongoing criticisms of the rule have been based on the fact that the rule prevents effect being given to the parties' intention, despite this being a fundamental principle of the classical model. Moreover, the growth of numerous exceptions to the rule has meant that the law in the field has become very complicated. But whilst the rule can be circumvented, doing so can involve a plethora of technicalities.

The law in this field has been radically altered by the introduction of the Contracts (Rights of Third party) Act 1999. This allows that a person who is not a party to a contract may in their own right enforce a term. They may do this if the contract expressly provides that they may or a term purports to confer a benefit on them and the parties appear to have intended this. A third party who seeks to enforce the agreement must be expressly named, be a member of a named class, e.g. offspring, or answer a particular description. The fact that they need not be in existence at the time the contract is made seems to be designed to allow for inheritance provision.

The issue of whether the Act completely abolishes the doctrine of privity or simply creates a very large exception to it has been mooted by some scholars. Reported cases which raise issues under the Act have been few and those that have been decided appear to be relatively uncontroversial. This legislative reform seems to have been universally accepted as a positive development as it allows the aims of the parties to be fully adhered to and provides relief from a rather draconian doctrine.

CONCLUDING REMARKS

In this chapter we have visited the doctrines which, in addition to the law relating to offer, acceptance and agreement, determine how the making of an enforceable contract is evidenced. It is clear from the doctrines and cases analysed that there are a number of tensions which have arisen and that different visions of contract have emerged. We have looked at the notion of exchange and bargain, but made clear that these notions, founded on the classical model, have been challenged by the idea of reliance. These competing ideas about what needs to be evidenced before the courts are prepared to recognise and enforce a contract have considerable repercussions for the subject as a whole. Challenges have come from the equitable doctrine of promissory estoppel but the courts in *Williams v Roffey* have shown an ongoing commitment to fitting agreements which make sense in the business community into a traditional framework of analysis. I shall leave you to draw your own conclusions about whether this is an acceptable state of affairs until you have read the cases. But, in the chapter which follows, we shall turn once more to the notion of reliance and its close and developing relationship with the concept of contract.

REFERENCES AND FURTHER READING

Adams, J and Brownsword, R 'Contract, consideration and the critical path' (1990) 53 MLR 536.
Chen-Wishart, M (1995) 'Consideration, practical benefit and the emperor's new clothes' in Beatson, J and Friedmann, D (eds) *Good Faith and Fault in Contract Law*, pp. 123–150.
Denning, Lord (1979) 'High trees' in *The Discipline of Law*, Part Five, Butterworths, London.
Dugdale, A and Yates, D 'Variation, waiver and estoppel – a re-appraisal' (1976) 40 MLR 680.
Peel, E 'Part payment of a debt is no consideration' (*Re Selectmove*) (1994) 110 LQR 353.
Phang, A 'Consideration at the crossroads' (1991) 107 LQR 21.
Tettenborn, I 'Commercial certainty: a step in the right direction' (1988) CLJ 346.
Treital, G (2002) 'Agreement to vary contracts' in *Some Landmarks of Twentieth Century Contract Law*' Oxford University Press, Oxford.
Unger, J 'Intent to create legal relations, mutuality and consideration' (1956) 19 MLR 96.
Wheeler, S and Shaw, J (1994) *Contract Law: Cases, Materials and Commentary*, Oxford University Press, Oxford.

? *QUESTIONS*

(1) 'Consideration is a perfectly adequate test of liability in contract, the so-called doctrine of intention to create legal relations is superfluous'. Discuss this statement in the light of decided cases.

(2) Can you apply what you know about the doctrine of consideration to the problems facing Angie and Georgie? For instance, are the following variations of contract supported by fresh consideration? Would they be upheld by the courts?

   (a) Kirsteen's claims that Angie and Georgie are obliged to pay her £500 commission for the help she gave them in finding a carrot supplier;

   (b) the reduction of Chelsea's wage;

   (c) Mister C's demand that they should pay him the 25 per cent of the rent he didn't collect while he was living with Missy J;

   (d) Marcus's demand for additional payment?

Continued

Please cite the relevant case law when giving your response. Do you think the variations should be upheld?

(3) Are there reasons why Georgie's medical insurance contract should be enforceable but the agreement between Angie and Georgie recorded in their tapestry should not?

(4) Explain the doctrine of promissory estoppel in terms of its being:
   (a) a moral principle;

   (b) the bending of a rule of higher generality;

   (c) good business sense.

CHAPTER 9

MISREPRESENTATION

INTRODUCTION

So far in this book we have looked at the big ideas which underpin the modern law of contract and then moved on to look at the doctrines, rules and ideas which govern the way we look at formation. Determining when the parties became legally obliged to each other and the detail of how they are bound is crucial and a point we shall return to again and again. The main reason litigation will commence about a contract is where a breach of contract is alleged. We cannot determine whether there has been a breach unless we understand what the parties have agreed. If one of the parties claims there has been a mistake during formation, we cannot determine the validity of their claim unless we determine what it is that each of the parties assumed about performance as they entered into the agreement.

In this section of the book we look at a number of problems which relate to formation which may allow one of the parties to have the contract set aside or to claim an extra-contractual remedy. Some of this behaviour is termed bargaining naughtiness and you will discover that many of the cases we turn to involve fraudsters. But in other instances agreement is defective because innocent misunderstandings have arisen or because one of the parties has been reckless in what they said. The main doctrines with which we are concerned here are those relating to misrepresentation, mistake, duress and unconscionability. These are all doctrines which operate in the 'twilight zone' of the law of contract.

MISREPRESENTATION AND PRE-CONTRACTUAL NEGOTIATIONS

During the course of pre-contractual negotiations people tend to make a variety of representations to each other. These might include comments about the condition of the thing being negotiated about, the standard of a service, the special characteristics of an item, and the price and method of payment. This is particularly the case in the business community where negotiations may be protracted. Many of these representations are sufficiently important that they will eventually become terms of the contract concluded between the parties. But it is also the case that negotiations break down or the parties do not expect all their statements to become contractual promises. This chapter focuses on whether negotiating parties can be found liable for the representations made before a contract is formed which do not become part of the contract.

In the previous chapter it was made clear that the judiciary are reluctant to impose unexpected obligations on the parties prior to them reaching agreement. This is in contrast to other jurisdictions, such as Germany, where a pre-contractual duty of good faith is proving increasingly popular. It has been argued that the traditional English approach increases market efficiency and benefits the business community. It protects the parties' freedom to negotiate at length, explore possibilities and exchange the sort of information on which efficient dealings are based prior to the moment of responsibility. The rationale for this position is that, when the parties are inhibited by legal regulations during the negotiation process, they may not feel so free to exchange information relating to the deal they plan to make. Traditionally then, the boundaries of contractual obligations have been set from the moment at which agreement is reached.

Judicial attitudes have changed and no longer accord with this approach. Atiyah (1979) has argued that the law relating to misrepresentation was one of the first areas of law to show signs of retreat from the high-water mark of Victorian individualism. In *The Rise and Fall of Freedom of Contract*, he sketched out the background to developments in this area:

> The older notion that a man could say what he liked to a prospective contracting party, so long only as he refrained from positively dishonest assertions of fact, seems to have come up against a new morality in the late nineteenth century. The courts began to insist on the duty of a party not to mislead the other party by extravagant or unjustified assertions ... in their determination to stamp out the laxer business morality.

Since Atiyah first expressed this view there have been a number of inroads into the traditional approach. The most notable of these has been the Unfair Terms in Consumer Contracts Regulations 1999 in which the European Union has subjected certain types of terms to the test of good faith. The treatment of pre-contractual tenders considered in Chapter 7 above also reflects an attempt to protect the legitimate expectations of negotiating parties in the run up to the formation of a contract. Misleading statements about the price of goods and services, quantity, composition, strength and fitness for purpose have also been singled out for regulation by legislation such as the Trade Descriptions Act 1968 and the Consumer Protection Act 1987. More recently the Consumer Protection (Distance Selling) Regulations 2000 require that the seller must provide clear and comprehensible information to a consumer such as their name and address, a description of the goods, the price including taxes, delivery costs where they apply, arrangements for payment, arrangements for date and delivery, the right to cancel the order and the length of time that the offer or price remains valid in order to enable them to decide whether they want to buy.

However, the overall approach has been to adopt piecemeal solutions in response to problems of unfairness rather than to adopt an *overriding* principle of good faith. On the whole, even the modern cases continue to reflect the hold which market individualism continues to have on the English law of contract. The approach adopted to these problems is not to impose a positive duty on negotiating parties to behave well but to declare certain types of behaviour unacceptable. The distinction may appear subtle but it has considerable connotations. This approach, which has dominated the development of contractual doctrine, can be compared with the law of tort which has not been so shy of intervening in the regulation of pre-contractual negotiations. Here, interference has been justified on the basis that dishonesty in the pre-contractual period can distort the market which relies on the exchange of *accurate* information for its optimal efficiency. Viewed in this way, it has been argued that deliberate and dishonest inducements to enter into a contract which incur expenditure for one of the parties abuse the notion of freedom to contract and standards of morality. However, the law remains a somewhat confusing mixture of tort and contract, common law and equity. Underpinning this confusion is ambiguity about the proper ambit of contractual principles and concern about whether they should be stretched to cover a pre-contractual period. Elsewhere in this book it will be argued that the courts and legislature have been prepared to step in to regulate the negotiation process where consumers are concerned but have continued to make certain assumptions about contracting parties who trade as businesses.

IS IT A TERM?

Since most contracts are made orally, or are a mixture of oral and written terms, it can be difficult to decide which pre-contractual representations become terms of the contract and which are excluded from the contract and become what lawyers refer to as 'mere' representations. Although the latter affect the contract, they do not become an integral part of it and, if untrue, do not give rise to a breach of contract. In practical terms the distinction is less important than it was before the Misrepresentation Act 1967, since the remedies available to those who are the victims of pre-contractual misrepresentations are now akin to, but not the same as, the remedies for breach of contract. However, there continue to be reasons why it is important for a lawyer to argue that a representation became a term of the contract. These include the fact that breach brings with it an automatic right to damages whereas this is discretionary in the case of mere representations. Moreover, there are different rules relating to the amount of damages that should be made available in the two cases which may affect the litigation strategy adopted.

Today, the test of whether a representation has become a term of the contract depends on an *objective* appraisal of whether the representor intended to be bound to the truth of the statement so as to render themselves liable to an action for breach? The courts have laid down certain guidelines when seeking an answer to this question, but the essential criterion adopted by the courts would seem to be that of fairness in the particular circumstances presented to them. So, for instance, in *Oscar Chess Ltd v Williams* (1957), Williams sold a car for £280 to a car dealer. He innocently described it as a 1948 model but, unbeknown to him, the logbook had been forged. In fact it had been registered in 1939 and was worth £175. The statement was held to be a misrepresentation but not a term of the contract. This was because the dealer might have bought the car anyway and was in a good position to discern the age of the car. Lord Denning LJ laid down a number of criteria to distinguish terms from mere representations. He argued that:

(a) the more important a statement made during negotiations, the more likely it is a term;

(b) the longer the time between the making of the statement and the agreement being concluded, the more likely that it is *not* a term;

(c) if an oral statement is not recorded in a written contract, it is evidence against a term being intended;

(d) the statement is more likely to be a term if made by a person possessing special skill or knowledge regarding its truth.

Whilst there are no hard and fast rules when trying to determine whether a representation is a term or not, the main theme running throughout the case law is a consideration of whether it was reasonable in the circumstances to rely on the representations made. Thus, in *Bentley v Harold Smith (Motors) Ltd* (1965), where the positions were reversed, a pre-contractual statement made by a dealer to a private purchaser was held to be a term of the contract. The dealer stated that a car had done 20,000 miles when it had in fact done almost 100,000. The statement by the dealer, who was in a much better position to check its truth, was held to be a term and contractual damages were awarded.

MISREPRESENTATION: THE GENERAL RULES

As attitudes towards pre-contractual negotiations have changed, the law has provided some relief through the doctrines of fraud and misrepresentation for those who have been misled in pre-contractual negotiations. As a general rule a party must not make any false and misleading statements to the other party which induces them to enter into a contract. If they do, they may result in successful claim of misrepresentation. The courts have defined misrepresentation as an untrue statement of existing fact made by one party to the other which, while not forming part of the contract, is nevertheless one of the reasons that induces them to enter into it. Figure 9.1 below shows what needs to be proved in pictorial form. As with promissory estoppel, the essence of the doctrine is reliance. Although there is no general duty to *disclose* material facts, a single word, a nod, a shake of the head or a smile may amount to a misrepresentation of fact if it is misleading and relied upon. A finding of misrepresentation will allow the misled party to avoid the obligations posed by the resulting contract, if the statement subsequently turns out to be untrue. In these circumstance, consent to enter the contract is said to be vitiated and the agreement false.

Although silence does not otherwise amount to misrepresentation, a partial non-disclosure may do so. A statement may omit facts which render what is actually said false or misleading. So for instance, a comment made during pre-contractual negotiations to the effect that a piece of machinery has run without any hitches for 10 years which fails to indicate that it has broken down repeatedly in its 11th year could be viewed as a misrepresentation. It is also the case that a statement may be made which is true at the time, but which to the representor's knowledge ceases to be true before the contract is entered into. Here, a failure to inform the representee of the change in circumstances will amount to misrepresentation. So, for example, in *With v*

Figure 9.1:   The elements of misrepresentation

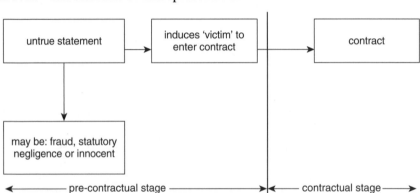

O'Flanagan (1936) a medical practice was stated to be worth £2,000 during negotiations for its sale. By the time the contract was entered into some months later, the practice had become worthless owing to the illness of the vendor. The contract was set aside as the changed circumstances had not been revealed.

STATEMENTS OF FACT, OPINIONS AND PROMISES

Much of the case law on misrepresentation is concerned with determining the sort of statements which it is reasonable for people to rely upon. In this context statements of fact, which are actionable, have been distinguished from other sorts of statement which cannot form the basis of an action. These include extravagant and unverifiable sales talk, statements of opinion, statements of intention and statements of law. The rationale behind the distinction remains sensible in most instances. It seems reasonable, for instance, to expect people to read contracts or get legal advice rather than rely on a statement of law made by a layperson. Similarly, statements of opinion and sales talk are commonly understood as 'puff' which should be believed with caution. For example, in *Bissett v Wilkinson* (1927), the vendor of land, which to the knowledge of both parties had not previously been used for sheep farming, stated that it would support 2,000 sheep. It was held that this was merely a statement of opinion which, when it proved to be unfounded, was not actionable. However, the courts have shown themselves less willing to apply the 'rule' relating to opinions where one party is in a position to know more than the other about the matter being discussed. So, in *Esso Petroleum Co Ltd v Mardon* (1976) an expert's inaccurate estimation of the future petrol sales of a filling station based on negligently prepared data was found to be a 'considered judgment' which was actionable.

A formulaic approach to distinguishing the sorts of statements which are actionable or not is dangerous as in some situations the distinction has become a rather subtle one. Indeed, it has been argued that the judicial distinctions between facts, opinions, intentions and other statements as to the future have now reached a state of oversubtle complexity. For example, it is a misrepresentation of fact for a person to say that they hold an opinion which they do not hold. Moreover, it could be argued that a pre-contractual statement about future intentions cannot be a misrepresentation if the party subsequently behaves differently as the statement of their intention may have been true when made. However, in *Quickmaid Rental Services Ltd v Reece* (1970) the company's representative, shortly before concluding a written rental agreement for a coffee machine with Reece, told him that they would not be installing another machine on the same road. Later another machine was installed and the representative's statement was held to be a promise in a contract partly written and partly oral (see also *Evans & Son (Portsmouth) Ltd v Merzario Ltd*, 1976).

An alternative to placing too heavy a reliance on distinctions of this type would be to ask whether, in all the circumstances, it was reasonable for the representee to rely on the statement rather than on their own judgment. As Collins (2003) has argued:

> These attempts to reduce to the form of rules the situations and contexts when it will be reasonable to rely upon pre-contractual statements looked doomed to failure for two reasons. In the first place, the reasonableness of reliance must depend upon numerous

features of the particular case, such as the relative expertise and knowledge of the parties, and the context in which a statement is made. For example, a statement about the legal effects of a document such as a Will might be reasonably relied upon if made by a qualified lawyer to a client, but not if made by someone without legal expertise .... We should also be aware that the issue of whether it was reasonable to rely on a statement is not simply a question of fact. It involves a normative judgment about which kinds of statements negotiating parties ought to be able to rely on.

INDUCEMENT AND RELIANCE

In order to lodge a successful claim for misrepresentation, the representee must also be able to show that they *relied* on the statement and that it *induced* the contract. Once it is established that the misrepresentation was calculated to induce entry into the contract, and that the representee has in fact entered, it is a fair inference that they were influenced by it. It used to be the case that it was defence to a claim of misrepresentation that the representee might have discovered its untruth by the exercise of reasonable care. But, since the coming into force of the Misrepresentation Act 1967, the judiciary have distinguished between those cases in which it was reasonable for the representee to make use of an opportunity to discover the truth and those in which it is not. Again, the courts have shown themselves willing to look at relative equality of bargaining power in these situations. So, for instance, in *Smith v Eric S Bush* (1990), the claimants relied on a negligent valuation of a house they were buying which was undertaken by a surveyor under contract to the building society they were using. Their claim against the surveyor succeeded even though they might have established the truth if they had employed their own surveyor. The House of Lords decided that it was not reasonable for them to take this step as the house was of modest value. Their decision might have been different had the house had a high value or if the case had involved commercial premises.

THE DIFFERENT TYPES OF MISREPRESENTATION

Three types of misrepresentation are currently recognised and can be classified according to the state of mind of the representor (see Figure 9.2). These are fraudulent misrepresentation (a dishonest assertion); negligent misrepresentation (not dishonest but careless); and wholly innocent misrepresentation (not dishonest or careless but nevertheless incorrect). All are capable of causing loss and are actionable but the remedies of the injured party are generally broadest in the case of fraud and much narrower for negligent and innocent misrepresentations. A party who proves that a misrepresentation induced them to enter into a contract, even if it was not the sole inducement, is entitled to rescind the contract or in certain circumstances claim damages. Rescission involves setting the contract aside and treating it as though it never happened. This means that both the parties must be able to return what they have exchanged.

Lord Herschell in *Derry v Peek* (1889) stated that 'fraud is proved when it is shown that a false representation has been made (1) knowingly, or (2) without belief in its truth, or (3) recklessly, careless whether it be true or false'. However, a person who

Figure 9.2:   The types of misrepresentation

type of misrepresentation	test	damages available?	rescission available?
fraudulent	deceit	special tortious–liable for all damage which flows directly from the misrepresentation even if not foreseeable	subject to usual bars
common law negligent	special knowledge	normal tortious–liable for all damage which was reasonably foreseeable	not applicable
statutory negligent	careless	special tortious–liable for all damage which flows directly from the misrepresentation even if not foreseeable	subject to usual bars
innocent	honest and on reasonable grounds	on discretionary basis	subject to usual bars

honestly believes their statement to be true, cannot be liable for fraud, however careless they might be. Thus, the claimant who alleges fraud must prove the absence of an honest belief, and although this burden is the same as in other civil proceedings, it is not easily discharged in practice. By way of contrast, innocent misrepresentation occurs in situations in which the defendant is able to establish that they had reasonable grounds to believe in the truth of their statement.

A misrepresentation is negligent if it is made carelessly and in breach of a duty to take reasonable care that the representation is accurate. It used to be argued that such a duty only arose in cases where there was an existing contract between the parties or a fiduciary relationship of some kind existed. But it became clear from the House of Lords landmark decision in *Hedley Byrne & Co Ltd v Heller and Partners Ltd* (1964) that, where a 'special' professional or business relationship, short of contract, existed, a duty of care was recognised in the law of tort as regards statements made and relied upon which caused financial loss. Significantly, in the case of such negligent misstatements, it is not necessary for the parties to enter into a contract following their negotiations.

These developments led up to a decision already referred to above. In *Esso Petroleum Co Ltd v Mardon* (1976), it was held that the relationship between the negotiating parties could be regarded as 'special' in the sense referred to in *Hedley Byrne*. Although the estimated throughput of 200,000 gallons a year was only a forecast, it was based on the superior knowledge of a senior sales representative who held himself out to be experienced in the field. Thus, it would seem that, if a person who has, or professes to have, a special knowledge or skill makes a representation in the form of advice, information or opinion with the intention of inducing the other party to enter a contract, they are under a duty to use reasonable care to ensure that what they have said is reliable.

The development of a common law doctrine of negligent misrepresentation was deemed largely irrelevant with the introduction of the Misrepresentation Act in 1967. Under s 2(1) of the 1967 Act a statutory liability for negligent misrepresentation was created which does not rely on any 'special relationship' (see Box 9.1). Significantly, the statute reversed the normal burden of proof in civil proceedings in which it is for the person making the claim to prove their case. Instead the duty is on the person making the representation to prove that they have reasonable grounds to believe, and do believe up to the time of making the contract, that the facts were true as

> **Box 9.1:   Section 2(1) of the Misrepresentation Act 1967**
>
> Where a person has entered into a contract after a misrepresentation has been made to him by another party thereto and as a result thereof he has suffered loss, then, if the person making the misrepresentation would be liable in damages thereof had the misrepresentation been made fraudulently, that person shall be so liable notwithstanding that the misrepresentation was not made fraudulently, unless he proves that he had reasonable ground to believe and did believe up to the time the contract was made that the facts represented were true.

represented. This makes an action under the statute much more attractive than an action under the common law doctrine of negligent misstatement. However, the *Hedley Byrne* principle will still be of use in situations in which no contract results from the parties' dealings or the party making the statement is not a party to the final contract.

THE REMEDY OF DAMAGES

Two remedies need to be discussed in the context of actions for misrepresentation. These are damages and rescission. Debate about the availability of damages in misrepresentation is difficult to understand without an appreciation of the different ways in which the law of tort and contract approach the subject of what the injured party should be compensated for. Liability for misrepresentation may arise in tort where the representation is made fraudulently or negligently. It will only arise in contract where the representation has also become a term. Where damages are assessed on tortious principles, the object is to put the misrepresentee into the financial position they would have been in had the tort not been committed. By way of contrast, where damages are assessed on contractual principles, the object is to put the party who has suffered as a result of breach in the position they would have been in had the contract been performed and their *expectations* fulfilled. Figure 9.3 compares these two positions in diagrammatic form but the fact is that, in practice, the distinction can be a difficult one to draw.

The general result is that tort tends to protect a bad bargain whereas contract protects a good one. This general rule should guide you when determining what arguments to pursue in a case. If your client has made a good deal, it would clearly be better to argue in the first instance that a pre-contractual representation had become a term. If, they have made a bad deal, then it would be more profitable to argue that it is a case involving fraud or negligence in relation to a non-contractual statement.

Figure 9.3: Damages

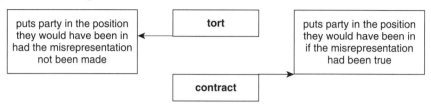

So for instance, a dress described as a 'vintage Dior black dress' has a market value of £1,000. I am prepared to pay £1,500 for it because I like it so much. In due course it transpires that it is not a vintage Dior and has a market value of £500. If I claimed tortuous damages I would be due £1,000 because I have lost £1,500 but still have a dress worth £500. This puts me back in the financial position I would have been in had I not purchased the dress. If I claimed contractual damages, I would be due £500 which is the difference between what it is actually worth (£500) and what I thought it was worth (£1,000).

However, the courts have tended to be more generous in cases involving fraudulent behaviour. In these instances the courts have allowed the claimant to recover for any damages which flow from the tort whether or not they are foreseeable; see *Doyle v Olby (Ironmongers) Ltd* (1969). In *East v Maurer* (1991), the court reconsidered whether 'all the actual damages flowing directly from the fraudulent inducement' covered loss of profits. This could be classified as an 'expectation' loss of a type usually found only in breach of contract. The facts of the case were that East bought one of Maurer's two hair salons in Bournemouth for £20,000 in 1979. Maurer fraudulently claimed in the course of negotiations that he did not intend to work in the other salon except in emergencies. In fact he continued to work full-time in that salon. The effect was that the claimants' business was never profitable. East sold it in 1989 for £5,000 and sued Maurer for fraudulent misrepresentation. At first instance, damages were awarded to cover the difference in value of the business between the purchase price and its true market value. They also included an award of £15,000 for loss of profits more in keeping with the award of contractual damages. On appeal, it was held that 'all the actual damage' did include loss of profits in this case, on the basis that, where deceit is concerned, the law should compensate the claimant for all the loss suffered, so far as money can. The distinction made by the court between damages in tort and contract was that it was assessing the profit the claimant might have expected to make in another salon bought for a similar sum (tortious). They were not assessing the profit on the basis of the profits that the salon might have made if Maurer had *promised* that he would not work in the other salon (contractual).

The judgment suggests there is a very fine line between the contractual test and tortious test. It will be appreciated that, in this case, Maurer did not contractually bind himself not to work in the other salon. The statement he made was a pre-contractual statement of intention which was held to be a misrepresentation of *fact* because it was proved that he did not have this intention when he made the statement. But, significantly, however, the outcome was virtually the same as if he had bound himself by contract.

Some of the same issues have arisen in the context of statutory misrepresentation. Section 2(1) of the 1967 Act, reproduced above (Box 9.1), gives a statutory right to damages but considerable confusion has also revolved around the section. Whilst it makes clear that assessment is to be calculated on a tortious basis, opinion has been somewhat divided over whether it should be calculated according to the more generous level of damages under the tort of deceit or the less generous level used more generally in the tort of negligence. Until recently the weight of academic opinion was in line with Treitel's analysis in 1987:

> Where the action is brought under s 2(1) of the Misrepresentation Act, one possible view is that the deceit rule will be applied by virtue of the fiction of fraud. But the preferable view is that the severity of the deceit rule can only be justified in cases of actual fraud and that remoteness under s 2(1) should depend, as in actions based on negligence, on the test of foreseeability.

It will be recalled that the 'deceit rule', means that a representee can recover all loss flowing directly from the fraud even if the loss was not foreseeable. The 'fiction of fraud' referred to by Treitel is an allusion to the wording of s 2(1) itself where it states that the liability for damages should arise *as if* the statement had been made fraudulently. In the case of *Royscot Trust Ltd v Rogerson* (1991), the Court of Appeal held that s 2(1) liability gave rise to liability under the 'deceit rule'. The facts of the case were that a car dealer negligently misrepresented to the claimant finance company both the price of a car and the amount of deposit paid by a customer who wished to take the vehicle on hire-purchase (HP) terms. The company financed the deal but the customer (first defendant) sold the car in breach of the HP agreement and defaulted on his payments. The finance company brought proceedings against both customer and dealer for the loss suffered. It was held that the measure of damages under s 2(1) of the 1967 Act is tortious, not contractual, and that the dealer's liability was such that, in the judgment of Balcombe LJ, 'the finance company is entitled to recover from the dealer all the losses which it suffered as a result of entering into the agreements with the dealer and the customer, even if those losses were unforeseeable'. The finance company was awarded £3,625 plus interest. The literal interpretation of s 2(1) in this case means that, as regards the measure of damages, a negligent misrepresentor is in the same position as the fraudulent and that the more generous award applies in either case. However, it is difficult to appreciate why the traditional tort law distinction between intentional and negligent conduct should be disregarded in this way, so making the negligent misrepresentor liable beyond the bounds of forseeability; but see also *Naughton v O'Callaghan* (1990).

There is no *right* to damages for a wholly innocent misrepresentation under s 2(2) of the 1967 Act, but the court is given a *discretionary* power to declare the contract subsisting and to award damages in lieu of rescission if it would be equitable to do so. The court must bear in mind the nature of the misrepresentation and the loss caused to the representee if the contract were upheld and the loss caused to the representor if the contract were set aside. This discretionary power extends to negligent misrepresentation so making available the remedies of rescission *and* damages under s 2(1) or, if appropriate, rescission or damages under s 2(2) in cases of this kind. However, the court's power to award damages in lieu of rescission, where this remedy is not barred (see below) is more likely to be used where the representor is not at fault and compensation is an adequate remedy. The assessment of damages under s 2(2) is the normal tortious measure which excludes consequential loss.

THE REMEDY OF RESCISSION

Rescission is an equitable remedy which is available in *all* cases of misrepresentation. If the representee chooses to rescind the contract, and the court so orders, the contract is treated as if it never existed. It can be gleaned from this that the remedy is a drastic one and it is for this reason that the courts are sometimes reluctant to use it as it involves both the parties giving back what they have exchanged. A party who wishes to rescind should, if possible, take active steps against the representor as soon as possible such as seeking a cancellation of the contract. But legal proceedings will be necessary if, say, money paid by the victim (representee) is claimed and the representor refuses to pay it back.

It is also important to understand that here are four bars or limitations to rescission. Firstly, if the representee continues with the contract in the knowledge of the other party's misrepresentation, as happened in *Doyle*, then the contract is treated as affirmed and will be allowed to continue. Secondly, it may be impossible to put the parties back into their original positions before the contract was made. This may be because the representee has made changes to the subject matter causing its value to decline or it may be a wasting asset such as a cargo of fruit. However, a representee who can make substantial, though not precise, restitution can still rescind the contract if they return the subject matter and make allowance for its deterioration. Thirdly, the right to rescind will be lost through the intervention of third-party rights. So, a person who has been induced by fraud to sell goods on credit cannot rescind the contract after the goods have been bought by an innocent third party; see further *Lewis v Averay* (1972) in Chapter 10. Finally, in cases of *non*-fraudulent misrepresentation, a lapse of time may bar rescission. This point was illustrated in *Leaf v International Galleries* (1950) in which a five-year delay in a case of innocent misrepresentation was held to bar the claimant's claim. In cases of fraud, lapse of time is merely evidence of affirmation, as time runs from the discovery of the truth.

EXCLUSION OF LIABILITY FOR MISREPRESENTATION

A sensible option for a smart lawyer trying to protect their client is to incorporate a clause in a contract excluding or restricting liability for misrepresentation. However, any such clause would be subject to the rules regarding incorporation and construction. It is also subject to s 3 of the 1967 Act, as amended by s 8 of the Unfair Contract Terms Act 1977, which applies the requirement of reasonableness, as laid down by s 11(1) of the latter Act, to the clause. This use of this test was looked at in *South Western General Property Co Ltd v Marton* (1982). In this case, Marton, an experienced builder, bought land at auction. It was described in the particulars of sale as building land for which planning permission had previously been refused because the proposed house was out of character. The sale was subject to an exclusion clause which stated that 'any intending purchaser must satisfy himself by inspection or otherwise as to the correctness of each statement contained in the particulars'.

Marton, who had bought the land as a site for his own residence, later discovered that planning permission had been refused in terms that made any further application futile. The court held that the description in the particulars was misleading because it implied that the land could be used for building if the house was in character and this was untrue. The defendant had relied on the description, which 'failed to tell more than a part of the facts which were material to the whole contract of sale'. Moreover, the attempt to exclude liability was held to be unreasonable in the circumstances. It is extremely important to look at the context of each case when determining whether this precedent might help. In cases involving experienced dealers and an individual, an exclusion may be found to be unreasonable, whereas the same clause might be regarded as reasonable if found in a contract with a property speculator.

CONCLUDING REMARKS

The issues raised in the chapter are important as they encourage us to think about the role of private laws in encouraging appropriate rather than just commercially acceptable behaviour. What is clear from the chapter is that a range of standards apply depending on the intentions and behaviour of those disclosing information in pre-contractual negotiations and the characteristics of the contracting parties. It is evident that different standards apply depending on the relative bargaining strengths of the parties. The last few decades have witnessed an increasing use of legal devices to protect consumers with little power in the market place or experience of commerce. But the case law in the field of misrepresentation also displays a sensitivity towards inequality of bargaining power in intra-business relationships. The influence of tortious principles is clear as the courts have had to turn their attention to notions of superior knowledge. It is within this context that the notion of reliance rather than bargain, discussed in the last chapter, begins to make sense. Many of the debates touched upon in this chapter will continue to have resonance as discussion of the effect of information asymmetry continues to trouble economists in their attempts to improve market efficiency. The judiciary and academics are also under much greater pressure than ever before to take the concept of good faith seriously in their discussions of pre-contractual negotiations.

REFERENCES AND FURTHER READING

Atiyah, P (1979) *The Rise and Fall of Freedom of Contract*, Part III, Clarendon Press, Oxford, particularly Chaps 14–16, 21 and 22.
Atiyah, P and Treitel, G 'Misrepresentation Act 1967' (1967) 30 MLR 369.
Bishop, W 'Negligent misrepresentation through economists' eyes' (1980) 96 LQR 360.
Cartwright, J (1991) *Unequal Bargaining*, Oxford University Press, Oxford.
Collins, H (2003) *The Law of Contract*, 4th edn, London: LexisNexis Butterworths.
Teubner, G 'Legal irritants: good faith in British law or how unifying law ends up in new divergences' (1998) 61 *Modern Law Review* 11.
Treitel, G (1987) *The Law of Contract*, Sweet and Maxwell, London. See, more recently, Peel, E and Treitl, G (2007) *The Law of Contract*, Sweet and Maxwell, London.

? *QUESTIONS*

(1) In the example of the Dior dress given above, reference is made to how a bad deal is better compensated in tort. Can you draft an example which demonstrates that a client who has made a good deal would be better advised to argue that the representation had become a term of the contract and that contractual damages could be claimed?

(2) In 'The Sad Tale of Angie and Georgie', could it be argued that any of the following are guilty of misrepresentation:

(a) Ned and Monkfish;

(b) Claude;

(c) Angie and Georgie?

What would the parties to any action have to prove before their action was successful?

(3) Discuss critically the following statement:

Some academic commentators have expressed concern that good faith could work practical mischief if ruthlessly implanted in our system of law'. Others have welcomed good faith as a healthy infusion of communitarian values, hoping that it will cure the ills of contractual formalism and interact productively with other substantive elements in British contract law.

PART FOUR:

BARGAINING NAUGHTINESS AND FORMATION PROBLEMS

CHAPTER 10

MISTAKE

INTRODUCTION

We have already discovered that, if two people appear, according to an objective test, to have intended to reach an agreement supported by consideration, they are bound by it. But in certain limited circumstances the courts have been prepared to set contracts aside on the basis that there is no true agreement because one or both of the parties were mistaken about something which strikes at the root of the contract. However, the mistake doctrines discussed in this chapter remain narrow despite the attempts of some members of the judiciary to expand them. In part this is because the judiciary has expressed discomfort with an expansive doctrine aimed at setting contracts aside. They have preferred instead to see themselves primarily as upholders of agreements and expectations.

The limited rationale for allowing certain contracts to be set aside came into the English common law from continental jurisprudence in the second part of the nineteenth century. Like the notion of intention to create legal relations, it grew out of strict 'consensus' or 'will' theory which insisted that obligations must be voluntary. If there were any factors present which vitiated consent, then this was considered fatal to the binding nature of the parties' agreement. Contrary to the objective test which places emphasis on what the parties actually say and do rather than what they intended, the will theory required a 'real' meeting of the minds and true intention.

This subjective approach to agreement has now been almost entirely superseded by the objective view of agreement which is concerned with what appears to have happened rather than the actual state of the parties' minds. However, it is still the case that the vestiges of the will theory remain in cases relating to mistake more than in any other contractual doctrine. So, for instance, in *Bell v Lever Bros Ltd* (1932), Lord Atkin suggested that true consent is still required when he said that: 'If mistake operates at all, it operates to negate or nullify consent'.

The subject is one which is rife with old decisions that are difficult to reconcile and in addition there is a wealth of 'explanatory' academic theory and counter-theory on the issue. A disproportionate amount of time can be spent on mistake which will be of little use in the day-to-day world of business. The possibility of mistake being pleaded might be discussed by lawyers but it is unlikely to be favoured as an excuse to avoid a contrast. This is because the threshold for proving mistake is extremely high. As a result there is little modern case law. Moreover, that which exists raises a number of difficult issues about how the courts should respond to mistakes, none of which have been comprehensibly resolved. Should the law prevent a party from profiting from the mistake of another? Can the courts impose a duty to correct an obvious mistake when they are so reluctant to recognise a general duty of good faith in pre-contractual negotiations? Should commercial transactions be conducted on the assumption that business people have fully appraised themselves of all the circumstances surrounding the transaction, regardless of whether they have made a mistake? Many of the decided cases involve the mistaken party seeking to avoid the 'agreement' they have made. What should the law do in instances in which they seek to enforce an agreement on the basis of the terms that they *thought* had been decided upon?

Two main types of mistake are discernible from the case law but in this chapter we are only concerned with the first type, which can be labelled 'agreement mistake'. The second type of mistake, known as 'common' mistake or 'possibility mistake', has traditionally be dealt with alongside agreement mistake despite the fact that it deals with circumstances which are conceptually different. For that reason it is discussed in the chapter on impossibility where it is considered alongside the related doctrine of frustration. In the remainder of this chapter we focus on agreement mistake. This occurs where the parties are at cross-purposes or one party is deceived by the other.

AGREEMENT MISTAKES

The doctrines of mistake discussed in this section and the next are very closely related to those concerning offer and acceptance. They are mistakes which occur in pre-contractual negotiations and at the moment of responsibility. Many of the cases involve instances in which the parties are at cross-purposes. So for instance, Fantasy Trains might offer to sell its fleet of excess trains to Europa Snail, a new rail operator. But it may be that in the negotiation Fantasy are referring to old rolling stock, whereas Europa Snail think they are negotiating about the latest models which they believe are no longer needed by Fantasy when a branch line is shut down (see Figure 10.1).

Figure 10.1:   Agreement mistake: cross purposes

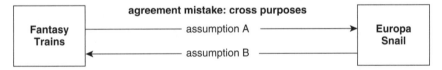

In such instances, disputes arise when the mistaken party realises that an error has been made and refuses to perform their part of the bargain. In *Scriven v Hindley* (1913) a man had bid at an auction for bales which he thought were hemp as a result of the misleading description given by the seller. When sued for the price he claimed mistake and was successful. In another 'cross-purposes' case, *Raffles v Wichelhaus* (1864), Raffles agreed to sell a consignment of cotton which was to arrive on a ship called *The Peerless* from Bombay. However, there happened to be two ships called *Peerless* sailing from Bombay. One was due to sail in October and the other in December. Raffles sent the cotton on the December voyage when the purchasers understanding was that it would be sent on the earlier one. Judgment was given for Wichelhaus.

The cross-purpose cases seem to suggest that the courts are prepared to make judgment on the basis of what the parties might be expected to know rather than what they actually know and understand. This is particularly relevant in industries and trades where certain ways of dealing have been adopted as standard practice. The case of *Hartog v Colin & Shields* (1939) illustrates this point. This case involved a unilateral mistake in which one party made a mistake which the other was aware of but does not correct. The facts were that the defendants offered to sell the claimants a batch of hare skins and quoted a price per pound weight, when they meant to quote a price per skin. The formal offer represented a very cheap price and the claimants accepted the offer. However, when the defendants realised their mistake, they refused to deliver the skins. They claimed that it was obvious that a material mistake had been made and that the claimants were trying to take advantage of the fact. It was made clear in the course of proceedings that it was the custom in the trade to quote the price per skin. Moreover, it was shown that in earlier stages of negotiations the defendants had asked a much higher price and had always expressed their offers in terms of the price per piece. These factors led the court to the conclusion that a mistake had been made and that anyone with knowledge of the trade would also have realised it. It was held that the claimants could not reasonably have supposed that the offer reflected the intention of the defendants. As a result the contract was void. This meant that it was treated as though it had never existed.

The courts have made clear that a mistake by one of the parties as the quality of the subject matter of the contract, rather than the subject matter itself will not render the contract unenforceable on the grounds of mistake. This rule is well illustrated by the case of *Smith v Hughes* (1871) in which the defendant sold a batch of oats to the claimant, after giving him an opportunity to inspect a sample of them. The claimant subsequently argued that he had made clear that he wanted old oats and that he had been sold young oats. The defendant argued that he had not specified old oats and that the oats delivered had the same quality as the sample which the claimant had inspected. Cockburn CJ agued that, whilst there appeared to have been no true agreement as to the age of the oats, there was a clear agreement about the sale and purchase of some oats (see further, *Frederick Rose (London) v Pim*, 1953).

THE PROBLEM OF MISTAKEN IDENTITY

A number of the mistake cases which have come to be considered by the courts involve issues about mistaken identity. The law in this particular area has the potential to be of considerable contemporary significance. As Lord Millett made clear in the House of Lords in *Shogun Finance Ltd v Hudson* (2003), mistaken identity is far from being an esoteric issue which only troubles academics. In the modern age of e-shopping and 'identity theft' impersonations and fraudulent purchases are on the increase. Mistaken identity cases involve fraudulent deception about the identity of one of the parties. A mistaken identity case might arise, for instance, where someone dishonestly pretends to be the Chief Executive of Fantasy Trains and Europa Snail enter into a contract with her as a result (Figure 10.2). It differs from the type of case outlined in Figure 10.1 because mistaken identity cases involve unilateral mistakes rather than mutual ones. That is to say, only one of the parties is mistaken.

Figure 10.2: Agreement mistake: unilateral

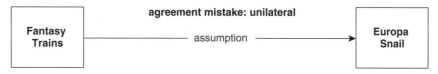

What tends to happen in mistaken identity cases is that a fraudster obtains valuable goods on credit by representing themselves as someone else, often against a worthless cheque. The fraudster then disposes of the goods to an innocent third party, for cash. The dilemma for the judges hearing such cases is whether they should place priority on protecting the interests of the first person deceived or the innocent third party to whom the goods have been sold on.

In such cases the first person deceived often has a choice to have the contract set aside on the basis that it was founded on a mistake or to bring an action for fraudulent misrepresentation. Unilateral agreement mistakes involving fraudsters bear many similarities to fraudulent misrepresentation discussed in Chapter 9 and the two heads are often pleaded in the alternative. In the cases in Chapter 9, the misrepresentation related to the attributes of the contractual subject matter such as a filling station's annual turnover of petrol. By way of contrast, the mistake cases tend to focus on the notion of identity, of who a party is. The differences can be difficult to discern in practice and some have argued that the distinction is meaningless, that a person cannot be distinguished from their qualities or attributes. However, the remedies available can differ considerably depending on whether fraudulent misrepresentation or mistaken identity is pleaded and this is something that students should remain sensitive to as the doctrine you use should be selected on the basis of what it is that you want to achieve.

Either way, the remedies available for fraudulent mistake or misrepresentation are often of little use because the fraudster will have disappeared without leaving a forwarding address! For this reason, the case before the courts is usually brought by the person first deceived against the innocent third party from which they wish to recover their property. However, it is important to understand that the action is *not* based directly on contract as there is no contractual relationship between the person first deceived and the third party (see Figure 10.3 below).

Figure 10.3:   Mistaken identity

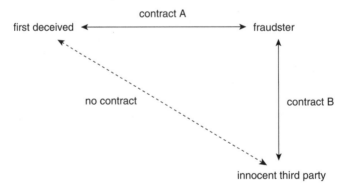

Instead, the first deceived has to bring an action in the *tort of conversion* for recovery of the goods or their value. This action is based on the claim that the innocent third party cannot own the goods because ownership of them never passed to the fraudster. To be successful in this claim, the first deceived has to prove that their contract with the fraudster was based on a fundamental mistake. When the contract between the fraudster and the first deceived was based on a fundamental mistake, it is argued that ownership did not pass to the fraudster. It follows that, as a result, they cannot have transferred ownership to the innocent third party. The dilemma faced by the courts is clear: which of the two innocent parties should suffer for the dishonesty of the fraudster?

Understanding of the issues at stake also relies on an appreciation of the difference between contracts rendered void and those which are merely voidable. The position is relatively simple if only the fraudster and the person first deceived are involved. If the deceived can prove mistaken identity, their contract with the fraudster is void. In other words, it is treated as never having existed. The result is that neither the fraudster nor innocent third party can obtain ownership of the goods. By way of contrast, if the action rests on fraudulent misrepresentation, then the deceived's contract with the fraudster can, at best, be declared voidable. The situation is more complicated when an innocent third party is involved. The involvement of a third party can stop the deceived from avoiding the first contract if the contract between the deceived and fraudster was unchallenged when the fraudster passed on ownership to the innocent third party. In this situation the court protects the interests of the innocent third party and will not upset the second contract. As a result it is the innocent third party who is able to retain the goods.

The factors which motivate the courts to set aside a contract on the basis of mistaken identity are illustrated in the leading case of *Cundy v Lindsay* in 1878. The claimants, Lindsay, received an order for goods from a fraudulent person, Blenkarn, who gave his address as 37 Wood Street, Cheapside. He signed his letter in such a way as to make it appear that the offer came from Blenkiron & Co, a firm known by reputation to the claimants whose address was 123 Wood Street. The goods were despatched to Blenkiron and Co, 37 Wood Street. Blenkarn took possession of them but, without paying the claimants, sold them to the defendants, who were sued by the claimants for conversion. It was held that there was no contract between the claimants and Blenkarn, therefore no title to the goods passed to Blenkarn or consequently to the defendants who were accordingly liable.

The court inferred that the claimants intended to sell to Blenkiron & Co and not to the person who traded at 37 Wood Street. In other words they thought they were accepting Blenkiron & Co's 'offer', as Blenkarn knew full well. As a result there was no 'concurrence of minds', consent was negated and no agreement arose between the claimants and Blenkarn. Lord Cairns opined:

> ... how is it possible to imagine that ... any contract could have arisen between the respondent Lindsay and Blenkarn, the dishonest man? Of him they knew nothing, and of him they never thought. With him they never intended to deal. Their minds never, even for an instant of time, rested upon him, and as between him and them there was no consensus of mind which could lead to any agreement.

If, alternatively, the court had inferred that the claimants, though misled by Blenkarn's fraud, had intended or at least were content to deal with the person at 37 Wood Street from which address the offer had come and to which the goods were sent, then there would have been a contract between the claimants and Blenkarn. It would have been voidable for fraudulent misrepresentation but the defendants' title to the goods would have been secure since they would have acquired a good but voidable title from Blenkarn before the claimants had avoided their contract with Blenkarn. In this way they would have defeated any re-transfer of title.

However, the reasoning in the case has not received universal support. Cheshire and Fifoot, for example, felt that 'it is permissible to regret the inference which their Lordships drew from the facts' (p. 174). They, and others, have been concerned that a finding of mistaken identity in such circumstances unnecessarily prejudices third parties who later deal in good faith with the fraudulent person.

Cundy v Lindsay was decided during an era in which the subjective test was used to determine whether there had been a 'true' concurrence of minds. For the case to remain relevant today, we must ask from an objective viewpoint whether the claimants had clearly shown that their intention was only to deal with Blenkiron & Co who were known to them. Thus, in line with what is now the basic test for establishing agreement, we must answer the following questions. Did Lindsay so conduct themselves that a reasonable person would think that they were accepting an offer from Blenkiron & Co? Moreover, did Blenkarn the rogue know, or ought he reasonably to have realised that Lindsay were prepared only to contract with Blenkiron & Co?

It is clear from the decision in *Cundy* that the main stumbling block in the claimant's case is their need to overcome the legal presumption that, despite a mistake, the parties entered into a binding contract. In order to rebut the presumption, the claimant must prove that the person whose identity is assumed is a definite and identifiable person. In other words, the claimant must show that they intended to deal with a specific person other than the fraudster with whom they apparently made a contract. If there is no confusion between two distinct entities, there is no fundamental mistake. In addition, the claimant must prove that the other party was aware of their intention to deal with some person other than himself. This requirement is easily met where it is a fraudster who has induced the alleged mistake. In *King's Norton Metal Co Ltd v Edridge, Merrett & Co Ltd* (1897). Here a fraudster obtained goods from the claimant by business letter using the alias 'Hallam & Co'. Since the fraudster and 'Hallam & Co' were the same person, the claimant could not be said to have made a mistake of identity. The claimant did mistakenly believe that 'Hallam & Co' existed as a separate entity but was unable to show that they meant to contract with 'Hallam & Co' and not with the fraudster. They had taken a risk as to the credit-worthiness of the letter writer. It was determined that they had made a voidable contract on the basis of fraud but that the contract was not void for mistake.

More recently, there has been a trend against finding an operative mistake in similar cases. The courts have preferred to find a contract between the claimant and the rogue which is only voidable for fraud. There are a number of reasons for this. Firstly, unlike the judges in *Cundy v Lindsay*, the courts are now primarily concerned with the objective 'outward and visible signs' of agreement and not with the presence of an 'inward and mental assent'. Moreover, in the significant 'mistake' cases since *Cundy v Lindsay*, the claimant and the rogue have dealt with each other face-to-face rather than through the medium of writing. In line with the objective view of agreement, a strong presumption has developed that when dealing face-to-face, the claimant intended to contract with the person physically present before them and identified by sight and hearing. So, for instance, in *Citibank NA v Brown Shipley & Co Ltd* (1991), Waller J stated that: 'The no contract situation, as opposed to a voidable contract, only arises if it is fundamental to the contract that one party to the contract should be who he says that he is. That is easier to establish where contracts are made entirely by documents and is less easy to establish in an *inter praesentes* position'.

Law Reform Committee Report of 1966 recommended 'that contracts which are at present void because the owner of the goods was deceived or mistaken as to the identity of the person with whom he dealt should in future be treated as voidable so far as third parties are concerned'. This recommendation has, however, never taken legislative effect. Whether these arguments render *Cundy v Lindsay* irrelevant or distinguishable from 'face-to-face' cases is debatable. What is clear is that modern courts are more likely to place the claimant's behaviour under closer scrutiny. Situations in which the claimant has been careless in his or her dealings with the rogue are more likely to prompt the courts to decide in favour of third party rights. So for instance, it has been argued that one should get a cheque cleared before parting with property worth several hundred pounds (see *Lewis v Averay*, 1972 and *Gallie v Lee*, 1971). Further, it is established that the claimant must also prove that, during negotiations and before entering into the contract, they regarded the 'identity' of the other contracting party as being of vital importance and indicated as such. They must also demonstrate that they took all reasonable steps to verify that 'identity'.

The outcome of judicial analysis is that a mistake of identity occurs where the victim confuses the attributes of two particular persons. But the expectation is that, to be successful, the claimant must be independently aware of some of the attributes of the person the rogue is pretending to be. So for instance, they must be aware of the existence of a famous tennis player with the name being used by the rogue or that a reputable company called Blenkiron exists. This is one of the reasons why the claimant in *King's Norton Metal* failed. Moreover, the attributes being claimed or inferred must be very important in the context of the deal. So, for instance, if a tennis wear designer was giving substantial discounts to anyone who approached them, then they could not rely on the doctrine of mistake to help them set aside a contract with the bogus tennis player. What the cases discussed below seem to show is that the claimant's mistake as regards the attribute of creditworthiness is not one which can be relied upon to negate consent. This is because the creditworthiness of a party can be checked. What has tended to happen in a number of cases is that the claimant relies on their own personal and mistaken judgment to assess creditworthiness and so takes a deliberate business risk. The result is that the courts have decided that they, and not an innocent third party, must bear the loss.

When we come to the actual decisions and the reasoning of the various courts in the mistaken identity cases, there are problems of reconciling one decision with another and of establishing the principles upon which the courts proceed. It is useful to start with a key case, *Lewis v Averay*, decided by the Court of Appeal in 1972. In that case, Lewis advertised his car for sale and was approached by a fraudster who falsely claimed to be Richard Greene, a film and television actor. When the fraudster wrote a cheque for £450, Lewis, on asking for proof that he was Greene, was shown a film studio pass with the name 'Richard A Green' and the fraudster's photograph. Lewis took the cheque signed 'RA Green' and the fraudster took the car. The fraudster then sold the car to Averay who bought it in good faith. The cheque was subsequently dishonoured and Lewis sought to recover the car from Averay. It was held that the contract was not void for mistake and that title in the car had passed to Averay.

The reason for this outcome was that the presumption was that the claimant intended to contract with the person physically before them. However, the contract was considered to be voidable for fraud. In his judgment, Lord Denning took into account the rights and needs of innocent third parties. He contrasted the position of the innocent third party, who knew nothing of what had passed between Lewis and the fraudster, and the position of Lewis 'who let the rogue have the goods and thus enabled him to commit the fraud'. Lewis's mistake was as to creditworthiness and it is clear that he did less than was reasonable to establish that the fraudster was Greene. Moreover, even if the fraudster was Richard Greene that was no guarantee that the cheque would be honoured. In order to reinforce his approach, Denning also expressed agreement with the Law Reform Committee's recommendation of 1966 to the effect that contracts entered into in these circumstances should be voidable so far as the acquisition of title by innocent third parties was concerned.

Similar issues have arisen in other cases. In *Phillips v Brooks Ltd* (1919), a rogue entered the claimant's shop and selected pearls worth £2,550 and a ring worth £450. He wrote a cheque for £3,000, stating that he was Sir George Bullough of St James' Square, a wealthy man known by name to the claimant. Phillips checked the address in a directory and, at the rogue's request, allowed him to take away the ring. The rogue pawned the ring with Brooks Ltd and the cheque he gave to Phillips was subsequently dishonoured. Horridge J held that Phillips had 'contracted to sell and deliver [the ring] to the person who came into his shop ... who obtained the sale and delivery by means of the false pretence that he was Sir George Bullough'. In his analysis, the judge started by considering the *prima facie* legal presumption about face-to-face dealing. He argued that the claimant's intention was 'to sell to the person present and identified by sight and hearing'. Moreover, the jeweller had failed to prove that he intended to contract with Bullough and with nobody else. His looking up the address was scarcely sufficient to verify the rogue's claim. In summary, the claimant took a risk as regards creditworthiness and his case failed. The contract was voidable for fraud rather than void for mistake and had not, in this case, been avoided in time to defeat the defendant getting good title (see also *Shogun Finance Ltd v Hudson* 2003 on this point).

The importance of placing emphasis on distinguishing between the type of action proven and whether this rendered the contract void or voidable has been criticised. Adopting a different approach in *Ingram v Little* (1961), Devlin LJ expressed the view in his dissenting judgment that:

> the relevant question in this sort of case is not whether the contract was void or voidable, but which of two innocent parties shall suffer for the fraud of a third. The plain answer is that the loss should be divided between them in such proportion as is just in all the circumstances ... if the fault or imprudence of either party has caused or contributed to the loss, it should be borne by that party in the whole or in the greater part.

This suggestion, with its relevance to apportionment was found to be 'plainly attractive at first sight' by the Law Reform Committee in 1966. Nonetheless it was rejected by them as leading, in some cases, to 'uncertainty' consequent upon 'a wide and virtually unrestrained judicial discretion'. Problems were seen in particular where the goods passed from the rogue to an innocent purchaser and then on to subsequent innocent parties.

CONCLUDING REMARKS

It is clear from this chapter that the law of mistake is a complex and intricate subject. Given the paucity of cases on the subject, it is questionable as to whether it is essential to study the topic in any depth in an introductory text of this kind. As a result, this chapter has aimed to introduce some key themes which will encourage students to think about the subjective and objective tests of agreement, the extent to which third-party rights should effect the remedies of the main parties to the contract, the ways in which issues relating to formation of contracts overlap and the issue of how risk should be allocated between the parties when something goes wrong. In the chapter which follows we shall go on to develop some of these themes in the context of fairness in the bargaining process.

REFERENCES AND FURTHER READING

Greig, D 'The passing of property and the misidentified buyer' (1972) 35 MLR 306.

Jackson, B (1988) *Law, Fact and Narrative Coherence*, Deborah Charles, Liverpool.

Sutton, P 'Reform of the law of mistake in contract' (1976) *New Zealand Universities Law Review* 40.

Wheeler, S and Shaw, J (1994) *Contract Law: Cases, Materials and Commentary*, Oxford University Press, Oxford.

Williams, G 'Mistake as to party in the law of contract' (1945) *Canadian Bar Review* 271, 380.

 QUESTIONS

(1) Could any of the contracts in 'The Sad Tale of Angie and Georgie' be set aside on the grounds of agreement mistake? What would the disadvantages of bringing such an action be?

(2) Appraise critically the argument that mistake is not to be used as an excuse for bad bargains and nor should it be allowed to jeopardise the security of market transactions.

CHAPTER 11

THE IMPOSSIBILITY DOCTRINES

INTRODUCTION

The vast majority of business agreements proceed to satisfactory completion without disputes or claims that there has been a breach arising. But some commercial ventures may be thwarted because of something happening which is beyond the contracting parties control. So, for instance, the goods contracted for may have perished, making performance impossible. Alternatively war may unexpectedly break out in a country in which components are being made for a UK-based computer company. This may make it difficult for the manufacturer to make or deliver the components. If the war is with the UK, what constituted a legal and legitimate contract for the supply of the components on Monday suddenly becomes trading with the enemy on Tuesday and is rendered unlawful. Events of this kind may make performance of the contract impossible, difficult or illegal. How do the courts respond to such unexpected circumstances? Are the parties absolved from responsibility to perform their contract or do the courts hold them to it? What happens where the parties have already begun performance or been involved in a significant financial outlay in anticipation of performance?

COMMON OR POSSIBILITY MISTAKE

In Chapter 10 we looked at the problems surrounding agreement mistakes. This is the term used to describe situations involving a fraudster and a unilateral mistake or instances in which the parties are at cross-purposes. It was made clear in that chapter that another category of mistake exists which involves a situation in which both parties share the same misapprehension. This would be the case, for instance, where oranges have, unbeknown to either party, perished while their sale was being negotiated, or if Slapper Trains's whole fleet is destroyed by fire as the talks about their sale are ongoing. For this reason, this type of mistake is often referred to as common or possibility mistake, although the use of nomenclature differs considerably between commentators (see Figure 11.1).

The problem which arises in such instances is that it is impossible to perform the contract. What distinguishes this type of impossibility from the doctrine of frustration discussed in later sections is timing. Possibility mistake occurs because the contract has been negotiated on a mistaken assumption about the existence or quality of the thing being exchanged. In cases of frustration, the contract is capable of being performed at the time it is made but a subsequent event renders it impossible or futile. However, the main problem with possibility mistake, as in cases of frustration, lies in deciding when an incorrect assumption is sufficiently fundamental for the courts to justify setting the contract aside. As regards mistake, the weight of opinion is that a contract will only be void, that is considered to have never existed, where there is nothing to contract about and the agreement is devoid of all content.

Figure 11.1: Possibility mistake

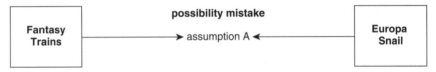

For some years there has been disagreement between commentators and members of the judiciary as to whether there is a second doctrine of common mistake founded in equity which allows the courts to intervene in circumstances where the contract would not be rendered void by the common law. The decision in *Bell v Lever Bros Ltd* (1932), suggests that this is not the case but Lord Denning argued in *Solle v Butcher* (1950) that the court did have this power and that common mistake could also render a contract voidable. In contrast to void contracts, those rendered voidable can be set aside at the discretion of the courts. The more recent decision of the Court of Appeal in *Great Peace Shipping Ltd v Tsavliris Salvage (International) Ltd* (2002) makes clear that this is not an appropriate statement of law. Applying *Bell v Lever*, the judges argued that there was no equitable jurisdiction in cases of common mistake and that the judgment in *Solle* had been an attempt to usurp the common law. The equitable doctrine envisaged by Denning was seen as bearing no difference to the common law doctrine and could not be used to revive a contract which the common law considered never to have existed. However, they argued *per curiam* that there was scope for the legislature to intervene to mitigate the harshness of the common law. We wait to see whether the legislature will take up the challenge.

In the *Great Peace* case, the defendants offered salvage services to a vessel in distress. The offer was accepted and the defendants approached a merchant ship which they both believed to be 35 miles from the vessel in distress. They entered into negotiations to use the ship for salvage purposes and concluded a contract to do so. They then discovered that the merchant ship was actually 410 miles away. However, the defendants did not cancel the contract until they had found an alternative ship to undertake the work. When challenged, they pleaded fundamental mistake of fact and that the contract was either void or voidable at law. The court found in favour of the merchant vessel, the owners of which were suing for breach of contract.

The judgment makes clear that the test for common mistake is extremely narrow. They contended that a common mistake would not allow the parties to avoid a contract unless it rendered the subject matter of the contract essentially and radically different from that the parties believed to exist. It was considered telling that the defendants did not want to cancel the arrangement until they knew whether they could find a nearer vessel. The judges rejected the argument that the doctrine was based on the notion of an implied term that the contract would be rendered void in the circumstances which had occurred. It was made clear that the circumstances were far removed from the contemplation of the parties and that, as a result, it was something of a falsity to imply agreement about such a term. In finding for the merchant shipowners they, were influenced by the fact that the ship could still have played a part in the rescue operation even though it was so far away, whereas the test for common mistake was that the circumstances had to render performance impossible rather than something which was just substantially different.

THE DOCTRINE OF FRUSTRATION

It has been argued that the security of contract is increasingly affected by the spread of political, economic and social upheavals, such as war, strikes, revolution or rampant inflation. Globalisation of markets has contributed to such modern disruptions, as more and more businesses form links with contractors in other states. The courts can respond to such problems through the doctrine of frustration, known elsewhere as the impossibility doctrine. Like the doctrine of mistake which deals with a pre-existing impossibility problem, the doctrine of frustration is a narrow one. This is because the courts have been reluctant to allow the parties to escape their obligations to each other in anything but the most extreme circumstances. A claim that a contract has been frustrated will not be successful, for instance, when one party merely finds performance difficult or unprofitable. However, frustration is often pleaded in such circumstances in an attempt to avoid contractual obligations. The courts have preferred to see the doctrine as one of *last resort* which should be used rarely and with reluctance.

There are few modern authorities that deal with the doctrine and trainee lawyers will not hear frustration being discussed with clients on a regular basis. Neither are there any empirical studies of the doctrine which allow us to place the formal law in its social, political or economic context. However, the doctrine of frustration remains important because it provides an example of the importance of planning contractual performance in advance. The allocation of commercial risk is something that all contractors are interested in and often bears a close relation to the price to be paid. Careful drafting and allocation of risk prior to performance means that the parties can often avoid the need for costly litigation should something unpredictable happen to disrupt the contract.

THE BASIC TENETS OF THE DOCTRINE

Taylor v Caldwell (1863) is generally acknowledged to be the first case which saw the introduction of a general principle of frustration and provides a good example of the use of the doctrine as a defence to a claim of breach of contract. In this case, Caldwell agreed on 27 May to let Taylor have the use of the Surrey Music Hall at £100 per day for four concerts. The first of the concerts was to be held on 17 June but on 11 June the hall was accidentally burnt down and it became clear that the parties had made no provision in the contract for such a contingency. Taylor claimed damages in respect of wasted advertising expenses but it was held that the contract was discharged by frustration and that Caldwell was not liable. Blackburn outlined the reasons for the decision:

> Where, from the nature of the contract, it appears that the parties must from the beginning have known that it could not be fulfilled unless ... some particular specified thing continued to exist, so that, when entering into the contract, they must have contemplated such continuing existence as the foundation of what was to be done; there ... the parties

shall be excused in case, before breach, performance becomes impossible from the perishing of the thing without the fault of the contractor. (p. 27)

Subsequent leading judgments were keen to make the point that the doctrine is a restrictive one. In *Davis Contractors Ltd v Fareham Urban District Council* (1956), Davis agreed to build Fareham Urban District Council 78 houses in eight months for £92,000. Serious shortages of labour and materials resulted in the contract taking 22 months to complete and costing Davis £18,000 more than estimated. Davis claimed that the contract had been frustrated by economic conditions and that, as a consequence, he was not bound by the agreed price. Instead he claimed a larger sum for services rendered on a *quantum meruit* basis. The House of Lords held that the delay caused did not mean that the basis of the contract was displaced. Lord Radcliffe famously explained the basic tenets underpinning the doctrine when he said that:

> ... frustration occurs whenever the law recognises that without default of either party a contractual obligation has become incapable of being performed because the circumstances in which performance is called would render it a thing radically different from that which was undertaken by the contract ... The court must act upon a general impression of what its rule requires ... But, even so, it is not hardship or inconvenience or material loss itself which calls the principle of frustration into play. There must be as well such a change in the significance of the obligation that the thing undertaken would, if performed, be a different thing from that contracted for. (p. 160)

In this case the thing contracted for was 78 houses. These had been built so in the circumstances, the court considered it appropriate that the risk fell upon the builder and rejected the claim of frustration.

In 1981, in *National Carriers Ltd v Panalpina (Northern) Ltd*, the House of Lords upheld Lord Radcliffe's 'radical change in the obligation' test, which was restated by Lord Simon as follows:

> Frustration of a contract takes place when there supervenes an event (without default of either party and for which the contract makes no sufficient provision) which so significantly changes the nature (not merely the expense or onerousness) of the outstanding contractual rights and/or obligations from what the parties could reasonably have contemplated at the time of its execution that it would be unjust to hold them to the literal sense of its stipulations in the new circumstances; in such a case the law declares both parties to be discharged from further performance. (p. 175)

In the same case, Lord Hailsham identified a number of different ways of justifying the setting aside of the contract in such circumstances. These included the inclusion of an implied term in the contract to the effect that if the parties had known what was going to happen they would have assumed that the contract should have been terminated. Alternatively he said it could be argued that the contract should be set aside because of a total failure of consideration. He noted that broader concepts employed by the judiciary to rationalise such interference included a requirement that justice be done in these exceptional cases or the assumption of an obligation to search for the real 'meaning' of the contract.

Unfortunately, the vast majority of frustration cases are not clear-cut. They frequently concern pleas of commercial futility brought about by a wide variety of political, economic or other disabling factors rather than the more obvious physical impossibility of the type in *Taylor v Caldwell*. So, for instance, in *Krell v Henry* (1903),

Henry hired rooms in Pall Mall at a high price for the purpose of viewing the coronation procession of Edward VII. The procession was cancelled owing to the King's illness but Krell sued for the hire charge and the doctrine of frustration was pleaded in defence. The court held that Krell's claim failed. The contract had been frustrated and was therefore void. In their opinion it was the coronation procession and the relative position of the rooms which was the basis of the contract rather than the value of having a hired room (see also *Amalgamated Investment & Property Co Ltd v John Walker & Sons Ltd*, 1976).

However, in another 'coronation case', *Herne Bay Steam Boat Co v Hutton* (1903), Herne Bay Steam Boat Company hired a boat in order to offer cruises on coronation day. The aim of the trip was to see the royal naval review which had been organised to celebrate the coronation together with a day's travelling around the fleet at Spithead. In contrast to *Krell v Henry* which involved the same frustrating event, the contract was held not to be frustrated when the royal review was cancelled because of the King's indisposition. The reason given by the court was that, in this case, the royal review was not the sole basis of the contract. As Sir Frederick Pollock said: 'In point of fact the fleet was still there and it was very well worth seeing without the review'.

At first glance the cases seem difficult to reconcile but it has been argued that they can be distinguished by reference to the relative economic positions of the parties. In *Krell v Henry* it was a consumer who would have suffered had the contract not been frustrated. In the latter case it was a businessman taking advantage of a commercial opportunity and charging a high price for the cruise who would have had to bear the risk. Moreover, Brownsword (1985) has argued that the real problem Hutton was trying to avoid was the fact that insufficient people were willing to pay high prices for the boat trip. The cases demonstrate the point that the doctrine of frustration will not be invoked to allow a party to escape from a contract which has merely become a bad bargain for him or her.

A number of frustration cases also arose as a result of the closure of the Suez Canal in 1956. In these cases a fine distinction was made between the main purpose of the contract and *the way* in which the seller was to carry out this basic obligation. So, for instance, in *Tsakiroglou & Co Ltd v Noblee Thorl GmbH* (1962), Tsakiroglou agreed to ship groundnuts to Noblee Thorl in Hamburg from Port Sudan. The agreement was made in line with international standard form contracts known as 'cif' contracts. It was agreed that shipment was to be made during November and December 1956 but no specific delivery date was named. Following the closure of the Suez Canal in early November, Tsakiroglou made no effort to ship the goods and, when sued for damages, pleaded frustration. It was held that the closure of the canal did not fundamentally alter the contractual obligation into one of a different character. The carrier could still ship goods from Port Sudan to Hamburg, albeit under the changed circumstances, by a lengthier and more expensive voyage round the Cape of Good Hope. As a result, the court held that Tsakiroglou was liable to pay £5,600 damages to Noblee Thorl for breach of contract. It has been said that it would require circumstances such as a contract to carry perishable goods from Port Sudan to Alexandria to bring about frustration in such a case.

Delay is frequently a factor in frustration cases. It may be, for example, that goods cannot be shipped on time because flooding prevents them reaching the port of loading, a strike holds up their movement, or the government requisitions the delivery vessels. But again, delay only frustrates a contract when it defeats the commercial venture. As Lord Roskill made clear in *The Nema (Pioneer Shipping Ltd v BTP*

Trioxide Ltd) (1981): 'Whether or not the delay is such as to bring about frustration must be a question to be determined by an informed judgment based upon all the evidence of what has occurred and what is likely thereafter to occur' (p. 1047). This exercise involves the court in trying to determine how long the delay is likely to occur and whether one of the parties can reasonably be asked to wait for a delayed performance. The task is an extremely difficult one as judges, like the contracting parties themselves, can not see into the future. This point is illustrated in *Tamplin SS Co Ltd v Anglo-Mexican Petroleum Co Ltd* (1916), where a five-year delivery by sea agreement signed in December 1912 was disrupted when the government requisitioned the vessel for war service in February 1915. The majority of the court felt that it was likely *at the time the case was decided* that the vessel would be released in time to render further substantial services under the contract. On that basis the contract was not held to have been frustrated even though the contract was in fact delayed for longer.

In an effort to clarify the position, distinctions have been made between indefinite delays and temporary interruptions. In *Metropolitan Water Board v Dick, Kerr & Co Ltd* (1918), Dick Kerr agreed in 1914 to build a reservoir at Staines for the Metropolitan Water Board. The work was to be completed in six years but in 1916 the Ministry of Munitions ordered the work to stop and Dick Kerr to sell all disposable plant. It was held that the interruption created by the statutory order was of such a character and probable duration as to make the contract, if resumed, a different contract from that entered into. It would seem then that where indefinite delay, as opposed to temporary interruption, is all that can be envisaged for the parties from the time of the intervening act, then the contract is discharged by frustration. It is not the case that the contract is definitely impossible to perform some time in the future, such as when peace is restored, but that, in the circumstances, it is not reasonable to hold the parties to their obligations in the new circumstances.

The discharge of a contract through supervening *illegality* is justified on different grounds. Where, for instance, war breaks out between the two states in which the contracting parties are based or a statutory ban is placed on trading certain produce, such as red meat, then the use of the doctrine is explained by reference to public policy and not by physical impossibility or even a radical change from the original obligation. Instead it is reasoned that there cannot be a contractual default if one is merely complying with the law. So, for instance, in *Fibrosa Spolka v Fairbairn etc Ltd* (1943), the export of textile machinery to Lithuania via the port of Gdynia was held to be frustrated by the occupation of that port by German troops in September 1939.

LIMITATIONS ON THE DOCTRINE

We have already seen that the doctrine does not apply in situations where the alleged frustrating event does not displace the basic obligation of the contract but merely makes its performance more onerous or expensive for one party. But other limitations also apply. The doctrine does not operate where the alleged frustrating event is the result of a party's own voluntary act or negligence. So, for example, in *The Eugenia* (1964), it was stated that a charterer who ordered a vessel into a war zone, with the result that she was detained, could not rely on the detention as the basis for frustration of a contract of hire. This was because the detention was due to the charterer's action, which was interpreted as a breach of contract and an instance of 'self-induced frustration'.

The leading case on the notion of 'self-induced frustration' is *Maritime National Fish Ltd v Ocean Trawlers Ltd* (1935). In this case Ocean Trawlers operated five trawlers for fishing with otter trawls. Three of the trawlers were owned by Ocean Trawlers and of the other two were chartered. In order to use the otter trawls, a licence was required from the Canadian government. As a result of a change in government policy, Ocean Trawlers was granted only three licences and did not allocate one to the chartered vessel owned by Maritime National Fish. When challenged, Ocean Trawlers argued that the charter of Maritime National Fish's vessel was frustrated. This claim was rejected by the Privy Council because the frustration was taken to be 'self-induced'. In the court's view it was Ocean Trawler's choice of vessels to be awarded licences which prevented Maritime National Fish's vessel from being used rather than the action of the government. In other words, Ocean Trawlers could have allocated one of the three licences to it rather than to one of their own vessels. The supervening event was not beyond their control and so did not frustrate the contract.

The rather harsh rule has been applied elsewhere. In *The Super Servant Two (Lauritzen AS v Wijsmuller BV)* (1990), a shipowner lost one of his two vessels capable of transporting oil drilling rigs. This meant that a contract for the transportation of the claimants' rig from Japan to Rotterdam could not be performed. The defendants claimed that the contract was frustrated but the claimants argued that the impossibility sprang from the defendants' own decision regarding their 'election' to use their remaining vessel for other contracts. The Court of Appeal held that, although the defendants were neither negligent nor in breach of contract as regards their allocation of duties, the problems were not sufficient to render the contract frustrated. Such interpretations of events are not without their critics. It might be argued for instance that frustration should not be excluded by a party's choice where his or her only realistic option was which of two contracts to frustrate; see *Constantine (Joseph) SS Line Ltd v Imperial Smelting Corporation Ltd* (1942).

The courts have also refused to apply the doctrine where the parties have clearly foreseen the precise risk but have nevertheless gambled on its non-occurrence. The doctrine does not generally apply where the parties have made express provision for the event which occurs. Here it is the contract which will govern the position. However, the fact that the parties foresee and provide for a possible delay does not prevent frustration if the delay which actually occurs is of a totally different order of magnitude than that foreseen. Also, where the contract is rendered illegal as a matter of public policy, foreseeability does not prevent frustration if to allow continuance of the contract would, as seen in the *Fibrosa Spolka* case, involve giving assistance to an enemy economy.

THE LAW REFORM (FRUSTRATED CONTRACTS) ACT 1943

Even where the contract is brought to an end by the operation of the doctrine of frustration, the aim of the law is to allocate or distribute the loss brought about by the supervening event. The Law Reform (Frustrated Contracts) Act 1943 improved on earlier common law rules and now governs such circumstances. According to the Act, the court's decision that a frustrating event took place means that the contract is automatically brought to an end *from the time of frustration*. What was a binding contract becomes void and the parties are excused from further performance by operation of law. The Act also deals with liabilities arising in the period in which the contract subsisted, between agreement and the time of the frustrating event. During this time work may have been undertaken, expenses incurred, and advance payments made. In these circumstances, the Act seeks to achieve a just settlement between the parties. The effect of the Act is that:

(1) Money *paid* before the frustrating event is recoverable whether performance is total or partial.

(2) Money *payable* before the frustrating event, but not in fact paid, ceases to be payable.

(3) A party who has incurred *expenses* in performance of the contract prior to its discharge may, at the court's discretion, be awarded those expenses. In exercising this discretion, the court or arbitrator can split the loss in such proportions as they think just. They will be influenced by the extent to which the expenses have been used to produce something rendered useless following the frustration. So, for instance, very little will be awarded if the expenses have been incurred in manufacturing machinery for one party which can readily be sold to another.

(4) A party who has gained a *valuable benefit* other than money under the contract before the frustrating event may be required to pay a just sum for it. In *BP Exploration Co (Libya) Ltd v Hunt* (1982), Robert Goff J explained in the Queen's Bench Division that 'the fundamental principle underlying the Act itself is prevention of the unjust enrichment of either party to the contract at the other's expense'. (p. 937)

However, the Act does not apply to all contracts. Excluded from its remit are voyage charterparties and other contracts for the carriage of goods by sea, contracts of insurance and certain contracts for the sale of goods where the goods have perished. This is because common law rules which were well known and respected in these areas have been preserved. Most importantly for present purposes, section 2(3) of the Act provides that, where the parties have included a clause in the contract which determines what should happen if an event renders performance impossible or difficult, then this clause will take precedence over the Act. As Lord Denning made clear in *The Eugenia* (1964):

> To see if the doctrine [of frustration] applies, you have first to construe the contract and see whether the parties have themselves provided for the situation that has arisen. If they have provided for it, the contract must govern. There is no frustration. (p. 239)

However, there are exceptions to this provision. The first is where frustration renders a contract illegal. The second, as Lord Denning implies, is where the clause is incomplete or narrowly construed and cannot, on the reading of the contract, be said to cover the situation which has arisen.

CONTRACTUAL PLANNING AND THE ALLOCATION OF RISK

Risk is far from an alien concept in the business community. Business people deal with risks on a day-to-day basis and the allocation of risk is a crucial part of the bargaining process. Risk can never be eliminated. A person planning a contract can never be certain that they will be able to perform it when the time comes. While a frustrating event or circumstance may be beyond their control, it is nonetheless possible for them to use the contract to plan what arrangements may govern the aftermath. The prudent business person may well consider it wiser to introduce a clause into their contract defining *in advance* the rights and duties of the parties if certain events beyond their control occur. A clause should also provide an agreed basis for assessing the allocation of risk and expense following delay or cancellation. Alternatively, the question of risk and additional expense or loss may be covered by an appropriate clause relating to insurance coverage. Such a clause is generally known as a 'force majeure' clause and it is the prime example of what Macaulay (1963) describes as planning for contingencies. The practice of including such clauses in contracts has gained official recognition in the International Institute for the Unification of Private Law (UNIDROIT) Principles of International Contracts which sets out what is considered to be best practice in modern international contracts. According to article six non-performance is excused if one party can prove that it was caused by an unpredictable impediment.

The expression 'force majeure' has been judicially defined to cover all circumstances which it is not in the power of contractors to control, and which justify the non-execution of a contract. Although the wording of these clauses varies according to the nature of the contract, as regards contracts for the international sale of goods, they usually contain a list of possible 'force majeure' events capable of impeding or preventing performance, together with

> **Box 11.1: Example of a force majeure clause**
>
> Strikes, lockouts, Box labour disturbances, anomalous working conditions, accident to machinery, delays en route, policies or restrictions of governments, including restrictions of export and other licences, or any other contingency whatsoever beyond seller's control, including war, are sufficient excuse for any delay or non-fulfilment traceable to any of these causes.

a 'sweeping up' phrase designed to ensure that there are no gaps in the formula. An example of such a clause can be seen in Box 11.1.

The purpose of these clauses is not to have the contract set aside immediately. Instead it is typical for force majeure clauses to suspend performance for an agreed period of time whilst requiring that each party is under a duty to keep each other notified as regards their respective positions. Once this agreed period of time has elapsed, one party will then have a right to exercise an option to cancel the contract. This can be invoked on the occurrence of a contingency which might or might not call for frustration in the legal sense.

Case law suggests that careful planning does not always keep you out of court. In *Czarnikow Ltd v Rolimpex* (1979), Rolimpex, a Polish foreign trading organisation, agreed to sell 200,000 tons of sugar to Czarnikow as part of the annual export quota. In Polish law, Rolimpex had a separate legal entity, distinct from the government, although it was subject to ministerial directions. The rules of the Refined Sugar Association were incorporated into the contract and rule 18(a) provided that, if delivery was prevented by 'government intervention beyond the seller's control', the contract would be void without penalty. The seller was made responsible for obtaining the requisite export licence under rule 21. The contract stipulated that failure to obtain such a licence was not 'sufficient grounds for a claim of "force majeure" if the regulations in force ... when the contract was made, called for such licences to be obtained'. The 1974 crop was poor and was needed for domestic consumption. A ministerial resolution imposed an immediate ban on all sugar exports. On the same date, a formal decree was issued giving legal effect to the ban though it did not revoke the export licences already ordered in compliance with rule 21. In reliance on the 'force majeure' clause, Rolimpex informed Czarnikow that the contract could not be fulfilled and the dispute was referred to arbitrators in London. Relying on rule 18(a), the arbitrators found in Rolimpex's favour.

On appeal it was held that the arbitrators had established that Rolimpex was not an organ of the Polish Government but an independent state organisation. The contract was therefore frustrated by 'government intervention' within rule 18(a) and was *not* self-induced, as it would have been if they had been part of the government. Rolimpex was accordingly relieved of liability under the contract. In addition, it was decided that the obligation under rule 21 to 'obtain' the requisite export licence implied no obligation to maintain it in force. As a result Rolimpex was not precluded from relying on Rule 18(a).

In *Toepfer v Cremer* (1975), the seller sold the buyer 5,000 tons of soya bean meal. The contract was made using the Grain and Feed Trade Association standard form No 100, which contained a 'force majeure' clause. This entitled the seller to an extension of time for shipment and stated that, in the event of default by the seller, the damages were to be based upon the actual or estimated value of the goods 'on date of default'. The goods were to be shipped by 30 April 1973 but the worst floods on the Mississippi for over 20 years caused great delays to shipping. On 16 May the seller invoked the 'force majeure' clause, and by an extension notice informed the buyer that he intended to ship the goods from 'Mississippi port(s)'. The date of shipment was thereby extended to 31 May, with a further extension, at the buyer's option, to 30 June, which was the latest date for shipment. If the goods had been shipped by 30 June, the seller could have fulfilled their contract, provided the buyer had been so notified by 10 July. The seller did not ship the goods. The buyer claimed damages for non-delivery and, the market price having risen, contended that the date of default was 10 July. The seller maintained that the date of default was another, earlier time and that their extension notice was bad because it did not state any definite port. The Court of Appeal held that damages would be assessed on the basis that the date of default was 10 July, for that was the last day for the performance of the contract. The extension notice was valid, for it was perfectly possible for the seller to intend to ship at one of the ports on the Mississippi. Further, since the seller had themselves invoked the 'force majeure' clause and had given the extension notice, they could not be permitted to say that the notice was bad.

It may be difficult to predict the unusual but it is possible to organise obligations in the contract in a way which makes it clear who shall bear the burden of contractual performance becoming difficult or impossible. It is also logical to suppose that, in most deals, the party who takes more risks can expect to negotiate a lower price. Indeed, one of the incentives for determining what will happen in the event that something unlikely or unpredictable occurs is that it will normally effect the price of the contract. So someone who is risk averse will prefer to pay more under the contract and be sure that their interests are protected whatever happens. Moreover, businesses are constantly sensitive to new risks. So, for example, after the 1956 closure of the Suez Canal, sellers began to stipulate for a 'Cape Surcharge' to be paid by the buyer if the Canal was closed again, as it was in 1967; see *Henry Ltd v Clasen* (1973).

Similarly, Davis Contractors were in a position to, and had tried to, protect themselves by a letter stating that their tender was subject to adequate supplies of labour and materials being available, or by the use of price fluctuation and extension of time clauses.

It would seem then, that this is an area of contract in which careful wording of contractual terms is of the essence. So for example, a seller who needs an export licence in order to ship goods assumes a greater risk if they agree to 'deliver as soon as licence granted', which would be interpreted as an absolute undertaking, than if they agreed to a conditional obligation to 'deliver subject to licence'. In the first instance, if the seller fails to get a licence, they will be liable in damages for the buyer's lost expectations. In the second, if they fail after reasonable efforts to obtain a licence, they will not be liable. Where the parties expressly allocate risk and loss in the contract, or apportion it between them, their agreed terms will govern the situation if the contingency arises. For this reason, the doctrine of frustration is properly limited to contingencies not specifically provided for in the contract. If the change in circumstances could lead to a successful plea of frustration, but the parties have nevertheless properly provided for the supervening event which has arisen, then their contractual terms will govern the situation; see s 2(3) of the Law Reform (Frustrated Contracts) Act 1943. As Lord Wilberforce has argued when outlining the policy behind the Unfair Contract Terms Act 1977:

> in commercial matters generally, where the parties are not of unequal bargaining power, and where risks are normally borne by insurance, not only is the case for judicial intervention undemonstrated, but there is everything to be said ... for leaving the parties free to apportion the risks as they think fit and for respecting their decision.

'Hardship' clauses are also used in the business community to manage unforeseen events which radically change the context in which the contract is performed. These serve a different purpose from a 'force majeure' clause which deals with instances in which performance is rendered impossible. By way of contrast, hardship clauses deal with situations where performance is rendered much more onerous. They are commonly used in long-term contracts such as those involving the construction of major building works, or in the crude oil or natural gas industries. The long-term nature of these relationships makes them vulnerable to unforeseen changes. Moreover, as both the parties may have invested a considerable amount in the contract, abandoning the contract is often an unattractive option. As Trakman (1983) has explained:

> Businessmen often prefer to modify rather than to terminate their arrangements in the face of disruptions of trade. They choose to increase or decrease their contract price ... or alter the quality of their performance because part-performance is usually better than non-performance. They modify their promises because salvaging segments of a contract is preferable to salvaging no segments at all. (p. 49)

The problem is that, in comparison with many civil jurisdictions, the English courts have shown themselves unwilling to intervene to adapt the terms of long-term contracts in such situations. But they are more sympathetic where the parties have undertaken comprehensive and detailed drafting of the contract and introduced a clause which allows them to re-negotiate certain terms in certain instances. By introducing a term variously labelled a 'hardship', 'escape' or 'adaptation' clause, the parties can make allowance to re-negotiate their contract so as to minimise losses and avoid undue hardship. Box 11.2 provides an example of a hardship clause taken from the case of *Superior Overseas Development Corporation v British Gas Corporation* (1982). In considering the clause, Lord Justice Donaldson argued:

In my judgment, [the hardship clause] is an ultimate safety net. To adopt an analogy which is perhaps appropriate to North Sea gas, the parties contemplated that in most foreseeable economic conditions the course of the joint venture would be dictated by the automatic price revision mechanisms contained in [other clauses] (the agreed price autopilot). But the parties realized that over a period of 25 years economic storms could arise of such severity that the price autopilot would not be able to keep the venture on course. [The hardship clause] provides for a manual override if this occurs and the venture goes so far off course as to cause one of the parties to suffer substantial economic hardship ...

> **Box 11.2: Example of a hardship clause**
>
> If at any time or from time to time during the contract period there has been any substantial change in the economic circumstances relating to this Agreement and (notwithstanding the effect of the other relieving or adjusting provisions of this Agreement) either party feels that such change is causing it to suffer substantial economic hardship then the parties shall (at the request of either of them) meet together to consider what (if any) adjustment in the prices then in force under this Agreement or in the price revision mechanism contained in [the contract] ... are justified in the circumstances in fairness to the parties to offset or alleviate the said hardship caused by such change.

and, if appropriate, revise the settings on the price autopilot.

But it should always be kept in mind that in the absence of such a clause the parties should not expect to obtain relief from the English courts.

CONCLUDING REMARKS

In this chapter we have looked at two doctrines which practitioners will have little cause to use. Not only are the disastrous array of events detailed in the case law unlikely to happen on a regular basis but the doctrines are designed to deter excessive use of the power of the court to set a contract aside. Regular attempts have been made to expand the doctrines in an attempt to help parties, who through no fault of their own find themselves to have suffered loss, but these attempts, though understandable, have met with mixed success. However, the most important aspect of the discussion in this chapter has been the focus on risk and planning which are central to an understanding of the interface between law and economics. The fact that contracts, no matter how carefully planned, can not anticipate everything that will happen is an important reminder of the need for flexibility in contractual relations discussed in earlier chapters.

REFERENCES AND FURTHER READING

Brownsword, R 'Rules and principles at the warehouse' (1977) 40 MLR 467, case note on
    Amalgamated Investment v John Walker (1977).
Brownsword, R 'Henry's lost spectacle and Hutton's lost speculation: a classic riddle
    solved?' (1985) 129 *Solicitors' Journal* 860.

Cartoon, B 'Drafting an acceptable force majeure clause' (1978) JBL 230.

Colinvaux, R 'Suez survey' (1964) JBL 176 (and see also the detailed analysis of the *Suez Canal* cases by Mocatta J: [1970] 2 Lloyd's Rep 21).

Cornwell-Kelly, H 'The community concept of force majeure' (1979) NLJ 8 March at 245.

Frug, M (1992) 'Rescuing impossibility doctrine: a postmodern feminist analysis of contract law' in *Postmodern Feminist Jurisprudence*, Routledge, New York.

Hedley, S 'Carriage by sea: frustration and force majeure' (1990) CLJ 209, case note on *The Super Servant Two*.

Lasok, K 'Government intervention and State trading' (1981) 44 MLR 249.

McKendrick, E (ed.) (1995) *Force Majeure and Frustration of Contract*, 2nd edn, Lloyds of London Press, London.

Schmitthoff, C 'Hardship and intervener clauses' (1980) JBL 82.

Schmitthoff, C (1990) *Schmitthoff's Export Trade. The Law and Practice of International Trade*, 9th edn, Stevens, London, Chapters 12 and 34 on hardship clauses.

Stannard, J 'Frustrating delays' (1983) 46 MLR 738.

Trakman, L 'Frustrated contracts and legal fictions' (1983) 46 MLR 39.

Treitel (1994) *Frustration and Force Majeure*, Sweet & Maxwell, London.

? QUESTIONS

(1) Do you agree with Collins when he argues that the doctrine of possibility mistake is not only inconsistent with the objective test of consent and based upon little authority, but that the problems in such cases are better handled through construction of the express and implied terms of the contract? Give reasons for your response.

(2) Could any of the parties in 'The Sad Tale of Angie and Georgie' rely on the doctrine of frustration? What would the barriers to pleading their case be?

(3) Ali agreed to allow Lin and her family the use of Ali's holiday villa for a week for £1,000. Lin paid a deposit of £400, with the balance payable the day before the holiday was to commence. Two days before the holiday was due, Lin's children were taken ill with measles and she sent a doctor's certificate to this effect to Ali, saying that the holiday would have to be cancelled. Ali expressed regret, but demanded the balance of the agreed sum. Advise Lin.

What difference would it make if:

(a) The villa was washed away the day before the holiday was to start.

(b) The previous occupiers of the villa had left the place filthy and Lin refused to stay and booked hotel accommodation which cost £500 for the week.

(c) The children had contracted smallpox instead of measles.

(4) 'The subject of frustration of contract has been associated, or confused, with various subjects, such as mistake, impossibility of performance, breach of contract, failure of consideration, illegality, failure of what is referred to as the common venture, and general considerations said to depend on reason and justice': Latham CJ in the Australian case of *Scanlan's New Neon Ltd v Toohey's Ltd* (1943). Discuss.

CHAPTER 12

UNFAIRNESS AND COERCION

INTRODUCTION

The standard of fairness is central to much of what is discussed in this book. In one sense we have learnt that according to the classical model the common law does not investigate whether an exchange is fair as that is for the parties to determine. But considerations of what is fair cannot be avoided by the judiciary. When the courts come to determine what is reasonable in the circumstances or determine the fate of a fraudster, it is inevitable that notions of fairness will come into play. Ideas of what constitutes a fair deal or negotiation process differ considerably but there is no doubt that the matter is important to contract lawyers.

While discussion of the issue is pervasive, debate about the concept has also continued in a number of specific contexts. In the last section we looked at misrepresentation and in next section we will be concerned with the idea of unfair and unreasonable contract terms. In this chapter, we will look at a number of particular doctrines which the courts have tentatively developed in order to mitigate the most extreme types of unfairness in contract and the illegitimate use of power. We will be examining ideas around inequality of bargaining power, unconscionablility and duress. The chapter raises a number of important questions. Is there a universal notion of unfairness? Should we look to what the parties think is fair or is there a general standard that can be applied? Can any one agreement between the parties be analysed alone or should we look to the backdrop of circumstances such as age, intelligence, norms in the industry or market position? Does our concern amount to anything more than value for money? When is intervention justified?

Many different approaches to the mitigation of gross unfairness are revealed by the doctrines discussed in this chapter. In some cases the approach is to look at the victim and to ask whether their consent to the contractual terms can be considered genuine when unacceptable levels of pressure have been put on them. Another standpoint is to look at the position of the oppressor and to impose particular duties on them because of their specialist knowledge or economic power. A third approach, less discernible in the English doctrines discussed, is to look at the terms of the contract in the search for oppression and unfairness. In each of these cases the most pressing issue is how we separate the acceptable from the unacceptable.

We have already considered the ways in which nineteenth century rules of contract were developed in the context of *laissez-faire* and a free-market economy. The parties' capacity to bargain freely and equality of bargaining power were often assumed. Fierce competition and commercial pressure were taken for granted and the courts generally declined to recognise a requirement for a general legal standard of fairness in transactions. The concepts of freedom and sanctity of contract inevitably led the courts to assume a primary role as upholders and enforcers of contracts rather than agents of their destruction. The judiciary were not prepared for the courts to be used to relieve parties from the type of risk-taking which was deemed inevitable in the commercial world.

However, even the most conservative judicial statements regarding freedom and sanctity of contract were qualified. The courts, then as now, would set aside contracts and grant relief to parties where agreement was clearly not genuine. Agreement mistakes and fraudulent misrepresentation are examples of this. Similarly, some parties, such as infants and persons of unsound mind, were afforded protection against those who would take advantage of their lack of business acumen. The fundamental idea that agreement or consent to a contract must be free and voluntary also allowed for a number of narrow rules to set aside agreements in which improper pressures had been applied. Such pressures ranged from actual physical violence to the improper use of a position of trust, such as that existing between solicitor and client.

GENERAL STANDARDS

A key question to be resolved in this area is whether relief should be granted to parties in such cases because the voluntary nature of the undertaking was called into question or because there is a general standard of fairness which pervades all contractual doctrines. The first of these possibilities was not necessarily offensive to proponents of the classical or neo-classical contract model because of the emphasis on the inadequacy or lack of true agreement. But the second suggests a more interventionist approach to the policing of bargains than traditionalists would find acceptable. Case law in the area suggests that extreme caution has been exercised in relation to the suggestion that a general standard would be the most fruitful approach to concerns about improper pressure or unscrupulous conduct. This approach is reflected in the development of specific doctrines relating to particular types of behaviour. English courts have not committed themselves to one overriding principle such as good faith and the development of the law has been piecemeal. This lead has been followed by the legislature which has tended to concentrate on the needs of particular classes of people it assumes to be in a relatively weak bargaining position. The protection of consumers in sale of goods legislation is an excellent example of this. That is not to say that attempts have not been made to develop more generic standards of fairness. So, for instance, Waddams (1976) has argued that:

> Despite lip service to the notion of absolute freedom of contract, relief is every day given against agreements that are unfair, inequitable, unreasonable or oppressive. Unconscionability, as a word to describe such control, might not be the lexicographer's first choice, but I think it is the most acceptable general word. (p. 390)

Unfairness, protection against improper pressure and inequality of bargaining power were also linked together by Lord Denning in the case of *Lloyds Bank Ltd v Bundy* (1975), where he also argued that English law should give relief to people who, without independent advice, enter into contracts on terms which are very unfair or transfer property for a consideration which is grossly inadequate when their bargaining power is seriously impaired. In his words:

> There are cases on our books in which the courts will set aside a contract ... when the parties have not met on equal terms, when the one is so strong in bargaining power and the other so weak that, as a matter of common fairness it is not right that the strong should be allowed to push the weak to the wall. Hitherto these special categories have

been treated as a special category in itself. But I think the time has come when we should seek to find a principle to unite them.

In his analysis Denning reviewed the various doctrines considered in this chapter as all being examples of one doctrine of inequality of bargaining power rather than separate ones.

The development indicated by Denning appeared at the time to promise the emergence of a new judicial doctrine which would provide relief against harsh bargains where there existed a patent inequality of bargaining power between the parties. It was assumed by many commentators that later case law would allow the courts to define more clearly the scope of the emergent principle, whether expressed in terms of unconscionability or inequality of bargaining power. There was some support for Denning's approach in *Schroeder Music Publishing Co Ltd v Macaulay* (1974). However, for some, the difficulty with the judgment was that the idea of inequality of bargaining power outlined could be seen to be enunciating the rule that *any* exercise of abnormal market power is *prima facie* reviewable by the courts. Further clarification was not forthcoming beyond statements that the principle would not operate where the bargain was 'the result of the ordinary interplay of market forces'. Moreover, in *National Westminster Bank v Morgan* (1985), Lord Scarman argued that discrete doctrines dealing with unfair contract had not been sufficiently developed to need the support of a general principle of inequality of bargaining power (see also *Barclays Bank plc v O'Brien*, 1993 and *TSB Bank v Camfield* 1995).

It is important to emphasise that this narrow approach to unfairness is not evident in all common law jurisdictions. The inclusion of a clause relating to 'unconscionability' in the United States Uniform Commercial Code is perhaps the most widely cited example of an attempt to develop a general doctrine. Under the code, the courts are required to examine the commercial setting of the contract, and it has been said there that the doctrine attempts for the prevention of oppression and unfair surprise. The concept of good faith which sits alongside the notion of unconscionability as a macro doctrine designed to capture a variety of different types of unfairness has also become more commonplace elsewhere. For instance, the French and German civil codes require that agreements are to be performed in good faith as does the American Uniform Commercial code. It imposes a positive duty on contracting parties to 'play fair' and engage in open dealing. In a practical sense, this would mean, for instance, that terms are expressed fully, clearly and legibly, and that notice should be given of particularly onerous terms. Acting in good faith might also include not taking advantage of someone's lack of experience or weak bargaining position.

These ideas are not totally alien to the English legal system. The idea of a general standard of good faith has attracted some support amongst the judiciary (see, for instance, Bingham LJ in *Interfoto Picture Library Ltd v Stiletto Visual Programmes Ltd*, 1989) and amongst academic writers. Moreover, certain types of specialist contracts such as those used in the insurance industry make use of the notion of good faith. Finally, the Unfair Terms in Consumer Contract Regulations 1999 use a test of whether a term is contrary to good faith and there are many modern developments, such as negligent misrepresentation, which encourage good behaviour in the pre-contractual period.

However, despite these innovations, English lawyers have remained suspicious of a general doctrine of good faith and the judiciary's preference for pragmatic rather than principled decision-making has mitigated against the progression of the idea. Concerns that the introduction of this standard would introduce uncertainty into the law and call for difficult inquiries into contractual terms and negotiations have been widely expressed. Others have argued that the piecemeal solutions to specific instances of unfairness offer as adequate a solution as a general requirement. Adams and Brownsword (2007) outline the dilemmas:

> For, what precisely does 'good faith' mean? Does it simply mean that a party must act with a clear conscience or are there some external standards of good faith dealing? If the latter, are these external standards set by a particular commercial community, or is there a critical moral benchmark for good faith? Moreover, where are the boundaries of a good faith requirement to be drawn? (p. 110)

A conservative judicial approach was much evident in the case of *Walford v Miles* (1992). In that case, the claimants were in negotiations with the defendant over the purchase of a business and during the course of their discussions it was agreed that the sellers would not negotiate with another party. When the sellers broke off the discussions, the buyer claimed that there was a collateral contract to negotiate in good faith but the House of Lords rejected the argument. Indeed, Lord Ackner went so far as to say that the concept of a duty to carry on negotiations in good faith is inherently repugnant to the adversarial position of the parties in pre-contractual negotiations. The toleration of such opportunism clearly makes it difficult to introduce general standards of acceptable behaviour.

Commentators have suggested that the adoption of a general principle would allow the English judiciary to avoid the excessive contortion of specific doctrines to achieve fairness, a factor which has characterised much development in the field. More fundamentally, it has been suggested that discrete common law doctrines are ill-suited to regulate contracts and that a new approach is essential. Resistance to the concept of good faith is likely to be challenged as model contracts for international trade which contain good faith clauses are adopted and European legislation requires the adoption of such standards. Moreover, it is clear from the empirical studies visited in Chapter 4 that good faith is already an accepted norm within the business community where co-operative behaviour is much more common than Lord Ackner would have us believe, especially where a contract is likely to be long term. Collins (2002) has argued that, rather than imposing uniformity, 'open textured' standards, such as good faith, allow the judiciary to explore such conventions within the business community with a view to bridging the gap between formal law and practice.

PROCEDURAL AND SUBSTANTIVE FAIRNESS

Before going on to discuss the specific doctrines which have emerged to deal with particular types of unfairness, it is important to say a little about how instances of unfairness, unconscionability or inequality of bargaining power may be classified. In their treatment of the notion of unfairness, commentators have tended to make distinctions between two different types of unfairness which might manifest themselves in the field of contract. The first of these is *procedural unfairness*. This deals with unfairness during the making of the contract: what Leff (1967) has called bargaining naughtiness. Concerns about this type of unfairness are reflected in the doctrines of misrepresentation which allow relief to parties who have been deliberately or recklessly misled about the quality of the thing they are trying to obtain.

The second type of unfairness is substantive. Here, commentators have been concerned with the fairness of the deal which has come about as a result of the bargaining. We have already seen that, on the whole, the courts are not concerned with whether adequate consideration has been given. Peel and Treitel (2007) has explained:

> The reason for this is not that the courts cannot value the promise of each party: they have to do this when assessing damages. It is rather that they should not interfere with the bargain actually made by the parties …. Such problems are however, more appropriately dealt with by special legislation or by administrative measures than by the ordinary process of civil litigation. The courts are not well equipped to develop a system of price control, and their refusal, as a general rule, to concern themselves with the adequacy of consideration is a reflection of this fact.

This position places emphasis on the sort of respect for individual autonomy so valued in the classical model. It is assumed that the parties know their own minds, that they are the best judges of their own needs and circumstance, that they will calculate the risks and future contingencies that are relevant. It follows that unfair bargains are irrelevant. Once made, the contract is binding on the parties.

Viewed in this way, the parties' achievements and failures are their own responsibility. Another justification for the emphasis on procedural rather than substantive fairness is that it is assumed that fair process tends to lead to outcomes considered fair by the parties. But some commentators have offered a more sophisticated analysis of the possibilities. Leff, for example, outlines the various scenarios which are possible. These are summarised in Figure 12.1.

Figure 12.1:   The dynamics of procedural and substantive unfairness

fair process	——————→	fair result
fair process	——————→	unfair result
unfair process	——————→	fair result
unfair process	——————→	unfair result

According to this conceptualisation of the interface between process and substance, a fair process might lead to an unfair result. So for instance, an open and honest bargaining process may lead to the payment of consideration which would generally be considered to be an inadequate price for what has been acquired. Conversely, a bargaining process in which misrepresentations and posturing are rife may nonetheless lead to a deal in which the parties both get what they want. In practice, the notions of procedural and substantive unfairness are often intertwined when cases come before the courts. Moreover, although classical contract theorists are reluctant to look at the fairness of the deal entered into, the judiciary frequently uses unfair terms as evidence of a procedural impropriety. Closer scrutiny reveals that the cases in which the courts have been prepared to recognise procedural unfairness are invariably those where a bad deal has also been made. This is a theme to which we shall return as we review the discrete doctrines concerned with fairness.

SPECIFIC DOCTRINES

Duress

Duress is a much narrower concept than Denning's generic idea of inequality of bargaining power. It involves coercion or compulsion, as in the case of a contract entered into under a threat of physical violence. The idea is that the party's will must have been overborne during the bargaining process. Far from working against traditional contract principles, this concept complements it. The idea, like that of mistake, is that if consent to a contract is not given freely, then it cannot constitute true assent or a meeting of the minds. This might happen, for instance, if someone was induced to sign a contract because they had a gun held against their head or other physical violence was threatened. A successful plea of duress can have significant implications. When duress is proven, the contract can be avoided by the victim of the duress if they so elect.

Over the last three decades, the courts have extended the idea of duress to cover situations where excessive *economic* pressure is brought to bear on one of the parties. Economic duress arises where a contract is formed or varied following a threat to their economic well-being or financial standing. The courts have established the concept of economic duress based on the idea of *wrongful* commercial pressure involving coercion. The modern beginnings of this development are perhaps to be found in another judgment of Lord Denning's in *D & C Builders Ltd v Rees* (1966). Here, Rees, knowing that D & C were in desperate financial straits, put pressure on them to accept £300 in full settlement of a bill for nearly £500. In Lord Denning's view: 'No person can insist on a settlement procured by intimidation' (p. 265). Pressure is commonplace in the modern business world but the new concept demonstrates, however indistinctly, that there is now a legal limit which must not be exceeded. The task for the courts is to distinguish acceptable levels of pressure such as those in *Williams & Roffey Bros and Nicholas (Contractors) Ltd* from unacceptable levels. How then is economic duress, which is actionable and grounds for setting a contract aside, to be distinguished from the normal 'cut and thrust' of the commercial world?

In *The Atlantic Baron (North Ocean Shipping Co Ltd v Hyundai Construction Co Ltd)* (1979), Hyundai agreed to build a supertanker for North Ocean Shipping for $30 million. The dollar was devalued during construction and Hyundai, without any legal justification, demanded a 10 per cent increase in the remaining instalments of the price. They stipulated that otherwise they would terminate the contract. Being anxious to fulfil a very lucrative charter for the new vessel, North Ocean Shipping agreed to this demand but under protest. It was held that the shipbuilder's threat amounted to economic duress but, as the buyers had not taken the matter further, had paid the extra instalments and taken delivery of the ship, they had by implication affirmed the variation in price. As a result, it was held that they could not recover the extra payments. The shipbuilder's problems in this case began as a result of a failure to negotiate a fixed-price dollar contract. As a result, they accepted the risk of adverse currency fluctuations during the construction period. Their transfer of this risk to the shipping company was seen by the court as illegitimate; coercive opportunism founded on a strong bargaining position. It was only North Ocean Shipping's inaction which allowed Hyundai to retain the extra payments.

The idea of a doctrine of economic duress was approved by the Judicial Committee of the Privy Council in *Pao On v Lau Yiu Long* (1980), although it was not proven on the facts. In that case, Lord Scarman was of the opinion that

> ...there is nothing contrary in principle in recognising economic duress as a factor which may render a contract voidable, provided always that the basis of such recognition is that it must always amount to a coercion of will, which vitiates consent. (p. 636)

In other words, the effect of the coercion is to 'cancel out' the consent given. According to the judges in that case, drawing the line between mere commercial pressure and actionable duress is a question of fact in each case, but Lord Scarman identified four questions to assist the courts in future cases which have been reproduced in Box 12.1.

The matter was further considered in *The Universe Sentinel (Universe Tankships Inc of Monrovia v International Transport Workers' Federation)* (1983). In that case, Universe Tankships' vessel, which flew the Liberian flag, was prevented from leaving Milford Haven harbour by the International Transport Workers' Federation (ITWF) who were engaged in a campaign of blacking 'flag of convenience' vessels because it was felt they exploitated their crews. The

> **Box 12.1: Lord Scarman's four-stage test**
>
> - Did the person alleged to have been coerced protest at the time?
> - Did that person have an alternative course open to them, such as an adequate legal remedy?
> - Was that person independently advised?
> - Did they take steps to avoid the contract as varied?

union had threatened Universe Tankships that they would induce tug operators not to assist the ship until various union demands were met. As a result, the ship's passage was delayed for 11 days at great expense to the owners. In breach of the operators' contracts, tugs were not available until the demands were acceded to. Shortly afterwards Universe Tankships themselves demanded the return of payments made to ITWF as money paid under duress. The union did not dispute that their demands amounted to economic duress. In Lord Diplock's words: '...it is conceded that the financial consequences to the shipowners of the Universe Sentinel continuing to be off hire ... while the blacking continued, were so catastrophic as to amount to a coercion of this shipowner's will'. (p. 544)

However, ITWF argued that their threat had been made in contemplation or furtherance of a trade dispute, and that they were therefore protected by the immunity against actions in tort conferred by the Trade Union and Labour Relations Act 1974.

A majority of the House of Lords held that there was no trade dispute within the meaning of the Act and the pressure exerted by the union was illegitimate. The agreement regarding the payments in question was voidable and Universe Tankships could recover the payments made.

Responding to criticism from academic circles, Lord Scarman conceded that duress should not be seen as negating the existence of consent on the part of the person coerced. He argued instead that the victim's decision is better seen as intentional and voluntary, but that they consciously choose only what they see as the lesser of two evils. In his words, the victim has no practical choice but to submit to the duress. A factor that may influence the court in coming to a conclusion that the victim had no other practical course but to submit to the duress is the extent of the loss they would have suffered if they had not submitted. In the court's view, the coercive effect of the pressure must be 'sufficiently great' in the circumstances to render it illegitimate.

Subsequent cases have not really made the meaning of 'illegitimate' clear in this context. Treitel (2002) states that 'the threat must be illegitimate either because what is threatened is a legal wrong ... or because the threat itself is wrongful' (p. 406). In *The Universe Sentinel*, there would appear to have been intimidation by threats to induce, breaches of contract by third parties upon whom the victim relied heavily. Cartwright (1991) has explained the position as follows:

> So we have only limited guidance on the circumstances in which economic pressure will be illegitimate for the purposes of duress. If the thing threatened, or the circumstances in which the pressure is exerted, amount to a crime or a tort, it appears from *The Universe Sentinel* that the coercion will be illegitimate; if the pressure was overwhelming, so as to give the coerced party no choice but to submit, then economic duress is likely to be held to have been established. Moreover, the threat of a breach of contract may be 'illegitimate', and so the question will be whether the threat was sufficiently overwhelming to constitute duress.

Where one party to the contract exerts pressure on the other by threatening breach of the contract, it has been suggested that such a threat is only illegitimate if accompanied by bad faith or malice, or the deliberate exploitation of difficulties of the other party. Again, it has been said that the party threatening must be exploiting a 'situational monopoly', which gives the victim no realistic alternative but to comply. This point was considered in *Atlas Express Ltd v Kafco (Importers and Distributors) Ltd* (1989). The facts were that Atlas discovered that they had badly underpriced a contract to transport Kafco's goods to retailers throughout the country, particularly to Woolworths, with whom Kafco had a valuable, long-term contract. Shortly before Christmas, Atlas demanded an increase in the carriage charges. They said that unless a new agreement, drawn up by them, was signed by Kafco, no deliveries would be made. Fearing being in breach of their contract with Woolworths and with no alternative transport available, Kafco signed but only under protest. When Atlas sued to recover the increased charges, Kafco pleaded economic duress. It was held that Kafco were not obliged to pay the additional charges.

An application of Lord Scarman's four questions in *Pao On v Lau Yiu Long* readily substantiates the decision in *Atlas Express*. The possibility of losing the Woolworths contract presented Kafco with the gravest financial consequences and an action against Atlas for breach of the original contract would not have compensated them for the loss of their lucrative business relationship with Woolworths; see also *CTN Cash and Carry v Gallaber* (1994). Despite these deliberations, the ambit of this common law doctrine has not yet been fully determined and it could be argued that there is a need to make its conceptual basis more clear.

Undue influence

The more expansive equitable doctrine of undue influence has developed alongside duress to prevent bargaining unfairness. Undue influence covers situations which fall short of duress but which are nonetheless inequitable. There are two types of undue influence which have been recognised by the courts. The first group of cases fall under the heading of *actual* undue influence. This arises where one of the parties to a contract can prove that they entered the transaction as a direct result of undue influence from the other party. So for example, in *Bank of Credit v Aboody* (1990), a husband bullied his wife into signing some documents which she did just because she wanted some peace. The emphasis in the cases has tended to be on procedural fairness (see *CIBC Mortgages v Pitt*, 1994) but the case law is not settled, and in *National Westminster Bank v Morgan* (1985) Lord Scarman argued that substantive unfairness or 'manifest disadvantage' is also a threshold requirement.

The second category of cases falls under the heading of *presumed* undue influence. This arises when the parties have the type of pre-existing relationship in which one party places their trust in the other. The types of relationship to which this doctrine addresses itself are those where one party displays a particular vulnerability or the other can be expected to display altruism in a relationship of care. Relationships covered are often professional and are seen as needing to transcend standards in the commercial world with its focus on pure economic exchanges. In *National Westminster Bank v Morgan* (1985), the House of Lords argued that it must be obvious to any independent and reasonable person that the relationship has special elements and the transaction is explicable only on the basis that the stronger party dominated the weaker. But again the law is far from clear as, in *CIBC* (1994), Browne Wilkinson argued that this formula might have to be reworked (see also *Barclays Bank plc v Coleman* (2001) QB 20).

The significance of being able to argue under this heading is that, once a presumption is raised, it is for the stronger party to prove that they have not taken advantage of the weaker party. Claimants attempting to raise a presumption have to prove that the contract between them 'calls for explanation' (see *Etridge no 2*). This significantly reduces the evidential burden placed on a claimant. The defendant can however rebut the presumption of undue influence by showing that there was procedural fairness and that, as a result, the claimant entered into the contract freely. This is usually done by establishing that independent advice was taken. But it is important to stress that the gaining of independent advice does not necessarily save the transaction nor is its absence fatal (see *Royal Bank of Scotland plc v Etridge (no 2)*, 1998 *per* Stuart Smith LJ).

The relationships of trust with which the courts are concerned in cases of presumed influence are called fiduciary relationships and may emerge in one of two ways. Firstly, there are some relationships in which it is automatically presumed to arise. These include contracts involving parent and child, religious adviser and disciple, guardian and ward, solicitor and client, trustee and beneficiary or doctor and patient. These cases raise an *irrebuttable* presumption. Alternatively, where the relationship does not automatically fall under one of these headings, the presumption can be established or rebutted on the facts. In theory, any type of relationship could fall within the remit of this type of undue influence, it all depends on the circumstances of the case. It is because of this that cases which fall under this second category have tended to be contentious.

One of the most widely cited examples of cases in which a fiduciary relationship arose on the facts is *Lloyds Bank v Bundy* (1974). In that case, the claimant and his adult son both used the same bank. The son ran into business difficulties and his father was asked to secure his son's overdraft and to put his farm up as security. He did this but, when the son was unable to pay the bank, they tried to re-possess the farm. The father claimed undue influence. He argued that he had banked with Lloyds for a long time and placed considerable trust in them. It was his contention that they had abused the confidence he placed in them by not making an effort to warn him fully that it was not in his financial interests to put up the farm as guarantee. The Court of Appeal agreed that the presumption of undue influence should be raised in this case, as there was a relationship of trust on the facts and the transaction was obviously disadvantageous. Moreover, the bank was unable to rebut the presumption.

Looking to both process and substance, Denning outlined the specific factors which needed to be proved. He reasoned that: (a) the relationship between the bank and the father was one of trust and confidence; (b) the relationship between the father and son was one in which the father's natural love and affection had much influence on him; and (c) that, on the facts, the consideration moving from the bank was grossly inadequate. The court also found that since the bank would derive an interest from the transaction, there was a conflict of interest. In their view, Lloyds was under a duty to advise the farmer to seek independent advice and that, as they had failed to do that, they had breached that duty.

The types of relationship capable of coming under this category are constantly expanding and being reviewed. In the past 20 years, for instance, the House of Lords has laid down no fewer than three sets of rules to determine in which circumstances a mortgagee will be bound by a transaction obtained through undue influence. *National Westminster Bank v Morgan* (1985) was the first case to recognise the undue influence of a husband on a wife in respect of their shared matrimonial home and this point was further discussed in *Barclays Bank plc v O'Brien* (1993). One of the most interesting aspects of the O'Brien case was that Browne Wilkinson accepted that a relationship of trust and confidence may arise on the facts where there is an emotional relationship between cohabiting parties who are not married. His deliberations were taken further in *Etridge (no 2)* which has now extended the rule to encompass *all* non-commercial relationships (see also *Massey v Midland* (1995), *Banco Exterior* (1997) and *Credit Lyonnais v Burch* (1997)).

Unconscionability

The idea of unconscionability has already been discussed in the introduction to this chapter where it was suggested that it has the potential to be used as an overarching term to describe the various doctrines being considered in this chapter. This is certainly the case in other jurisdictions where it has become synonymous with general doctrines of good faith and unfairness. But in the UK the notion has been used instead to describe a very narrow and longstanding equitable doctrine. Many of the early cases concerned with the doctrine involved 'expectant heirs' who borrowed money at extortionate rates and secured the loan on their future inheritance. These claimants were generally taken to be weak because of their youthful ignorance and desire to get advance on money they were due to inherit. Another group of cases in which the concept has been used involve emergency salvage operations, such as those involving sinking ships, in which the ability of someone to give meaningful consent has been questioned because of the urgency involved. In *The Port Caledonia and the Anna* (1903), a captain whose ship was in trouble agreed to pay £1,000 for a tug to rescue it. Bukhill J said:

> I have to ask myself whether the bargain that was made was so inequitable, so unjust and
> so unreasonable that the court cannot allow it to stand … I hope that those who perform
> such grand services in tugs from time to time, in worse weather than this, and in peril
> of their own lives, save property around the coast, will note that this Court will keep a
> firm hand over them if they attempt to do what has been done in this case. p. 190–191

More recently, the decision of *Cresswell v Potter* in 1978 suggests that the doctrine of unconscionability is alive and well, and capable of being applied to modern-day transactions. In that case, a wife left her husband and conveyed her half share in the matrimonial home to him so that she would not be liable for mortgage payments. She later sought to recover her share when the husband sold the property. In the words of Megarry J:

> What has to be considered is first whether the [claimant] is poor and ignorant; second whether the advice was at a considerable undervalue and third, whether the vendor had independent advice ... the euphemisms of the 20th century mean that the word poor has to be replaced by 'lower income group' and the like and the word ignorant by 'less highly educated'.

However, there are also clear indications that, by the mid-nineteenth century, the judiciary began to be concerned that the doctrine was too broad and that certain judgments brought with them the danger of too many transactions being set aside (see, for instance, *Earl of Aylesford v Morris*, 1873). The result is that there have been very few modern cases on the topic. The task of limiting the doctrine has been made easier by the fact that the legislature has shown itself willing to legislate for unfairness. For example, consumer credit legislation permits extortionate credit bargains to be reopened by the courts and affords a right to consumers who sign certain types of credit agreements at home to cancel then within a 'cooling-off' period. As we shall see in subsequent chapters, the Unfair Contract Terms Act 1977 concentrates it efforts on consumers and European Directives also allow for the setting aside of certain types of terms in contracts.

CONCLUDING REMARKS

The doctrines considered in this chapter go to the heart of the issues raised in this book. In particular, they pertain to issues surrounding the extent to which we desire a level playing field or general standards of positive behaviour in contracts. As they develop, the doctrines discussed begin to challenge the classical notion that rough equality between contracting parties can be assumed and that individuals are the best judges of what is in their interests. But whilst it is clear that courts in the UK are prepared to intervene in cases of unfairness in the worse types of exploitation, they have tended to do so in a piecemeal fashion. The challenge to contractual fairness has been muted by the fact that the emphasis has tended to be on bargaining naughtiness rather than substantive fairness, although the latter continues to influence decisions. This seems to reflect an ongoing commitment to the market philosophies underpinning the classical notion of freedom of contract. The area remains fraught with competing philosophies about the market and the practical difficulties in determining whether there is such a thing as a general standard of fairness. But what makes the topic so stimulating is an increasing willingness for these issues to be discussed.

REFERENCES AND FURTHER READING

Adams, J and Brownsword, R (2007) *Understanding Contract Law*, (5th edn), Sweet and Maxwell, London.

Auchmuty, R (2004) 'The rhetoric of equality and the problem of heterosexuality' in Mulcahy, L and Wheeler, S (eds) *Feminist Perspectives on Contract*, Cavendish Publishing, London.

Birks, P 'The travails of duress' (1990) LMCLQ 342.

Brownsword, R 'Good faith in contracts revisited' (1996) 49 *Current Legal Problems* 111.

Brownsword, R, Hird, N and Howells, G (eds) (1999) *Good Faith in Contract: Concept and Context*, Ashgate, Aldershot.

Cartwright, J (1991) *Unequal Bargaining: A study of vitiating factors in the formation of contracts*, Clarendon Press, Oxford.

Collins, H (2002) *Regulating Contracts*, Oxford University Press, Oxford.

Dalton, C 'An essay in the deconstruction of contract doctrine' (1985) 94 *Yale Law Journal* 997.

Halson, R 'Opportunism, economic duress and contractual modifications' (1991) 107 LQR 649.

Leff, A 'Unconscionability and the code – The Emperor's New Clause' (1967) *University of Pennsylvania Law Review* 485.

Millett, P 'Equity's place in the law of commerce' (1998) 114 LQR 214.

Peel, E and Trietel, G (2007) *Treitel on the Law of Contract*, Sweet and Maxwell, London.

Phang, A 'Whither economic duress?' (1990) 53 MLR 115.

Smith, S 'Contracting under pressure: a theory of duress' (1997) 56 *Cambridge Law Journal* 343.

Trebilcock, M (1980) 'An economic approach to unconscionability' in Reiter, B and Swan, J (eds) *Studies in Contract Law*, Butterworths, Toronto.

Trietel, G., (2002) '*The Law of Contract*, Sweet and Maxwell', London.

Waddams, SM 'Unconscionability in contracts' (1976) 39, MLR, 369.

? QUESTIONS

(1) In 'The Sad Tale of Angie and Georgie' identify aspects of behaviour which you find unacceptable? In how many instances do you think that the law of contract should get involved in mitigating such unfairness? Could existing doctrine be used to help Angie circumvent the agreement she made with St Ives Bank?

(2) Can you identify the advantages of limiting the concepts of economic duress and undue influence?

(3) The task of regulating the fairness of contracts is one which the judiciary is singularly ill-equipped to perform. Appraise critically this statement.

(4) In *Lloyds Bank Ltd v Bundy* (1975), a farmer guaranteed the bank account of his son's company and charged his farm to the bank as security. The Court of Appeal set aside the guarantee and dismissed the bank's claim against the farm. Why?

(5) 'In sum, for both market-individualists and consumer-welfarists, the doctrine of economic duress rightly shields contractors against unacceptable pressure for renegotiation, but … it is unclear how adherents of either approach will apply this central idea in individual cases' Adams and Brownsword, (2007). Discuss.

PART FIVE:

THE CONTRACT

CHAPTER 13

CONTRACTUAL TERMS

INTRODUCTION

So far in this book we have looked at the theories underpinning the law of contract, what happens in the course of pre-contractual negotiations and problems with formation. In this fifth section, we will focus on the contents of contracts. The ingredients or terms of a contract are not always easy to discover. You will already be aware from the earlier discussion of misrepresentation that certain statements made in the course of pre-contractual negotiations will become terms of the contract whilst others will be excluded from it. Even where a contract is written down and signed by both parties, you will discover that other terms may be added by the courts legislation. In the majority of cases, this will be done because the additional terms represent what the parties intended, but in other instances, the legislature have shown themselves willing to rewrite parts of the contract made by two autonomous and consenting individuals. The extent to which this offends the classical notion of freedom of contract has been the subject of much discussion. Judicial and legislative activity in this area reflects the way in which notions of contractual responsibility have changed and moved away from the political ideals of individualism and *laissez-faire*.

WHERE CAN TERMS BE FOUND?

The judiciary is not unduly concerned with the form into which the parties put their agreement. Many business agreements, such as export sales, building contracts and hire-purchase agreements, are based on standard printed documents. A contract may be entirely in written form or it may be partly written with the remainder orally expressed. Many agreements are wholly oral and certain contractual obligations may simply be implied from the parties' conduct whatever they have agreed on paper. So, for instance, if you take a magazine from an unattended pile at a newstand and place 60 pence into a tin on the counter, a contract has been formed without a word having been spoken or a form signed. A variety of factors such as economy, convenience, certainty, security or speed dictate how contracts are expressed and, as one aspect of freedom of contract, the law itself rarely demands a particular approach.

The multiplicity of forms that a contract may take is well illustrated by the case of *Evans & Son (Portsmouth) Ltd v Merzario Ltd* (1976). The facts of the case were that for several years Merzarui made the transport arrangements for the importation of machinery by Evans from Italy. The course of dealing between the parties was based on the printed standard conditions of the freight forwarding trade, clause 4 of which read: 'Subject to express instructions in writing given by the customer, the Company reserves to itself complete freedom in respect of means, route and procedure to be followed in the handling and transportation of goods'. It was not disputed that the terms of the standard form had, in the course of dealings, become part of each individual contract made by the parties. After eight years it was proposed that the machinery should be carried in containers, and Merzario's manager, in the course of discussions in Portsmouth with Evans's manager, assured him: 'If we do use containers, they will not be carried on deck where the machinery might go rusty'. Containers were used and invoices, referring as usual to the standard conditions and containing new charges, were sent. Nothing was put in writing about the containers being carried below deck. A container carried on deck fell into the sea and was lost. The court held that Evans was entitled to damages for breach of contract because the oral assurance amounted to an express term of the contract. It was held that the contract was partly in writing, partly implied by conduct and partly oral. Moreover, because the new oral term and clause 4 of the printed conditions were inconsistent, the court held that the individual assurance overrode the standard form.

This case was mainly concerned with express terms: what was written on the printed form or said by the parties. But it is important to understand that, more generally, *implied* terms are just as binding as express terms. Implied terms can be incorporated into contracts from a variety of sources. Although statute law is the most important source of implied terms, say as regards consumer protection, the courts themselves also possess the power to imply terms into a contract. The courts have long argued that they will not make a contract for the parties. So when and on what basis will they 'find' a term which has not been expressed? Judges and academics have gone to great lengths to identify certain categories or groups of implied terms. Opinions vary as to how many categories there are, probably because they are not so much distinctive categories as shades on a continuous spectrum. Moreover, you will see that certain terms added to a contract by the courts or legislature cannot in all honest be 'implied' at all but are *imposed* in the interests of social justice. In the remainder of this chapter we will look at the three key ways in which implied terms can be incorporated into contracts: custom, common law and statute.

IMPLIED TERMS

Terms implied by custom or trade usage

The courts have shown themselves prepared to imply terms to reflect common *business practice*. This is a clear illustration of the point that it may be unwise to regard a contract's express terms in isolation. The better course, in appropriate circumstances, is to set them firmly within an overall framework or context of business conduct and relationships. In this way evidence of commercial custom can be added to the contract as a type of 'annex' to the contract. The rationale for importing such terms into the contract is that the parties can be taken to assume that normal business practice applies where a contract is silent on a matter. If the parties object to certain types of trade practice, they can circumvent the imposition of implied terms by ensuring that an express term lays down alternative arrangements. In such circumstances, the courts will enforce the express term rather than impose trade custom on the parties where they have expressed a clear intention to avoid it. This reflects the judiciary's commitment to enforcing what was intended by the parties.

The approach of the courts can is illustrated in *British Crane Hire Corpn Ltd v Ipswich Plant Hire Ltd* (1975). The facts of the case were that British Crane supplied a dragline crane to Ipswich Plant. It being a matter of urgency, the agreement was made by telephone and nothing was said about the conditions of hire. Later British Crane sent their printed conditions to Ipswich Plant but, before they were signed, the crane sank in marshy ground. The conditions were similar to those used by all firms in the plant hire business and they laid down that the hirer was liable to indemnify the owner of equipment against all expense in connection with its use. When sued for the cost of recovering the crane, Ipswich Plant claimed they were not liable under British Crane's conditions because they had not been incorporated into the oral contract. The court held that, as Ipswich Plant knew that such conditions were in common use in the business, British Crane were entitled to conclude that Ipswich Plant were accepting the crane on their conditions. As a result the court treated these implied terms as having been incorporated into the contract, on the basis of the common understanding of the parties.

In this case, a term was implied or incorporated into a contract because it was in common use in a trade to which both parties belonged. Similarly, terms may be incorporated into contracts between parties who have established a regular, previous course of dealing, whether or not they are in the same line of business. In *Kendall & Sons v Lillico & Sons Ltd* (1969), Hardwick Game Farm sold poultry feeding stuffs by way of oral contracts on the Bury St Edmunds Corn Exchange to the Poultry Producers Association. The next day, Hardwick Game Farm sent a confirmation note to the Poultry Producers Association on the back of which were Hardwick Game Farm's conditions of sale, including one that the buyer took responsibility for latent defects. It was established that the parties had regularly contracted in this way over a period of years, and so it was held that the note's written terms could properly be incorporated into the oral contract. Similarly, it will be recalled that, in *Hillas & Co Ltd v Arcos Ltd* (1932), details from a previous contract between two parties engaged in the timber trade were available to 'fill out' and provide sufficient certainty for a subsequent agreement to be declared binding.

Terms implied at common law

Terms implied at common law are given force on the basis that we can assume that the parties *must* have intended them. Therefore such terms can only be implied if *both* parties, had they applied their mind to the matter now in issue, would have considered them to be necessary for the contract to work. In *The Moorcock* (1889), Bowen LJ argued that the importation of such terms was required to give a contract business efficacy. In a much cited attempt to reiterate this stance, MacKinnon LJ in *Shirlaw v Southern Foundries (1926) Ltd* (1939) suggested:

> *Prima facie* that which in any contract is left to be implied and need not be expressed is something so obvious that it goes without saying; so that if while the parties were making their bargain, an officious bystander were to suggest some express provision for it in the agreement, they would testily suppress him with a common 'Oh, of course!' (p. 124)

In *Banco de Portugal v Waterlow & Sons Ltd* (1932), a term was implied into a contract for the printing of bank notes for the Portuguese central bank which stated that the London printers should not allow use of the plates to get into unauthorised hands. These types of implied terms are often referred to as *terms implied in fact*. It is important to stress that the test which applies to the importation of such terms rests on necessity. The general approach has been that it must be necessary and common sense to imply the term because the parties themselves would have agreed to it. In other words, the test is, rather unusually in the modern law of contract, a subjective one.

By way of contrast, *terms implied by law* do not depend on the common intention of the parties. Instead, they should be seen as duties arising out of certain types of contracts. Terms are implied by law as a matter of policy and, in many instances, the implication of the term amounts to the *imposition* of a legal duty on an unwilling contractor. So, for instance, in *Liverpool City Council v Irwin* (1977), a 15-storey tower block of council flats had rapidly and drastically deteriorated, and tenants claimed it should be replaced by the council. The council's obligations under their 'conditions of tenancy' were absent from the document. The contract being incomplete, the court implied terms 'such as the nature of the contract itself implicitly required'. These included the council's duty to take reasonable care as regards the repair and usability of common parts. However, the tenant's appeal failed. Although the court was prepared to import such implied terms, the court did not think it had been shown that in this case the council was in breach of the implied duty. Giving judgment, Lord Wilberforce stated that:

> ... the court is here simply concerned to establish what the contract is, the parties not having fully stated the terms. In this sense the court is searching for what must be implied .... The question to be answered ... is what is to be the legal relationship between landlord and tenant as regards these [missing] matters. (p. 43)

In various sectors of business and commerce, terms implied judicially as legal duties have come to acquire the status of general rules. So, for instance, in building contracts, it is required that the contractor will supply good and proper materials; in contracts for the carriage of goods by sea, that the carrier will provide a seaworthy vessel; and in contracts for the sale of goods, that the goods sold must be reasonably fit for their purpose. As we will soon see, some of these 'standardised' implied terms have also been put into statutory form.

Finally, it is important to stress in this introductory text that there has been considerable debate about the different categories of terms which can be implied in the common law. Lord Denning has suggested that the overarching test should be one of reasonableness but this approach has not found favour. One reason for this is that it suggests that it is the judges rather than the parties that are determining what should go in the contract.

Terms implied by statute

We have already noted in Chapter 4 that there has been a tremendous expansion of the mixed economy and welfare functions of the state since the classical period of contract. Since the end of the Second World War in particular, this has led to vastly increased judicial and governmental involvement in business and social affairs and a multitude of terms substituted for, or added to, contractual terms agreed between the parties. It is this erosion of freedom of contract by the judiciary and legislature which it is argued has transformed certain types of contracting from a private to a public act. In a sense then, contract is now as 'mixed' as the economy itself. For a variety of social welfare reasons, statutes now compel us to make certain contracts, such as those for motor insurance coverage. Even more commonly, statutes now regulate the terms of many contracts, such as hire-purchase agreements, rent-controlled tenancies, contracts of employment and package holidays.

Intervention often stems from the need for Parliament to restore some semblance of balance to the contractual relationship in question. Where the ideal of freedom of contract has degenerated into the freedom of one party to oppress the other because of the imbalance of economic power between them, the courts and legislature have tended to move in on behalf of the weaker party by way of implied contractual terms. Interference has also been justified on the basis that there is a need to redress the imperfections of a free market in which traders lack incentives to supply quality products, and where meaningful appraisal of the quality of goods by consumers is not always possible.

The twin goals of regulating the market and balancing interests through the imposition of obligations on a party possessing stronger bargaining power has a long history in the sale of goods field. The ongoing importance of the ideals of the free market in this field are clear from the part that the notion *caveat emptor* has played in the development of law in this field. The maxim, which can be translated as let the buyer beware, has its English origins in the system of trading common to the markets and fairs of the Middle Ages. In these marketplaces, the goods were on open display and could be examined, tested and bought on the spot. It was reasonable in these circumstances for the buyer to rely on their own judgment. Professor Llewellyn has described later developments in this way:

> Western markets gradually developed into industrial economies which focused on predictability and standardization. Merchants began to trade with distant sellers as transportation improved and much more extensive use was made of credit. Contracts made by description, sample or specification, became common as did contracts made before production. The law of obligations was forced to change to reflect these transformations in the marketplace.

At the time of predominantly face-to-face contractual situations, a buyer might obtain a remedy if, on receiving defective or worthless goods, they could prove breach of an express promise made by the seller or fraud. But, as Llewellyn makes clear, goods later came to be purchased mainly by way of description. So a contract could be formed with a buyer who lived a hundred or a thousand miles away. This trend has developed to a point where, in the current age of 'globalisation' of markets, goods can be brought within minutes on the internet between contracting parties living in different continents.

Changes in the common law relating to seller's obligations as to quality did gradually change in response to such concerns and, in 1893, The Sale of Goods Act (1893) codified the common law rules that had developed. However, this landmark statute represented something of a halfway house between the opposing ideas of *caveat emptor* and consumer protection. The greatest stumbling block to the fulfilment of real consumer protection was to be found in s 55 of the Act which provided that: 'Where any right, duty or liability would arise under a contract of sale by implication of law, it may be negated or varied by express agreement'. The clause reflected an ongoing respect for the idea that implied terms should reflect what was the intention of the parties rather than an imposition of external statndards and a certain ambivalence about regulation of contracts which remains today. But reactions to the statute also suggest that, by clinging to the notion of freedom of contract, the legislature set its statutory seal of approval on the freedom to exploit. By means of tightly worded, small-print exclusion clauses in their contracts, economically powerful sellers of goods were able to negate whatever protection was afforded the buyer by means of s 14(1) and so deprive buyers of their legal remedies.

A shift in legislative approach has been signalled by subsequent statutes which have tended to favour greater consumer protection. It is now clear that exclusion clauses in contracts for the sale of goods which seek to negate or vary the seller's implied obligations as to such things as fitness for purpose will be of no effect in consumer transactions and in other cases will be subject to a test of reasonableness. The complex question of exclusion clauses will be fully examined in Chapters 14 and 15, but it is worth noting here that the increasing prevalence and severity of such clauses, particularly in the related field of hire purchase, meant that eventually Parliament was prevailed upon to introduce legislation on this specific topic. This was a major advance in the protection of buyers' rights and the implied term is no longer, for parties contracting as consumers, in the shadow of the exclusion clause (see now the Unfair Contract Terms Act 1977).

The Sale of Goods Act 1893 together with its subsequent amendments has now been consolidated in the Sale of Goods Act 1979 (as further amended in 1994 and 2002). Similar statutory implied terms regarding quality in such contracts as those for work and materials, exchange and hire are to be found in the Supply of Goods and Services Act 1982. Some of the most important provisions of the Sale of Goods Act are contained in sections 12–15, which have been reproduced in Box 13.1. As with all the other instances in which terms can be implied into a contract, the legislature have remained sensitive to the parties intentions. As a result, the provisions of

> **Box 13.1:   Key provisions in the Sale of Goods Act 1979 (as amended)**
>
> **Section 12:** The seller has the right to sell the goods.
>
> **Section 13:** Goods should correspond to their description.
>
> **Section 14:** The goods should be of satisfactory quality if sold in the course of a business.
>
> **Section 14:** The goods should be reasonably fit for the purpose for which the buyer requires them.
>
> **Section 15:** If the goods are sold after a sample has been supplied, then they should correspond to the sample.

the Sale of Goods Act will not generally be implied if the parties specifically exclude them. However, the Unfair Contract Terms Act has had a radical impact on this regime by making sections 12–15 mandatory in sales involving consumer sales and subject to the test of reasonableness in non-consumer sales.

CONCLUDING REMARKS

In this chapter we have introduced you to some of the key themes of this section of the book. Our consideration of implied terms demonstrates that this is an area in which the courts have looked at relational elements of contracts through the notion of previous courses of dealing and industrywide understandings of common practice. Whilst the judiciary has expressed reservations about writing the contract for the parties, they have also steered away from literal interpretations of words to try and give meaning to agreements made in a business context. However, they have been cautious of stepping over the threshold to become writers rather than interpreters. As Collins (2003) reminds us, invoking the implicit dimensions of contracts is of fundamental concern to those who wish to promote the efficiency of the market as well as those concerned about social justice. He argues that greater efficiency can be achieved through the observance of conventions that augment mutual trust and confidence. In this way, the legal system can make a profound contribution to the creation of trust in inter-firm relations which may help to reduce transaction costs, avoid disputes and reinforce the legitimacy of the law. In this sense, an understanding of the implicit dimensions of contracts can be used by the courts to understand how successful economic organisations are established and evolve.

REFERENCES AND FURTHER READING

Collins, H (2003) 'The research agenda of implicit dimensions of contract', in Campbell, D, Collins, H and Wightman, J *Implicit Dimensions of Contract: Discrete, Relational and Network Contracts*, Hart Publishing, Oxford.

Department for Business Enterprise and Regulatory Reform: http://www.dti.gov.uk/consumers/fact-sheets/page38311.html (last visited December 2007).

Macdonald, E 'Express and implied terms and exemptions' (1991) 107 LQR 555.

Phang, A 'Implied terms revisited' (1990) JBL 394.

Phang, A 'Implied terms in English law: some recent developments' (1993) JBL 242.

Sale of Goods Act 1979: http://www.opsi.gov.uk/acts/acts1994 (last visited December 2007).

Sale and Supply of Goods Act 1994: http://www.opsi.gov.uk/acts/acts1994

The Sale and Supply of Goods to consumers regulations 2002 SI 2002 No.3045: http://www.opsi.gov.uk/si/si2002/20023045.htm (last visited December 2007).

? **QUESTIONS**

(1) In 'The Sad Tale of Angie and Georgie', what terms, if any, would be implied into the contract between Chelsea and the company she booked a ferry ticket with?

(2) In Chapter 7 you were asked to identify the points at which agreements between the parties in 'The Sad Tale of Angie and Georgie' had come into place. Building on that analysis, can you now identify all the terms of such agreements? In addition to express terms, can you think of any terms which might be implied into the agreements?

(3) Is it still appropriate for the law of contract to place emphasis on the notion of negotiated agreement in the twenty first century? Discuss.

(4) Collins (2003) has argued that any legal system that enforces contracts must develop techniques for determining the legal significance of the context and conventions surrounding the social practice of entering into contracts. Can you think of any arguments which undermine this point of view?

CHAPTER 14

STANDARD FORM CONTRACTS

INTRODUCTION

The classical contract model developed at a time when most negotiations were conducted face-to-face by two parties. Doctrines associated with this model and its neo-classical offshoot continue to dominate the modern development of the law of contract despite the fact that a considerable number of legal agreements are now standard form contracts containing written express terms prepared in advance of negotiations and exchange by parties other than those contracting. Standard form contracts probably account for the bulk of contracts now made in inter-business agreements and consumer contracts. Most parking tickets, theatre tickets, package receipts, debit card purchase slips are standard form contracts. Although the Unfair Contract Terms Act 1977 recognises the existence of 'written standard forms of business', there is no statutory definition of a standard form contract in this country. However, all standard form contracts share certain characteristics. They have terms which are fixed in advance by, or on behalf of, the person supplying or buying the commodity or service. The intention is that the same contract be used in multiple transactions, with people who have not always been identified at the time of drafting the terms.

Standard form contracts are of two main types, and each category raises different issues to students of contract law. In *Schroeder Music Publishing Co Ltd v Macaulay* (1974), Lord Diplock set about describing the first category:

> Standard forms of contracts are of two kinds. The first, of very ancient origin, are those which set out the terms on which mercantile transactions of common occurrence are to be carried out. Examples are bills of lading, charter-parties, policies of insurance, contracts of sale in the commodity markets. The standard clauses in these contracts have been settled over the years by negotiation by representatives of the commercial interests involved and have been widely adopted because experience has shown that they facilitate the conduct of trade. Contracts of these kinds affect not only the actual parties to them but also others who may have a commercial interest in the transactions to which they relate, as buyers or sellers, charterers or shipowners, insurers or bankers. If fairness or reasonableness were relevant to their enforceability, the fact that they are widely used by parties whose bargaining power is fairly matched would raise a strong presumption that their terms are fair and reasonable. (p. 624)

The same presumption, however, does not apply to the other kind of standard form of contract. This is of comparatively modern origin. It is the result of the concentration of particular kinds of business in relatively few hands. The ticket cases in the nineteenth century provide what are probably the first examples. The terms of this kind of standard form of contract have not been the subject of negotiation between the parties to it, or approved by any organisation representing the interests of the weaker party. They have been dictated by that party whose bargaining power, either exercised alone or in conjunction with others providing similar goods or services, enables them to say: 'If you want these goods or services at all, these are the only terms on which they are available. Take it or leave it'. Standard form contracts of this kind are often referred to as 'contracts of adhesion'. This account of standard form contracts enables us to consider some important points about their uses and the extent to which they can be considered abusive.

USES, ABUSES AND BARGAINING POWER

The basic reason underlying the widespread use of standard forms of contract is the need to facilitate the conduct of trade in the most efficient way. Standard form contracts often run to a great many pages of detailed clauses and individual clauses to more than a page. There are undoubtedly thousands of such contracts in use at any time. Often standards form contracts are of use because the parties regularly enter into complex technical and legal relations. This is the case, for instance, in the construction industry, international trade and engineering. In other cases it is because the dealings in question involve transactions relating to standardised and mass-produced products, services or marketing techniques. The latter is a particularly common feature of modern business. In such cases the presence of a standard form contract such mean that standard conditions do not have to be re-negotiated for every transaction.

Many of the reasons for the development of standard written contracts are positive. In the inter-business field, they may be well established as exemplars negotiated by trade associations or professional bodies on behalf of parties of approximately equal bargaining power over a lengthy period of time. The cif international contract of sale and the JCT form of building contract, discussed below, are good examples of this. With these types of contracts there is a presumption by the courts that they are fair and reasonable. However, this does not mean that standard form contracts are without their problems. The 'battle of the forms' is an example of the problems which arise when use is made of standard form contracts by both parties to the deal. While standard form contracts can represent the intentions of the parties, it is clear that people often proceed without reading the details embodied in a standard form.

However, it is not uncommon for a powerful business organisation to impose its 'written standard terms of business' upon others who possess considerably less bargaining strength. Such inequality of bargaining strength is normally found to exist between businesses and consumers. It comes about as a result of a concentration of market power, be it monopolistic or oligopolistic, or because the interests of smaller firms are regulated by a trade association. Where the use of standard form contracts is accompanied by inequality of bargaining power, there is a greater likelihood of their being used as instruments of economic oppression because their terms can more easily be weighted in favour of the interests of the stronger parties who prepare them. Here there is no presumption by the courts that such contracts are fair and reasonable and, as a result, they are more likely to be subjected to judicial regulation. In such circumstances, the courts may well take into account the absence of genuine agreement and justify their intervention on that basis.

A number of problems with the use of standard forms when dealing with a consumer relate to the way information about the crucial rights and duties of the parties is communicated. All too often, this is contained in the 'small print' of standard form documents. A maze of small print usually means that onerous clauses are either not read or not understood. It is well known that the consumer may have no time to read standard form clauses which are often contained in another document elsewhere. Contracts with railway or bus companies are an excellent example of this. Tickets commonly refer to the fact that standard terms and conditions apply but these are often only available on posters near the booking office. However, practice is changing with greater use being made of the internet for buying and selling services. Many sites do not allow 'click and wrap' contracts to be concluded until the purchaser confirms they have read the standard forms which can be called up at the click of a mouse.

It also remains the case that, even if consumers did have time to read standard contracts, they would probably not understand them. And even if they did understand them, they would probably, as Lord Diplock suggested, have little choice but to 'take them or leave them'. When was the last time that you renegotiated the terms of a standard form contract with a major airline carrier or web-based bookseller? One approach to this problem would be to reject the assumptions about roughly equal bargaining strength made by classical or neo-classical theorists by encouraging judicial and statutory rewriting of contracts. Another would be to try and create the negotiating autonomy anticipated by traditionalists and to work towards increased consumer awareness of contracts.

Examples of both these approaches are evident in modern statutes and case law. Legislation passed in recent years has removed some of the more obvious causes of concern, such as high and hidden interest rates in credit transactions, by outlawing them. Changes have also been imposed relating to the form, layout and language of consumer documents in order to make them more accessible and comprehensible. The Unfair Contract Terms Act 1977 and European legislation have also played an important part in the legal struggle against unfair exclusion and liability in standard form contracts. These developments will be considered more fully in the chapter which follows.

CASE STUDIES

In an introductory book such as this, it is neither possible nor appropriate to attempt even a general survey of the law and practice of standard form contracts. However, it is important that students become familiar with some of the contexts within which they operate. In the remainder of this chapter, examples of building and engineering contracts are examined more closely. The prevalence of standard form contracts is such that the courts are regularly asked to interpret them. A dispute between the parties to a standard form contract may, for instance, require the court to establish the true meaning of an individual clause, the relationship between two printed clauses, or the standing of a printed clause and written addition. It may involve a question of whether or not a term may be implied into the contract, or the breadth of an exclusion or limitation of liability clause.

In broad terms, building and engineering standard forms display many similarities. Both reflect a high degree of planning of complicated technical operations. This planning attempts to establish the detailed nature and scope of the rights and duties of the principal parties and third parties involved in commercial networks of agreement. These can involve the commissioning body, the architect, consulting engineers and sub-contractors. As we saw in *Williams v Roffey Bros and Nichols (Contractors) Ltd* (1991), it is rare in building contracts for the contractor to be in a position to undertake all the work required. The result is that a number of sub-contracts spring out of the main contract and a network of contracts which are intricately connected with each other for the success of the project is born. It can be seen that the discrete model of contract anticipated by classical contract theory is an inadequate tool through which to understand what fuels each contract in this interconnected web of relationships.

The two most difficult problems relating to sub-contracts are delay and the weighing of a sub-contractor's possible liability against their contribution to the total venture if it fails. So, for instance, the component supplied by a sub-contractor engaged in the building of an aircraft may be of little financial significance on its own, but if defective, it may be the cause of a major disaster. For these reasons another third party, such as the consulting engineer or architect, is given extensive duties to supervise work under the sub-contracts. These professionals commonly issue instructions to the contractor and act as arbitrators in disputes between contractor and purchaser.

Delays are almost always inevitable in such contracts, but the problem of how to deal with them is not an easy one in a network of relationships expensive machinery, a large number of workers with a range of different skills. Litigation is rarely an option. The delay and cost of bringing an action not only disrupts completion of the contract further but is likely to lead to financial difficulties for all the parties involved. As a result, there is a considerable incentive to plan for contingencies in advance whilst building in a level of flexibility. It is often possible to settle a dispute arising out of the execution of the works on an *ad hoc* basis without reference to the courts. Alternatively, a party with supervisory functions in the contract, such as an architect, may on a relatively informal basis seek to come to an agreed interpretation of the standard form. If no agreed interpretation can be found, resort may be had to the contract's mediation or arbitration clause. The success of those who use the standard form describe contracts below is such that commentators have suggested that they have these standard form contracts simplified contracting procedures and led to the abandonment of litigation and arbitration throughout the industry. In the sections which follow, we will take a closer look at how this has been achieved.

STANDARD FORMS USED IN THE BUILDING TRADE

Established in 1931, the Joint Contracts Tribunal (JCT) has produced standard form contracts for the building industry for 75 years and it is estimated that two-thirds of projects in the UK are conducted according to their terms. It has been argued that the standard form contracts they produce are now so influential that they have come to resemble a 'legislative code'. The contracts produced have been devised and revised over a period of time by representatives of all interested parties in the building trade, such as builders,

> **Box 14.1: Membership of the Joint Contracts Tribunal**
>
> ○ Association for Consultancy and
>   Engineering
> ○ British Property Federation
> ○ Construction Confederation
> ○ Local Government Association
> ○ Royal Institute of British Architects
> ○ National Specialist Contractors Council
> ○ The Royal Institution of Chartered
>   Surveyors
> ○ Scottish Building Contract Committee

architects, surveyors, sub-contractors and local authorities. Representatives of all of these bodies form the Joint Contracts Tribunal (see further, Box 14.1). All new contracts and subsequent amendments are published with the advice and agreement of members.

A practice note produced by the JCT in 2007 claims that the contracts are generally considered to be fair and evenly balanced between the parties. But it also warns that this balance should not be put at risk by ill-conceived incorporation of substantive provision from another contract into the JCT form.

The JCT standard form contract rapidly assumed the status of an authoritative agreement as regards the building operations that it covers, although it has always been accepted that terms may be implied. Disputes about the terms are far from unheard of. Although managers and site operators are assumed to be familiar with the contract and work proceeds more or less in adherence to its terms, it is often the case that the task of resolving disputes arising out of the execution of the works brings out difficult questions of interpretation of the standard clauses. Rather than referring such matters to the court which are costly and take time to hear a case, the JCT standard forms give power to certain supervising professionals within the industry to adjudicate on disputes which arise in the course of a contract.

The idea which underpins the JCT contracts is that there is value in producing a mutually consistent set of documents to enable a suite of contracts to be used on the same project. As a result, there are common expectations and procedures in place whether the contract is for a consultant, constitutes the main contract, deals with the relationship between main contractor and sub-contractor or indeed between sub-contractors.

It is a key theme throughout this book that legal insistence on clarity and precision in a contractual document may well not wholly accord with the looser, more flexible approach to the implementation of the aims of such a document favoured by those in business. This is clearly the case as regards builders, architects and others on site. However, during the 1970s, the flexibility of some of the standard forms of contract being used was such that they began to be perceived of as too obscure. Standardisation caused problems because broad terms designed to fit all situations rendered the contract almost meaningless. As a result, a new

Box 14.2:   Examples of JCT contracts

- Standard Building Contract
- Intermediate Building Contract
- Minor Works Building Contract
- Design and Build Contract
- Major Project Construction Contract
- Construction Management
- Management Building Contract
- Prime Cost Building Contract
- Measured Term Contract
- Housing Grant Works Building Contract
- Adjudication Agreement
- Framework Agreement
- Generic Contracts
- Collateral Warranties

improved JCT80 standard form was published in six varying editions to suit the requirements of different sorts of parties and endeavours, and has since been further amended. The most recent suite of contracts, JCT05 consists of a family of contracts including main and sub-contractor standard forms together with a number of other documents which can be used to cover a range of scenarios in the construction industry. Box 14.2 gives some examples of the types of standard form contracts produced by the JCT. Even so, the benefits of standardisation are often lost in practice. Even the most recent editions of the JCT contract are rarely used exactly as they are printed. Amendments are made, unwanted clauses are deleted and new ones are added.

Following the government commissioned Latham Report in 1994, increasing emphasis has been placed in the industry on the need for increased collaborative working within project networks. In the 1990s it was argued that adversarial attitudes and confrontational relationships between contractors were proving detrimental to the construction industry. Project completion rates were poor and projects commonly ran over budget. The principles of collaborative working which the Latham report espoused included a number of measures aimed at getting the various contractors and sub-contractors on a project communicating more effectively. These included involving key contractors across teams in decision-making from the offset, working across contractors to agree mutual objectives, adopting common processes, using participants who have long-term, supply-chain relationships and dealing with risks through collaborative contracts. As a result of these developments, a new form of contract launched by the JCT in 2007 aimed to promote collaborative and integrated working within networks of people employed on the same construction project. The emphasis in this 'umbrella' contract is on encouraging the parties to view a project as a joint mission, with the stress being placed on collaboration, trust and fairness. Significantly, the Chief Executive of JCT was keen to emphasise at the launch that these values were not meant to reflect 'fuzzy terms' but rather were embedded within a rigorous legal framework. It is clear that these new approaches bear many of the hallmarks of relational contracts in which contracts are seen as more than isolated and discrete exchanges between two parties.

STANDARD FORMS USED IN THE ENGINEERING BUSINESS

The Institution of Mechanical Engineers (IMechE) has been producing a range of standard form contracts which deal with arrangements for the erection and installation of plant since 1903. In partnership with the Institution of Engineering and Technology (IET), it now produces four model forms and three commentaries. These are designed for use in home and overseas contracts for mechanical and electrical plant, goods and consultancy. The forms are produced by a Joint Committee whose members represent the various interests in the electrical and mechanical engineering industries. Box 14.3 gives some idea of the sort of terms which the model conditions contain.

The basic object of contracts governed by these terms is to enable the purchaser at an agreed date to take over and operate the plant which has been completed and tested in accordance with the contract. The approach to the formation of the contract varies from the JCT model above. In practice, engineering contracts are frequently of a complex technical nature and the time required for completion may be lengthy. As a result, there is a greater need for them to be governed by specially agreed 'tailor-made' contracts which are modelled on the general conditions. In contrast to arrangements in the construction industry, it is common for large-scale

Box 14.3: Joint IMechE and IET model forms – examples of terms

o Patent and other protected rights
o Assignment and sub-contracting
o Site conditions
o Variation orders
o Unforeseen site conditions
o Access to manufacturers' premises for inspection of plant
o Ownership of plant
o Temporary works and contractors' equipment
o Liquidated damages
o Currency of payment
o Dispute resolution
o Confidentiality

operators in the industry to produce their own 'in-house' models which follow the appropriate recommended model. These contracts become 'tailor-made' only by a careful process of incorporation, variation and addition of terms to suit the parties' project.

The work of contract lawyers in the engineering sector is dominated by the need to plan complex operations, interpret and periodically revise the model forms so that the rights and duties of the principal parties are clearly established. Clearly, it is essential for the main parties to the contract to be very clear about who is responsible for the various risks inherent in such enterprises and the mechanism of contract is useful for establishing the obligations of the parties who enter into it. But the nature of the projects being undertaken is such that obligations to third parties also need to be taken into account. It might be thought that a principal party to the contract is in no real position to incur liability for loss or injury to third parties because the contractor, or their sub-contractor undertaking the work is the party who is in all probability directly responsible for any injuries caused. However, the purchaser of services will probably be the owner or occupier of the site on which the work is being carried out and as such owes duties to others under such statutes as the Health and Safety at Work Act and the Occupier's Liability Act. Moreover, they may have their own employees working in connection with the contract for whom they are vicariously liable and they may even be vicariously liable in tort for the acts or omissions of the contractor themselves.

An example of how such problems could arise is provided by the case of *Murfin v United Steel Companies Ltd* (1957). The facts of the case were that United Steel engaged Power Gas on work at their factory. The latter were bound to indemnify the former

> against every claim against United Steel under any statute or common law for ...
> (b) death ... arising out of or in connection with the carrying out of Power Gas's work and from any cause other than the negligence of United Steel or their employees. (p. 23)

An employee of Power Gas' sub-contractor was electrocuted in the factory owing to the failure of Power Gas to install insulating screens. But because United Steel were owners of the factory it was held that they were liable in damages for breach of the Electricity (Factories Act) Special Regulations. However, United Steel was able to use the indemnity clause to argue that they were entitled to be indemnified by Power Gas. They did so on the basis that se United Steel's 'negligence' was not interpreted as including a formal breach of their statutory duty.

It can be seen from this example, why extensive use is made of indemnity clauses in the industry in planning for claims from injured third parties which may arise. Significantly, wherever liability eventually rests, this will or should mean that the insurance company of the party responsible will bear the loss. This means that the contractor's insurance company must indemnify the site owner's insurance company who have already met the site owner's liability for the damages awarded; see, for example, *Walters v Whessoe Ltd & Shell Refining Co Ltd* (1960).

CONCLUDING REMARKS

The importance of standard form contracts in the world of businesses cannot be overstated. More than any other factor, it is the growth of standard forms which has prompted the development of legislative and judicial forms of protection for those who suffer from inequality of bargaining power in the market place. Moreover, it is in this field that we have witnessed some of the worst abuses of economic power. But, alongside the popular vision of standard contracts as abusive, lies another model in which standard form contracts can be seen as facilitating the more efficient working of markets by saving time when the contracting parties are of roughly equal bargaining strength. They can be conceptualised as a private form of ordering in which industries are able to formalise shared understandings about what constitutes fair practice and sound economic sense. Viewed in this way, the use of standard contracts to plan future relations and allow for the flexibility needed in a field can be seen in a positive light.

In the chapters which follow, we shall look at how the judiciary and legislature have attempted to tread the thin line between efficiency and abuse. In the next two chapters, we shall be focusing on the use of clauses which attempt to exclude certain liabilities from contracts. Exemption clauses can be found in negotiated and standard form contracts, but it is their use in the latter which has most often troubled the judiciary and legislature. The UK government has legislated for regulation of certain types of exclusion clause for nearly three decades but European intervention in the field has returned the spotlight to standard form contracts.

REFERENCES AND FURTHER READING

Institution of Mechanical Engineers: http://www.imeche.org/
Joint Contracts Council: http://www.jctltd.co.uk
Joint Contracts Tribunal (2007) *Deciding on the Appropriate JCT Contract, Practice Note*, Sweet and Maxwell, London.
Kessler, F 'Contracts of adhesion: some thoughts about freedom of contract' (1942) 43 *Columbia Law Review* 629.
Latham, M (1994) *Constructing the Team*, HMSO, London.
McKendrick, E (2003) *Contract Law*, 5th edn, Palgrave Macmillan, Basingstoke.
Mouzas, S and Furriston, M (2008) 'From contract to umbrella agreement' *Cambridge Law Journal*, 7(1) pp. 37–50.
National Audit Office (2005) *Improving Public Services Through Better Construction*, National Audit Office, London.
Rakoff, T 'Contracts of adhesion: an essay in reconstruction' (1983) 96 *Harvard Law Review* 1173.
Slawson, W 'Standard form contracts and democratic control of law-making power' (1971) 84 *Harvard Law Review* 529.
Trebilcock, M (1980) 'An economic approach to unconscionability' in Reiter, B and Swan, J (eds) *Studies in Contract Law*, Butterworths, Toronto.

? QUESTIONS

(1) How would you distinguish between contracts of adhesion where market power is being abused and standard form contracts which benefit both parties?

(2) In your view, in 'The Sad Tale of Angie and Georgie' does Chelsea need consumer protection when booking the ferry ticket on the web? Can you find out what recent regulations say about these types of contract?

CHAPTER 15

JUDICIAL APPROACHES TO EXCLUSION AND LIMITATION CLAUSES

INTRODUCTION

So far in this section of the book we have concentrated on the terms of a contract and how these reflect the obligations the parties owe to each other. This chapter shifts the focus to look at how the judiciary has dealt with certain types of unfair terms in contracts which seek to exclude or limit liability. As in other chapters, it is important to start by making it clear that different approaches to unfair bargains are apparent from case law, and these reflect different conceptions of the role of contract law and notions of what is fair and reasonable. Whilst the classical model of contract recognises that unfairness occurs, the focus is on procedural rather than substantive unfairness. This means that traditionalists have been willing in some circumstances to intervene to upset a contract which has been negotiated in an unfair way but not to regulate unfair exchanges. Even with the introduction of legislation and the development of doctrines to protect the parties against manifestly unfair contracts, it remains the case that contractual terms are not set aside lightly. The courts and legislature will only intervene to mitigate the effects of extreme behaviour. Atiyah (1979) has likened the approach to a contest or game in which there are rules to protect how it is played, to outlaw fouls and so on, but there is no scope for revisiting whether the outcome was fair.

This mixed approach has become more contentious since the time when the classical model first came to dominate the law of contract. Moreover, it could be argued that the courts have always found it hard to separate questions of unfair negotiations from unfair terms. The growth of welfarism within the law of contract has encouraged the courts and legislature to intervene to limit the autonomy of contracting parties where significant inequalities of bargaining power are reflected in contractual terms. This approach to the subject has been particularly evident in the field of consumer contracts where there has been recognition that the growth of large-scale businesses and standard form contracts means that consumers have no power to either negotiate the terms of the contract or suggest alterations. The courts and legislature have been particularly diligent in their approach to the regulation of exclusion and limitation clauses which tend to restrict liability rather than define positive obligations. In this chapter we will look at judicial activity in this field and in the next we will turn to look at what the legislature has done to mitigate the harshness of certain contractual terms.

THE JUDICIAL ROLE

The judicial role in the regulation of unfair exclusion and limitation clauses has been somewhat overshadowed by legislation in the field in recent years, but it remains important to understand it. Judicial precedent is particularly important on the question of whether an exclusion or limitation clause is part of the contract in the first place.

Figure 15.1:   Elements of a contract – what goes in, what comes out

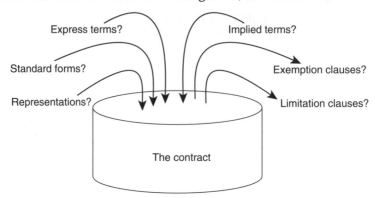

Moreover, even with the advent of legislation in the field, the judiciary has an important role to play in interpreting the meaning of exclusion clauses, legislative provisions, and giving context to the circumstances in which the exclusion clause is being used. It is also the case that many contracts in the field of insurance, land, intellectual property and securities do not fall within the ambit of major statutes regulating exemption clauses such as the Unfair Contract Terms Act 1977. Furthermore, legislative intervention cannot be understood fully without reference to the case law as it was the judiciary who first showed themselves to be active in the field. In the remainder of this section we outline the various common law rules which they have developed in their attempts to police terms.

So far, in this book we have focused on determining the positive obligations of the parties to a contract. In this chapter we will look at the ways in which exemption clauses can be used to exclude or limit liability.

It can be seen from Figure 15.1 that there are two types of clause which are of interest in this context. Exemption clauses seek to exclude a particular type of liability, whereas limitation clauses merely seek to limit liability. Beale, Bishop and Furmston (2008) have identified a number of different types of clauses which fall under this heading and these have been reproduced in Box 15.1.

The clear purpose of an exclusion clause in a consumer transaction is to enable the business person to eliminate

> **Box 15.1:   Types of exclusion and limitation clauses**
>
> o Limiting the compensation for a breach of contract
> o Limiting the remedies available
> o Limiting the time during which a remedy is available
> o Imposing a condition on obtaining a remedy
> o Excluding express or implied terms
> o Giving one party a broad discretion over the manner or substance of performance

the risk of financial loss as a result of having to pay damages to the other party for breach. Consequently, exclusion and limitation clauses are common in business–consumer contracts. In commercial transactions where bargaining strength is more likely to be equal, exclusion clauses are less common, although limitation of liability clauses are often found. These apportion the risk of loss between the parties who can insure accordingly. In fact, in standard form dealings between business organisations, there is a general tendency towards a more sophisticated and wide-ranging concern with risk and its apportionment than is to be found in consumer transactions. The parties, through the use of settled, agreed devices, often display a willingness to be very specific about what they are undertaking and to avoid or minimise common 'enemies' including the risks of litigation. To this extent, contrary to the classical approach, their contracts emphasise common interests rather than 'separation' and conflict.

As we have already suggested, approaches to attempts by the parties to exempt liability have changed considerably. Seventy years ago, a Miss L'Estrange (see further *L'Estrange v Graucob Ltd*, 1934) bought a cigarette machine under a sales agreement which contained a clause which stated that 'any express or implied condition, statement or warranty, statutory or otherwise not stated herein, is hereby excluded'. Although the machine soon jammed and became unworkable, she lost her action for breach because the clause was considered valid. This year, the author purchased a car under a sales agreement which stated that: 'Nothing in these conditions is intended to remove, alter or restrict any rights or obligations of either party arising under the Sale of Goods legislation'. On the face of it, many of Miss L'Estrange's expectations and remedies were removed by the exclusion clause. In the second transaction, the protection afforded by implied statutory obligations was apparently unimpaired. What is the explanation for this change? How has the common law approached the issue of unfair limitations and exclusions? How have they balanced the needs of autonomous individuals to make whatever deals they see fit with a desire to introduce more substantive notions of fairness?

Whenever faced with an exclusion or limitation clause, it is standard practice to divide analysis of it into five main questions. Firstly, is the clause which seeks to exclude or limit a party's liability incorporated into the contract? Secondly, if so, as a matter of judicial construction, does the wording of the clause satisfactorily cover the loss or damage at issue? Thirdly, if it does, is it a clause which is rendered ineffective under the Unfair Contract Terms Act 1977? Fourthly, if it passes this test, does the clause satisfy the requirement of reasonableness? Finally, if the term is contained in a standard form contract, is it subject to the test of fairness in European regulations?

The first two questions are addressed in this chapter and, in the next chapter, we go on to consider the remaining issues. But before moving on, it is useful to summarise the various questions which you will need to ask when determining whether an exclusion clause is effective and the limitations which might be placed on it. There is no doubt that the law surrounding exclusion clauses is complex as it involves a web of different types of regulatory controls.

The key questions which you should be asking are summarised in Figure 15.2 which you might like to help guide you through the sections which follow.

IS THE CLAUSE INCORPORATED INTO THE CONTRACT?

The issue of how terms become incorporated into contracts has already been touched upon in the section of this book concerned with pre-contractual negotiations and misrepresentation. The courts' dislike of attempts to exempt liability in contracts

Figure 15.2:   Is an exclusion clause effective?

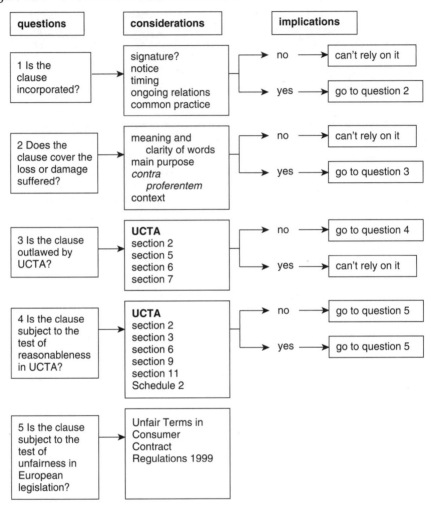

involving those in a relatively weak bargaining position has led to a number of particular rules being developed about limitation and exclusion clauses being developed. Despite the intervention of the legislature, the pre-statutory case law continues to provide guidelines in this area. It will soon become clear that the common law cases are almost exclusively concerned with situations in which one party seeks to rely on written terms contained in a document displayed at a place of business or on documents exchanged between the parties in the course of negotiations. In these cases, the courts have required that, if such terms are to form part of the contract, then they must have been brought to the attention of the party whose rights are being restricted. The case law reveals an increasingly restrictive approach to those who try to impose their standard conditions on others because of their market power or knowledge.

Signed documents

The case of *L'Estrange v Graucob Ltd* (1934) is authority for the proposition that a person who signs a contractual document is bound by its terms even though they have not read them. In this case, the claimant was bound by her signature although the exclusion clause was, in the view of the court, in 'regrettably small print'. Putting her signature to the document meant that she could not argue that she had no notice of the clause. This is a case which would now be decided on the basis of the 'reasonableness' of the clause under s 6(3) of the 1977 Act (see Chapter 16). It is relevant for present purposes because it reminds us that the court will *imply* that notice has been given in certain circumstances even if the signatory has not read the clause and has no working knowledge of it. If, however, the true purpose of the signed document has been misrepresented to the party signing, the absolute effect of their signature will not be enforced. So, in *Curtis v Chemical Cleaning & Dyeing Co Ltd* (1951), the restricted scope of an exclusion clause was taken to be as orally represented at the time the contract was being negotiated and not as written (see also *Couchman v Hill*, 1947 and *Evans & Son (Portsmouth) Ltd v Merzario Ltd*, 1976).

The 'rule' in *L'Estrange v Graucob* (1934) reflects the formalistic tendencies of English contract law and an early unsympathetic approach to the plight of those who contract with a stronger party on their standard terms and conditions. The rationale behind the decision is that the best way to prove that written terms on which you are seeking to rely have been brought to the notice of the other party is to ask them to sign the document in which they are contained. This is clearly something of a fiction. In modern-day society, we probably all sign contractual documents without reading the document fully. This does not necessarily reflect our stupidity or lack of business acumen. Rather, it is a reflection of the fact that, even if one did object to a particular clause, there is often no practical alternative and the agents with whom we contract are rarely in a position to re-negotiate terms. When was the last time that you heard of anyone re-negotiating a ticket price or exclusion clauses with a cinema or 'white goods' dealer?

Reasonably sufficient notice

In cases which do not involve signatures, it is necessary to prove that the party relying on the limitation or exclusion clause incorporated it into the contract by giving the other party notice. This is established if the other party was aware, or ought to have been aware, of the conditions that the other party was trying to incorporate. Most of the cases in this area involve attempts to incorporate written standard forms or clauses into the contract. One way in which the judiciary have approached this issue is to ask whether the document containing the conditions is a 'contractual' document. If not, the clause set out or referred to has no force. In *Chapelton v Barry UDC* (1940), for instance, a ticket handed to a customer after they have paid for the hire of a deckchair was held to be merely a 'voucher or receipt'. In general, whether a document is one which could reasonably be expected to contain contractual terms is a question of fact which may vary with business practice. This means that a 'receipt' may still have contractual force in other business contexts.

Other cases have focused on what constitutes reasonable notice of a restrictive term when documents containing it are not to hand. In 1930 in *Thompson v London, Midland and Scottish Rly Co Ltd*, the court was satisfied that reasonable notice had been given to a passenger of an exclusion clause found on p. 552 of the company's sixpenny timetable. The trail to the clause started with the words 'see back' on her ticket. Although a similar point would probably be decided differently today, incorporation by reference to a further document or by the use of a clearly exhibited printed notice may, in many situations, be the only feasible means of communication for the party relying on a clause. Interestingly, the increasing use of the internet to make contracts has improved the position as regards notice, as consumers using this medium are often given ample opportunity to read easily accessible written terms. Indeed, in many cases, a contract cannot be concluded until the terms have been called up on screen and the purchaser indicates they have read them.

Despite the general provisions relating to notice, the courts have been prepared to take a more interventionist stance where the clauses concerned are especially onerous. In *Thornton v Shoe Lane Parking Ltd* (1971), Lord Denning insisted on the need for *special steps* to be taken by a party wishing to incorporate unusual or unexpected protective terms into a contract. In that case, Thornton parked his car for the first time at Shoe Lane Parking's car park. A notice outside the entrance stated that: 'All cars parked at owner's risk'. At the entrance, Thornton received a ticket from a machine and an automatic barrier was raised. In small print on the ticket it was stated that: 'This ticket is issued subject to the conditions of issue displayed on the premises'. Inside the building was another notice which purported to exempt Shoe Lane Parking from any liability resulting from damage to the car or personal injury. When collecting his car, there was an accident and Thornton was injured, partly as a result of Shoe Lane Parking's negligence. The court held, that although bound by the exterior notice, the clause relating to personal injury had not been incorporated into the contract. They reasoned that Shoe Lane Parking had not taken sufficient steps to draw Thornton's attention to the 'less typical' personal injury disclaimer at the time the contract was made at the entrance.

The same approach to unfair terms was adopted in a more general commercial context in *Interfoto Picture Library Ltd v Stiletto Visual Programmes Ltd* (1989) which demonstrates the close relationship between substantive and procedural unfairness in practice. The term in question was not an exclusion clause but referred to holding charges for late return of photographs loaned to the defendants for promotional purposes. A two-week delay in returning them incurred a charge of £3,783, which was well above comparable rates elsewhere in the trade. The term was described as 'unreasonable and extortionate'. The court decided that, because the claimants had failed to take exceptional steps to bring the defendant's attention to their charges, the term did not become part of the contract for lack of reasonable notice and was disallowed as a result.

The courts have also been interested in the timing of the notice, particularly whether the clause had been brought to the attention of the other party before, or at the time of, making the contract. This was one of the issues discussed in the *Thornton* judgment but was also considered in *Olley v Marlborough Court* (1949). In this case, a contract for the hire of a hotel room was made at the hotel reception desk. However, a clause, relating to the safe custody of guests' valuables, was to be found in a notice on their bedroom wall. The court in that case barred the hotel from relying on the exclusion clause as contract formation had already been completed before notice of the clause was given.

The courts' recognition of relational elements to contracts is reflected in the expectation that a clause may be incorporated into a particular transaction because of a regular previous course of dealing. In these circumstances it is argued that it can be assumed that the parties have already been made aware of the existence of a term and had an opportunity to examine it. So, for instance, if the Olleys had regularly visited the Marlborough Court Hotel before and seen or had the opportunity to see the exclusion clause, the clause might have become part of the contract (see also *Kendall & Sons v Lillico & Sons Ltd*, 1969 and *British Crane Hire Corpn Ltd v Ipswich Plant Hire Ltd*, 1975).

THE JUDICIAL CONSTRUCTION OF EXCLUSION CLAUSES

Those attempting to rely on an exclusion clause will have passed the first important hurdle facing them if they are able to prove to the court's satisfaction that the clause has been incorporated into the contract. But even where the clause *is* incorporated as a term of the contract, the judiciary may interpret the wording of it restrictively so as to limit its scope. Long before the advent of legislation, the common law required that exclusion clauses be expressed clearly and without ambiguity if they are to be effective. An important offshoot of this rule is that the judiciary also expects that a clause must clearly cover the liability which it seeks to exclude. The tendency has been to adopt a literal approach to wording and this has favoured those disadvantaged by the clause. Moreover, if there is ambiguity as to the scope or meaning of an exclusion or limitation clause, the doubt will be resolved by construing it *against* the party who seeks to rely on it. This is known as the *contra proferentem* rule. So, for instance, in an inter-business contract for the sale of cotton thread, it was stipulated that: 'the goods *delivered* shall be deemed to be in all respects in accordance with the contract, unless the buyer complained within 14 days of their receipt'. It was held that this clause was no defence to a claim for damages for non-delivery. This was because the clause expressly mentioned only goods actually delivered. The courts have even been known to 'discover' ambiguity in order to allow them to interpret a clause in the interests of justice and the weaker party. In *George Mitchell (Chesterhall) Ltd v Finney Lock Seeds Ltd* (1983), Lord Denning reflected on the use of the *contra proferentem* rule and this period of judicial activism:

> None of you nowadays will remember the trouble we had – when I was called to the Bar – with exemption clauses. …It was a bleak winter for our law of contract …. Faced with this abuse of power – by the strong against the weak – by the use of the small print of the conditions – the judges did what they could to put a curb upon it. They still had before them the idol, 'freedom of contract'. They still knelt down and worshipped it, but they concealed under their cloaks a secret weapon. They used it to stab the idol in the back. This weapon was called 'the true construction of the contract'. They used it with great skill and ingenuity. They used it so as to depart from the natural meaning of the words of the exemption clause and to put upon them a strained and unnatural construction. In case after case, they said that the words were not strong enough to give the big concern exemption from liability; or that in the circumstances the big concern was not entitled to rely on the exemption clause. (p. 297)

However, the judiciary have also been shown to favour moderation in some circumstances. In the case of *Ailsa Craig Fishing Co Ltd v Malvern Fishing Co Ltd* (1983), the opinion was expressed that the rules of construction would not normally operate as strictly in the case of limitation of liability clauses as they did with exclusion clauses. This was because those using limitation clauses were not attempting to absolve themselves of all responsibility but merely to contain it. Moreover, many limitation clauses are considered acceptable in contracts where the point of the deal is to allocate risks between the parties. For instance, clauses which place a financial limit on compensation are generally found in inter-business transactions and are common risk-allocation devices backed by insurance.

Generally, it is true to say that, the more extensive the attempt to exclude liability, the clearer the words used must be. So, in applying the *contra proferentem* rule to attempts to exclude liability for negligence, the courts have required that extremely clear words must be required. Perhaps the best guide was established by the House of Lords in the indemnity case of *Smith v South Wales Switchgear Ltd* (1978) in which a business party seeking to exclude liability for negligence was advised to expressly use the word 'negligence' or a synonymous expression in his clause rather than a general phrase such as 'any liability, loss, claim or proceedings whatsoever' (but see *Scottish Special Housing Association v Wimpey Construction Ltd*, 1986). Moreover, it has also been argued that, if there is any doubt as to whether the words used cover negligent liability, it will be assumed that they do *not* unless there is no other liability to be excluded (see *Alderslade v Hendon Laundry Ltd*, 1945).

In addition to the *contra proferentem* rule, the courts have developed the 'main purpose' rule. This requires that, where exclusion clauses are inconsistent with the main purpose of the contract, then they can be rejected because they are in danger of rendering the purpose of the contract nonsensical. So, for instance, an exclusion clause which sought to exclude liability for the roadworthiness of a new deluxe model car would seem to defeat the object of entering into a contract to purchase one. The rule was endorsed by the House of Lords in *Suisse Atlantique Société d'Armement Maritime SA v NV Rotterdamsche Kolen Centrale* (1976) and was subsequently given statutory effect by s 3 of the Unfair Contract Terms Act 1977.

At one point it was argued by the some members of the judiciary that, if a party committed a 'fundamental' breach of a contract, they were not able to rely on any exemption clause in a contract. The rule had the effect of depriving a party in default of the benefit of their clause. This position was questioned by the House of Lords in *Suisse Atlantique*, where it was suggested that there is no rule of law that an exemption clause can never apply in these circumstances. In the *Photo Production Ltd v Securicor Transport Ltd* (1980) case the House of Lords re-affirmed that the efficacy or otherwise of an exclusion clause depends upon its construction, whether or not the contract has terminated. It was further argued that, although a breach may have occasioned dire consequences, this in itself did not bring into play *even harsher* construction of an exclusion clause than was usual. The court emphasised that business parties, assumed to be of equal bargaining strength, should be left free, through their use of exclusionary and other devices backed by insurance cover, to apportion risks of loss as they thought fit without judicial intervention. This position was reinforced by s 9 of the Unfair Contract Terms Act 1977.

CONCLUDING REMARKS

It is clear from the various doctrines discussed in this chapter that the judiciary has had a major role to play in the regulation of unfairness in contracts. This is nothing new. Many commentators have argued that the common law has always placed considerable emphasis on fairness and that this heritage is particularly obvious in the pre-classical period. But it is also clear that the growth in the use of standard form contracts has encouraged the judiciary in its interventionist tendencies. Nonetheless, the cases discussed raise some complex issues for contract lawyers. Doctrines relating to exclusion clauses have arguably the greatest potential to undermine the classical and neo-classical underpinnings of modern contract law. But the discomfort of the judiciary in overtly interrogating the actual terms of the contract rather than the making of it also marks out the boundaries of judicial regulation of contracts. The setting aside of contractual terms agreed between the parties has remained sufficiently contentious for it to require judicial intervention to outlaw particular types of abuse. It is to this issue that we turn in the next chapter which continues the story of regulation of unfair contractual terms.

REFERENCES AND FURTHER READING

Atiyah, P (1979) *The Rise and Fall of Freedom of Contract*, Clarendon Press, Oxford.
Beale, H, Bishop, W and Furmston, M (2008) *Contract Cases and Materials*, Oxford University Press, Oxford.
Nichols, A and Rawlings, R 'Note on *Photo Production v Securicor*' (1980) 43 MLR 567, also Guest, A (1980) 96 LQR 324.
Whittaker, S 'Judicial interventionism in consumer contracts' (2001) 117 LQR 215.

> **?** *QUESTIONS*
>
> (1) On what basis did the House of Lords in *Photo Production Ltd v Securicor Transport Ltd* (1980) overrule the Court of Appeal decision in *Harbutt's 'Plasticine' Ltd v Wayne Tank and Pump Co Ltd* (1970)? In preparing your answer, summarise the arguments made by Nicols and Rawlings (1980) and respond to them.
>
> (2) Connor goes to Brightpool for a week's holiday. While there he decides to visit the swimming pool. A notice at the turnstile says: 'The Management accept no responsibility for loss or damage to valuables unless left at the office'. Connor ignores this notice. In his cubicle there is another notice which reads: 'No liability for personal injury'. Connor ignores this notice and places his mobile phone on the ledge above it. As he runs to dive into the water, he trips over a brush negligently left on the floor by the attendant and breaks his arm. He later finds that his phone was stolen while he was at the hospital having his arm set. Discuss whether Connor has any claim against the management in respect of his phone or his injury.

CHAPTER 16

LEGISLATIVE REGULATION OF UNFAIR TERMS

INTRODUCTION

In the last chapter, we looked at how terms are incorporated into contracts and the various devices employed by the judiciary to limit the scope of limitation and exclusion clauses. Apart from isolated statutory measures, the legal struggle against such unfair terms was carried on until the 1970s by the judges, who as we saw in the last chapter, devised a variety of weapons to render such clauses inoperative. This is especially the case where they operated against the interests of consumers in contracts for the sale of goods or supply of services. The problem was that judicial regulation merely drove the drafters of exclusion clauses to renewed efforts to produce 'judge-proof' forms of words to which the judiciary did not always feel equipped to respond. The main problem was that the judges felt that they had no general power to strike down unreasonable exclusion clauses as being, for example, against public policy and therefore void. They felt that the concept of freedom of contract overrode such an approach. It was left, instead for Parliament to take up the challenge.

There are now hundreds of statutory provisions dealing with such issues as tenancies, consumer credit, hire purchase and package holidays. Following the lead of the common law, each of these interferes with the freedom to contract by regulating the terms of certain contracts and determining what sorts of liability can be excluded from them. It is not the purpose of this chapter to examine the whole body of civil and criminal law, the regulatory mechanisms and voluntary codes of practice which now exist to protect the consumer from unsafe products, qualitatively deficient goods and services, fraudulent trading practices and the other matters. The main aim is to concentrate on the legal response to unfair and oppressive terms in contracts made between businesses and consumers and others, which has culminated in the passing of the Unfair Contract Terms Act 1977 and the coming into effect of the European Community Directive on Unfair Terms in Consumer Contracts 1994 and Unfair Terms in Consumer Contracts Regulations 1999. One of the reasons for this emphasis is that this was the first legislative attempt to introduce standards about exclusion clauses into the general law of contract.

The common law approach to exclusion clauses is reflected in many of the provisions of the legislation which has been used in recent decades to complement or reinforce judicial precedent. However, the Unfair Contract Terms Act (UCTA) 1977 and European codes also go beyond the common law and have introduced additional hurdles to jump for those attempting to rely on exclusion clauses. These two pieces of legislation overlap substantially, with the result that some types of term are regulated by both and others by just one. Consequently, it is now open to consumers to challenge certain contract terms on the basis that they are void or 'unreasonable' under the UCTA or 'unfair' under the regulations. In many cases the result will be the same, but the fact that the concepts of reasonableness and fairness are different means that there is considerable scope for confusion.

Owing to the confusion caused by the parallel provisions of domestic and European Law, the Law Commission was asked by the government to review the law in the field with the aim of replacing existing provisions with a single Act written in plain, accessible language. A final report and draft Bill was produced by the Commission in 2005. Whilst the government has accepted the report in principle, it has committed itself to evaluating the potential impact of the reforms before attempting to implement them. Moreover, at the time of going to press, the draft Bill appears to have been caught up in a backlog of unimplemented reports that would benefit the consumer. As a result, the approach taken in this chapter has been to describe the law at it currently stands and outline the proposals for change which have been put forward by the Law Commission.

THE UNFAIR CONTRACT TERMS ACT 1977

Despite its title, the Unfair Contract Terms Act (UCTA) does not deal with all contracts or unfair terms, but focuses instead on exclusion clauses. This has been done in an effort to protect consumers and others from particularly unfair limitations of liability. The general thrust of the Act is to regulate those terms which enable one party to offer a performance which is substantially different from that expected. Legislative interventions have provided a hierarchy of protection depending on the type of liability which a party is attempting to exclude, the status of the person seeking to avoid the clause and the characteristics of the person seeking to rely on it. In order to understand fully the provisions of the Act, it is necessary to appreciate that it is based on the premise that there are two types of contracting party: those who are dealing as consumers and those dealing as businesses. Potentially, this allows for three different types of contract to be concluded and this point is illustrated in Figure 16.1.

Figure 16.1:   The three different types of contract

	contracting with	
business party	+	business party
business party	+	non-business (consumer)
non-business	+	non-business

The Act is limited in its application in that it only subjects certain contracts to scrutiny. These are contracts between two businesses or contracts between a business and a consumer. According to s 11, 'business liability' can only occur under the Act if one of the parties is acting in the course of a business or the occupation of business premises. On the other hand, s 12 makes clear that a person deals as a consumer if they do *not* make, or hold themselves out as making, the contract in the course of a business and the other party does make the contract in the course of a business. In other words, you cannot be a consumer under the Act unless you are dealing with someone who is acting in the course of a business. This means that, when one party deals with another outside a business environment, neither is treated by the Act as a consumer. It would seem then, that the conferment of the status of consumer depends on the circumstances rather than the person. This approach reflects the fact that the Act is primarily concerned with protecting the interests of consumers when dealing with businesses.

Outlawed clauses

One of the most interesting features of the Act is that it renders completely void certain types of clause, whatever the circumstances in which they were negotiated. The Act renders six main types of exclusion clause inoperative on the basis that they attempt to deny specific rights to contracting parties that social policy requires they should have. The ban is total, pays no heed to the intentions of the parties so valued by the classical model and gives the judiciary no discretion to amend the contract in any way where these clauses are present. The relevant clauses are summarised in Figure 16.2.

Figure 16.2:   Unfair Contract Terms Act 1977 outlawed exclusion clauses

outlawed exclusion clauses	section
negligence – any liability for *negligently* causing death or personal injury cannot be excluded by businesses	2(1)
manufacturers'guarantees – liability for negligence in the manufacture or distribution of goods usually supplied for private use cannot be excluded when the goods are used by a consumer	5
implied terms – statutory implied undertakings as to ownership to title in sale of goods and hire-purchase contracts	6(1)
implied terms – statutory implied undertaking relating to conformity with description or sample in sale of goods and hire-purchase contracts cannot be used against a person dealing as a consumer	6(2)
implied term – statutory implied undertakings relating to quality or fitness for purpose in contracts for sale of goods or hire-purchase cannot be used against a person dealing as a consumer	6(2)
other undertakings – relating to description, fitness, sample or quality cannot be used against a person dealing as a consumer	7(2)

Not all of the outlawed clauses detailed above relate to contractual liability. Section 2 relates to clauses or notices which purport to exclude business liability for negligence. According to s 1(1), negligence means breach of a contractual duty to take reasonable care or exercise reasonable skill *and* a breach of a tortious duty. The latter might arise, for example, in respect of a notice at a sporting event that spectators attend free of charge and for which there is no contract. Section 5 also extends the Act beyond the scope of contract law. It prevents the use of clauses which restrict or exclude liability for loss or damage that arises from manufacturers' negligent defects which manifest themselves when the goods are in 'consumer use'. The section is therefore concerned with the manufacturer–consumer relationship where there is no contract between the parties rather than the supplier–consumer relationship.

One of the most important provisions for the general law of contract is s 6(2). This establishes that in *consumer* transactions, business liability for breach of the statutorily implied obligations relating to the satisfactory quality and fitness for purpose of goods cannot be excluded or restricted by any contract term. This section follows the lead taken by the Sale of Goods and Supply of Services legislation in requiring that certain terms are implied into consumer contracts by the legislature. Since legislation requires that they be written in, it seems logical that the person dealing with a consumer should not then be able to exclude them. It would be on this basis that the exclusion clause in the *Karsales (Harrow) Ltd v Wallis* (1956) hire-purchase case could now be struck down by reference to the Act rather than the notion of fundamental breach.

The tests of reasonableness

The exclusion clauses which do not fall into one of the six categories rendered void by the Act may nonetheless be subjected to a second type of control, that of the test of reasonableness. Significantly, the burden of proof regarding reasonableness lies with the party seeking to rely on the clause, a factor which facilitates the undermining of such a clause by consumers. Wherever the Act provides that a contract term or notice must meet the requirement of reasonableness, the *time* for assessing its reasonableness is the time when the contract was made. This means that an assessment is made against the background of the circumstances which were, or ought reasonably to have been, known to the parties at that time. If a clause is considered to have been reasonable at the time the contract was made, then its effectiveness will not be impaired by subsequent events or conduct such as the effect of breach. It has been argued that to provide otherwise would amount to 'changing the rules in the middle of the game'. Figure 16.3 outlines the sort of terms which are subjected to this additional test.

Figure 16.3:   Unfair Contract Terms Act 1977 test of reasonableness

key exclusion clauses subject to test of reasonableness	section	can apply to
negligence – terms which attempt to exclude negligent liability for loss or damage other than personal injury or death	2	business and business business and consumer
standard form contract – terms which attempt to exclude or restrict liability for breach when party attempting to rely on clauses is in breach	3(2)(a)	business and business business and consumer
standard form contracts – terms which attempt to allow for a contractual performance which is substantially different from what was expected	3(2)(b)(i)	business and business business and consumer
standard form contracts – terms which attempt to allow for no contractual performance at all to be rendered	3(2)(b)(ii)	business and business business and consumer
implied terms – terms which attempt to exclude or restrict liability for breach of the statutorily implied terms in sale of goods or hire-purchase contracts	6	business and business
breach – exclusion clauses in contracts where the contract is justifiably terminated	9	business and business business and consumer

Whilst the provisions relating to outlawed clauses impose an evaluation of what is considered to be unacceptable on contracting parties, the thrust of the reasonableness test is to look at the fairness of the term in the context in which it was negotiated (s 11). So, for example, the Act recognises that contracts often reflect agreements as to risk allocation and the price paid. But it also requires that when a term or notice, required to be reasonable, places a maximum *financial limit* on the amount that may be recovered, the court must take account of the resources available to the party seeking the benefit of the clause to meet the liability if it arises (section 11(4)). It is also the case that the Act expects the judiciary to inquire into whether the parties were in a position to cover themselves by insurance.

We have already discovered that attempts to exclude certain implied terms in contracts between a business and consumer are outlawed. But the Act also has something to say about attempts to exclude liability where the contract is between two business parties. Here the approach has been to attempt to ascertain the extent to which the parties were in a position to make a rational choice about the limitation or exclusion of liability. In these cases, additional guidance is given about the application of the reasonableness test. This is contained in schedule 2 to the Act and suggests that the factors contained in Box 16.1 may be taken as relevant by the court.

These guidelines apply only to sale and supply of goods cases but they remain significant in other cases. Not only are they one of the first legislative attempts to specify the factors which should be taken into account when accessing what is reasonable in the general law of contract, they have also been found to have influenced the courts in other cases which are outside the ambit of the section (see later, *Smith v Eric S Bush*, 1989).

> **Box 16.1: Reasonableness test in non-consumer contracts**
>
> ○ The relative bargaining strength of the parties
> ○ Whether the claimant received an inducement such as a lower price, to agree to the exemption
> ○ Whether the claimant knew, or ought reasonably to have known of the existence and extent of the term, having regard to such things as a custom of the trade or previous course of dealing between the parties
> ○ Whether any condition for the enforcement of liability such as the need to bring a claim within seven days of performance could practicably be complied with by the claimant
> ○ Whether the claimant had the opportunity to enter into a similar contract with other persons but without having to accept a similar term
> ○ Whether the goods were specially made to the order of the claimant

Negligence liability – 'other loss or damage'

We have already considered the fact that the Act outlaws any attempt on the part of a business to exclude any liability for *negligently* causing death or personal injury. In addition to this, section 2(2) requires that a business can not in other instances of loss or damage exclude or restrict their liability for negligence, except in so far as the term or notice satisfies the requirement of reasonableness. The clause covers business–business agreements as well as consumer–business contracts. The application of the test can be demonstrated in *Wight v British Railways Board* (1983). In this case, British Railways Board lost Wight's suitcase but sought to rely on a clause limiting their liability to £1,500 per ton. The drafters of the limitation clause clearly had commercial consignments in mind rather than those of individuals. Wights's suitcase contained valuable jewellery but, according to terms on display and in the consignment note, the case was carried 'at owner's risk'. Satisfied that the clause had been incorporated into the contract, the judge moved to enquire whether the clause was fair and reasonable in the circumstances. It was held that it was easier for the claimant to insure than the carriers because, in the circumstances, there were no real means whereby British Railways Board might ascertain the value of the goods consigned. As a result, the clause was considered reasonable (see also *Waldron-Kelly v British Railways Board*, 1981).

The fact that the question of reasonableness depends on the facts of each individual case was brought home in the *Phillips Products Ltd v Hyland* (1987) decision where the Court of Appeal stated that appellate courts should not readily overturn decisions at first instance where the full facts of the case had been considered. In *Smith v Eric S Bush* (1989), a surveyor was employed by a building society to inspect and value a house. The surveyor's contract disclaimed responsibility to the purchaser to whom the report would eventually be passed. The purchaser was paying the fee for the survey. In the House of Lords, Lord Griffiths stated that, whatever else, the following matters should always be considered.

(1) Were the parties of equal bargaining power? In this case it was decided that the purchaser ... has no effective power to object to the surveyor's terms.

(2) In the case of advice, would it have been reasonably practicable to obtain the advice from an alternative source taking into account considerations of costs and time? Here the house was 'at the bottom end of the market' of a type typically bought by young, first-time buyers who were financially not well placed to pay for a second opinion.

(3) How difficult is the task being undertaken for which liability is being excluded? The court found that in this case, the work was 'at the lower end of the surveyor's field of professional expertise'.

In their deliberations, the judges considered the practical consequences of the arguments before them. More specifically they asked whether the risk was one against which the surveyor could easily have insured, but which would have serious consequences for a claimant who was required to bear the loss. It was held that the clause relied upon by the surveyor in this case was not reasonable, but Lord Griffiths also stressed that the decision would have been different if the purchase had concerned 'industrial property, large blocks of flats or very expensive houses'.

Other case law reiterates the importance of determining who is in a position to insure against risks in commercial relationships. *Photo Production Ltd v Securicor Transport Ltd* (1980) concerned a business–business agreement which was not decided under the 1977 Act but in conformity with it. Securicor were contracted to guard Photo Production's factory but, in the course of doing so, one of their employees burnt it down. Despite this, the House of Lords found in Securicor's favour because Photo Production was in a better position to insure its factory against such a contingency but had failed to do so.

Phillips Products Ltd v Hyland (1987) also involved business parties and damage to property. In this case, Phillips Products hired a JCB extractor and its driver. The contract was based on the Contractors' Plant Association model conditions for plant hire. Clause 8 of these conditions stated that the *hirer* was responsible for claims arising from the negligent operation of the plant by the driver. The driver negligently drove the JCB into Phillips Products' premises and damaged them. Finding for Phillips Products, it determined that the clause did not satisfy the test of reasonableness. On the facts, it was found that the hirers did not regularly hire plant and drivers, had no control over the driver and no opportunity to arrange insurance.

Non-consumer sale of goods and hire purchase

Under s 6(3) of UCTA, a business–business sale of goods or hire purchase contract in which an attempt is made to exclude or restrict liability for breach of the statutorily implied terms is also subject to the requirement of reasonableness. Two cases are instructive here. Although neither was decided on the basis of the 1977 Act and the guidelines in Schedule 2, the legislation on which the cases are based had a similar effect to the 1977 Act. *RW Green Ltd v Cade Bros Farms* (1978) concerned the reasonableness of a clause in a contract for the sale of 20 tons of seed potatoes which limited claims for compensation to a refund of the price. The potatoes were infected by a virus in breach of s 14 of the Sale of Goods Act but the limitation clause was found to be reasonable. Firstly, the contract was concluded on standard terms, based on trade practice and agreed over many years by both merchants and farmers. Secondly, certified virus-free potatoes could be bought at a higher price. Finally, the parties had regularly done business together on such terms. However, a further clause requiring complaints to be made within three days of delivery was declared unreasonable as the defect was not discoverable on inspection within the time allowed.

Reasonableness in the context of a contract for a sale of goods was also considered by the House of Lords in *George Mitchell (Chesterhall) Ltd v Finney Lock Seeds Ltd* (1983). In that case, Finlay Lock Seeds supplied cabbage seed to the claimants, George Mitchell at a price of £192. The seed was planted but the crop failed with a loss to the farmers of an estimated £63,000. The parties had dealt with each other for some years and the contract was on the supplier's standard terms. It contained a clause limiting liability for defective seeds to the contract price. On the facts of this particular case, the Court of Appeal and the House of Lords both adopted an interventionist approach to this business–business transaction. It was held that the clause was unreasonable. In the Court of Appeal, Kerr LJ stated that:

> The balance of fairness and reasonableness appears to me to be overwhelmingly on the side of the [claimants] …. Farmers do not, and cannot be expected to, insure against this kind of disaster; but suppliers of seeds can …. I am not persuaded that liability for rare events of this kind cannot be adequately insured against. Nor am I persuaded that the cost of such cover would add significantly to the cost of seed. Further, although the present exemption clause has been in existence for many decades, the evidence shows that it was never negotiated. In effect, it was simply imposed by the suppliers, and no seed can in practice be bought otherwise than subject to its terms. To limit the supplier's liability to the price of the seed in all cases, as against the magnitude of the losses which farmers can incur in rare disasters of this kind, appears to me to be a grossly disproportionate and unreasonable allocation of the respective risks. (pp. 313–314)

Standard forms and further consumer protection

Section 3 of the Act extends control of exclusion clauses to cases where one party deals as consumer or on the other's written standard terms of business. The section aims at both unequal bargaining situations and non-negotiated contract situations which may or may not involve a consumer. Where a consumer or a party dealing on another's standard terms is involved, then the other party cannot rely on a contractual term to limit or exclude liability for breach or claim to be entitled to render a contractual performance substantially different from that which was reasonably to be expected of him, or render no performance at all, except in so far as the term is reasonable.

The section came into play in a non-consumer context in *St Albans City and District Council v International Computers Ltd* (1994). In this case, International Computers Ltd supplied the council with a database for its community charge register. The contract was on International Computers's standard terms and limited its liability for loss to £100,000. An error in the software resulted in an overstatement of the city and district population by almost 3,000. The community charge was in consequence set too low with a loss to the council of £1,314,846. Section 3 applied because the contract was made on International Computers's 'written standard terms of business'. The court held that the determining factor was that the parties were of unequal bargaining power, as International Computers were dealing on their terms and conditions. They also felt that the figure of £100,000 had not been justified in relation to potential risk and actual loss, as International Computers were insured to the extent of £50 million worldwide. In short, they determined that in practical terms it was better that the loss should fall on International Computers and its insurance company than on the local authority and local population by way of increased charges or reduced services.

Section 9 of the Act confirms an injured party's right, in the face of a serious breach, to elect to terminate or to affirm the contract. Section 9(1) makes it clear that if, by election, the contract is justifiably terminated, an exclusion clause survives such termination and it *may*, if not rendered ineffective by the Act, protect the party in breach. Statements in *Photo Production* indicate that, in any event where business parties of equal bargaining power are involved, the courts should not strain to defeat clearly expressed exclusionary terms. In Lord Diplock's words:

> In commercial contracts negotiated between business people capable of looking after their own interests and of deciding how risks inherent in the performance of various kinds of contract can most economically be borne (generally by insurance), it is, in my view, wrong to place a strained construction upon words in an exclusion clause which are clear and fairly susceptible to one meaning only. (p. 851)

Section 9(2) has the effect of allowing that, in the less likely event of a party affirming a contract, their affirmation does not eliminate the need for a clause to satisfy judicial construction and the reasonableness test.

THE EUROPEAN COMMUNITY DIRECTIVE ON UNFAIR TERMS IN CONSUMER CONTRACTS (COUNCIL DIRECTIVE 93/13)

In addition to the Unfair Contract Terms Act 1977, UK contracts have more recently been regulated by European legislation. The provisions of the European Community Directive on Unfair Terms in Consumer Contracts 1993 and the Unfair Terms in Consumer Contracts Regulations 1999 generally act in parallel with UCTA, although there are some overlaps. The European approach to the regulation of contracts appears to offer a regime which is conceptually distinct from that of the common law, although many of the same concerns underpin the two pieces of legislation. In the sections which follow, we shall review the European approach to unfair contracts and compare it to that adopted by the UCTA.

According to Recital 5 of the directive, the removal of unfair terms from consumer contracts will facilitate the development of the European single market by giving consumers the confidence to contract outside their own states and by doing so increase choice and facilitate competition. The directive and regulation provide for a *minimum* level of protection throughout the European Union and make clear that member states are free to provide additional protection on the basis of their own national law. This has already happened in the UK with the UCTA 1977. In contrast to the Act, the regulations of 1999 focus on *all* contractual terms in contracts between 'consumers' and 'sellers or suppliers' which have *not* been 'individually negotiated' by the parties.

A term in such contracts which is adjudged unfair is not binding on the consumer. The concept of unfairness in the regulations is wider than in the 1977 Act, because it is not confined to exclusion and limitation of liability clauses. In another sense it is narrower, as the regulations do not apply to business–business transactions. The regulations have met with a considerable amount of criticism and speculation, mainly as regards difficulties of interpretation and the complexity created by having the regulations stand alongside the 1977 Act. It is for this reason that the Law Commission was asked to review the area with a view to consolidation.

Key characteristics of the regulations

Like UCTA, the regulations identify two key players with whom regulation should be concerned. These are 'consumers' and 'sellers or suppliers'. Regulation 3 defines a 'consumer' as 'a natural person who … is acting for purposes which are outside his business, trade or profession'. According to this definition, 'consumers' protected by the regime may be individuals of considerable means (see, for instance, *Standard Bank of London Ltd v Abelowolakis*, 2000). By way of contrast, the seller or supplier is defined as 'a person who sells goods and who … is acting for purposes relating to his trade, business or profession'. The scope of the term 'business' is similar to that in the 1977 Act. Just as it is impossible under the Act for a business to 'deal as consumer', so there is European Union case law to the effect that a business cannot be regarded as a consumer. The effect of the regulations is that a term which is found by the court to be *unfair* will not be binding on the consumer. However, the remainder of the contract will continue to bind the parties, if it is capable of continuing without the term in dispute.

The regulations apply to terms which have 'not been individually negotiated'. In essence then it concentrates on standard form, non-negotiable contracts rather than the broader range of contracts which come under the ambit of UCTA. Regulation 5(2) states that 'a term shall always be regarded as not having been individually negotiated where it has been drafted in advance and the consumer has not been able to influence the substance of the term'. However, the regulations also adopt a technique unknown to the Act. Under Regulation 6(2) certain 'core' terms are *insulated* from regulation. In short, they are not subject to the test of fairness as long as they are in 'plain, intelligible language'. The terms that come within this provision are those which define the main subject matter of the contract, or concern the adequacy of the price or remuneration

Figure 16.4:   The scope of European regulations when compared to UCTA

	wider provision	narrower provision
European Regulations	1 Concerns go beyond exclusion clauses to all unfair terms in standard form contracts	1 Only relates to terms in *contracts*
	2 Introduces broader concept of good faith?	2 Only relates to contracts which have not been individually negotiated
	3 Allows for the insulation of certain terms	3 Limited to dealings between consumers and sellers/producers

(see, for instance, *Director General of Fair Trading v First National Bank plc*, 2002). Collins (1994) has argued that the objective of this provision is to preclude judicial review of terms of which the consumer was fully aware.

Before turning to some of the specific concepts employed in regulations, it is useful to summarise the ways in which they can be seen to be wider and narrower than domestic legislation. Figure 16.4 attempts to do this in succinct form and should be used to guide you through the provisions discussed.

Unfair terms

Regulation 5(1) states that 'unfair term' means any term which, contrary to *the requirement of good faith*, causes a *significant imbalance* in the parties' rights and obligations under the contract *to the detriment of the consumer*. In common with the Act, the test of fairness is to be made against the background of all the circumstances at the time the contract was entered into. Since no general principle of good faith is explicitly recognised in English contract law, this is a new concept with which the English judiciary has had to grapple

> **Box 16.2:   Schedule 2 - Factors to be considered when judging good faith**
>
> (a) The strength of the bargaining positions of the parties
>
> (b) Whether the consumer had an inducement to agree to the term
>
> (c) Whether the goods or services were sold or supplied to the special order of the consumer
>
> (d) The extent to which the seller or supplier has dealt fairly and equitably with the consumer.

and was described as 'one of fair and open dealing' by the House of Lords in *Director General of Fair Trading v First National Bank plc* (2001). However, some indications of what factors should be taken into account when assessing whether a term meets the requirement are contained in the regulations and these are reproduced in Box. 16.2

A non-exhaustive list of terms which *may* be regarded as unfair is to be found in Schedule 2 to the regulations. One example is a term which provides for the price of goods to be determined at the time of delivery without giving the consumer the right to cancel the contract if the final price is too high. Other examples deal with provisions relating to negligent liability and death or personal injury; the exclusion or limitation of the consumer's rights in the event of total or partial non-performance; and inadequate performance by the seller or supplier of any of the contractual obligations.

However, the list of 17 different types of potentially unfair terms are not automatically unfair nor presumed to be unfair. The question of finding 'a significant imbalance ... to the detriment of the consumer' is left to the courts, proceeding on a case-by-case basis.

Plain, intelligible language

As regards the drafting of terms, Regulation 7 states that: 'A seller or supplier shall ensure that any written term of a contract is expressed in plain, intelligible language', and that 'if there is any doubt about the meaning of a written term, the interpretation most favourable to the consumer shall prevail'. 'Plain and intelligible' will presumably be tested objectively from the point of view of the reasonable consumer and the outcome in cases of doubt is to be determined on the basis of the *contra proferentem* rule of construction. It is reasoned that obscure drafting may be indicative of an absence of fair and equitable dealing and therefore of good faith. In one sense this provision does little more than was already expected in the common law. But the important difference is that this should now become a core standard for the *drafting* of consumer contracts.

Regulation 8: general use of unfair terms – member states' duties

In contrast to domestic legislation, the European approach has been to take the position that standard form contracts are *presumed* to be undesirable. Under Article 7(1) of the directive, member states are to provide 'effective means to prevent the continued use of unfair terms'. Moreover, the collective interest in achieving this goal is reflected in Article 7(2) which states that such 'means' should include 'provisions whereby persons or organisations having a legitimate interest under national law in protecting consumers may take action ... before the courts ... for a decision as to whether contractual terms drawn up for general use are unfair'. Under clause 10(1) of the regulations, the Director General of Fair Trading must consider any complaint made to him that a term drawn up for 'general use' is unfair. He cannot act on his own initiative but there is no doubt that he will receive numerous complaints from the Consumers' Association and others.

The Director General has a discretion as to whether to seek an injunction 'against any person appearing to [him] ... to be using, or recommending use' of unfair terms. The Director General will presumably decide not to seek an injunction if he is satisfied with voluntary undertakings he receives regarding discontinuance of unfair terms in general use. Any injunction sought may relate not only to the particular term but also 'to any similar term, or a term having like effect', so as to forestall evasion by re-drafting. According to Regulation 12(3), the court may grant an injunction on such terms as it thinks fit.

REFORM OF THE LAW RELATING TO UNFAIR TERMS IN CONTRACTS

In 2001, the Department of Trade and Industry asked the Law Commission to review the law of unfair contract terms with a view to producing a single regime which was less complex than current provision. There is clearly scope for consolidation. As Brownsword and Howells (1995) have argued:

> Generally speaking … the underlying pattern of the protective regime ushered in by the Directive will closely resemble that under the reasonableness test of UCTA. In both regimes, certain sorts of contractual terms are singled out as potentially unfair. Under UCTA it is terms that exclude or restrict liability (and their cognates); under the Regulations, it is terms that involve a significant imbalance (as elaborated by the indicative examples given in Schedule 3). Under UCTA, once a term is subject to the reasonableness test, attention largely focuses on whether it is plausible to assume that there has been free agreement to the provision; under the Regulations, once a term is seen as involving a significant imbalance, attention turns to whether the dealer has acted contrary to the requirement of good faith – which, we have suggested, is largely a matter (as under UCTA) of satisfying oneself that there has been free agreement to the term.

As part of their review the Law Commission was also asked to consider whether the regulatory framework should be expanded to cover the interests of small business, which were often no better placed than consumers to object to terms imposed upon them. In their report in the subject, published in 2005 the Law Commission supported the initiative by arguing that the 1977 Act was dense in style and so complex that even specialists found it difficult to follow. At the same time there were difficulties with the European Regulations because they use concepts such as good faith which are unfamiliar to the English legal system.

The aim of the Unfair Contracts Bill which is appended to the Law Commission's report (2005) is to produce a single unified regime that preserves existing levels of consumer protection. Where the Act and regulations differ, the approach adopted has been to include the most far-reaching or interventionist provisions from each scheme. As a result, in relation to consumer contracts, the Bill extends to all terms covered by the European Regulations rather than just exclusion clauses; continues to render ineffective limitations for death or personal injury or statutory implied terms; negotiated and standard form contracts; and maintains the expectation that the burden of proof to demonstrate fairness remains with the business.

Significantly, the Bill also brings improved protection for small businesses. At present, challenges to standards terms in business–business contracts are limited to exclusion clauses. Whilst not wanting to interfere with business contracts that are genuinely negotiated, the Law Commission has argued that problems exist where on large business imposes its standards terms on a more vulnerable business which may not have the bargaining strength to challenge it. As a result, the Bill introduces new special protections for 'micro' businesses of nine or less staff which do not receive the protection of other regulators. It now provides that small businesses can challenge any standard term of the contract that has not been altered through negotiation other than clauses relating to subject matter and price.

The final achievement of the Bill is that it undermines current provisions relating to business–business negotiated contracts. At present, the courts can review any term which limits the effect of implied undertakings in the Sale of Goods Act as regards description, quality and purpose. In the view of the Commission, it is very unlikely that a court would find a genuinely negotiated clause to be unfair. As a result, the Bill allows business–business contracts which are negotiated rather than on standard forms to limit contractual liability.

CONCLUDING REMARKS

The discussion in this chapter reveals that significant inroads have been made into the regulation of contracts in the last three decades. This is especially true of consumer contracts leading some to argue that we have, in part, returned to the notion of a 'status' contract which relies for its enforceability on the characteristics of the parties rather than the circumstances of the actual deal which has been negotiated. No regard is paid to the business acumen or bargaining power of those dealing as a consumer: they are assumed to be in need of protection in both domestic and European legislation. It is clear, however, that the Law Commission's Bill heralds a slightly different approach. Sensitive to the many nuances of power, it recognises that micro-businesses may be in need of protection just as much as consumers. There is also an assumption in the provisions relating to limitation of implied terms in business–business contracts that business parties are well able to protect their own interests. To my mind, this suggests a much more nuanced approach to the problem of how contract law responds to assumed imbalances of power and the realities of the business–business contracts in which limitation and exclusion clauses are not always perceived as a threat, but rather as an opportunity for sophisticated planning about the extent of liability.

REFERENCES AND FURTHER READING

Adams, J and Brownsword, R 'The Unfair Contract Terms Act: a decade of discretion' (1988) 104 LQR 94.

Adams, J and Brownsword, R 'Double indemnity – contractual indemnity clauses revisited' (1988) JBL 146.

Beale, H 'Unfair Contract Terms Act 1977' (1978) 5 *British Journal of Law and Society* 114.

Brownsword, R and Howells, G 'The implementation of the EC Directive on unfair terms in consumer contracts – some unresolved questions' (1995) JBL 243.

Collins, H 'Good faith in European contract law' (1994) 14 OJLS 229.

Dean, M 'Unfair contract terms: the European approach' (1993) 56 MLR 581.

EC Council of Ministers, Council Directive on Unfair Terms in Consumer Contracts: 93/13/EEC (1993) *Official Journal* L95/29, 21 April.

Law Commission for England and Wales: http://www.lawcom.gov.uk

Law Commission, (2005) *Unfair Terms in Contracts*, LC no 292, Law Commission, London.

Office of Fair Trading: http://www.oft.gov.uk/

Macdonald, E 'Mapping the Unfair Contract Terms Act 1977 and the Directive on Unfair Terms in Consumer Contracts' (1994) JBL 441.

Peel, E, 'Making more use of the Unfair Contract Terms Act 1977: *Stewart Gill Ltd v Horatio Myer and Co Ltd*' (1993) 56 MLR 98.

? QUESTIONS

(1) What is meant by an 'unfair term' in the Unfair Terms in Consumer Transactions Regulations 1999? Look through the terms of the contracts made by Angie and Georgie. Do you think any of them would fall foul of the regulations? If so, why?

Continued

? *QUESTIONS (Continued)*

(2) Comment on the validity or otherwise of the following exclusion clauses or notices in 'The Sad Tale of Angie and Georgie':

   (a) A notice on the signpost which narrowly misses Georgie which reads: 'The owners of this car park accept no responsibility for damages to property or personal injury which occurs in this car park. The car park is used at the car owner's risk'.

   (b) The effect of the exclusion clause on Earth2Earth!'s Charter of Standards on the potential liability to Dipti.

   (c) Clause 2 of Angie and Georgie's agreement with the Wacky Machine Company.

   (d) Clause 6 of Angie and Georgie's agreement with Claude.

PART SIX:

WHAT HAPPENS WHEN THINGS GO WRONG

CHAPTER 17

BREACH OF CONTRACT

INTRODUCTION

So far in this book we have focused on how contracts are made and performed. We have looked at how the courts and legislature have sought to regulate what is included within the contract as well as what ought to be excluded from it. In this final substantive section, we will look at the issue of what happens when things go wrong. We will consider what constitutes a breach of contract and the remedies which flow from it. In the final chapter on dispute resolution, we will review the different methods and processes of dispute resolution which the parties can invoke when they need the help of a third party to resolve their disagreement. It is worthy of note that most books on contract do not actually include a chapter on dispute resolution processes. In this book the decision has been made to incorporate one because, in the lived world of contract, the advice that lawyers give to a client will be very dependent on the channel through which the dispute is likely to be resolved. Moreover, in the commercial sector, the number of dispute resolution procedures is burgeoning and preference for one form of dispute resolution over another is one of the vital terms which should be included in the contract at formation stage.

Before we go on to discuss these matters in some detail, it is important to stress that, if you have read all the chapters which precede this one, then you already know something about breach of contract. A claim that one party is in breach is the trigger for a legal claim and none of the many cases reviewed in earlier chapters would have even been considered by the courts unless one party had made this allegation. The issue before the court in each contractual claim is whether or not the behaviour of the party in breach is significant enough to allow remedies to flow from it. Clearly this issue cannot be looked at in isolation. In order to assess whether the behaviour was unacceptable, the court needs to understand the nature of the agreement between the parties. It is for this reason that an action for breach so often involves the courts in a consideration of whether a contract was formed in the first place, how different terms should be interpreted, the obligations they impose, whether variations to the contract have complied with the appropriate formalities or whether liability for the behaviour complained of has actually been excluded.

We have seen in earlier chapters that contract planning often covers four main issues: the definition of performances, the effect of defective performance, the effect of contingencies and the use of legal sanctions. Cases which come before the courts are those where the parties' planning and co-operation have broken down completely. Some would consider these to be failed contracts, not only because an irreconcilable division has developed between the parties but also because they have failed to plan in advance for the problems which have arisen. It is also important to remember, however, that many disputes are resolved by negotiations between the parties. The empirical studies visited in Chapter 4 provide us with a salutary reminder of the limitations of law in addressing the needs of disputing parties. It is within this context that we must study breach and the tensions the cases reveal between the need to balance the parties' understanding of the contract, the normative frameworks which define what constitutes good practice in a particular industry and the need to impose external standards of fairness on the parties.

JUDICIAL APPROACHES TO BREACH OF CONTRACT

When looking at terms in the context of breach, the courts' approach has been to introduce a hierarchy between two different types of term. Terms which describe performance are considered to be of primary or substantive nature because they indicate what the contractual obligations are and how they will be fulfilled. In addition, they also imply or express the required quality of performance. Clauses in a contract which relate to defective performance, contingencies and sanctions are taken to be of a secondary or procedural nature. These might include clauses to the effect that 'if there is a strike then …' or 'the parties agree to arbitrate any dispute arising …'; for a discussion of primary and secondary rights in the context of breach, see Lord Diplock in *Photo Production Ltd v Securicor Transport Ltd* (1980).

Determining the status of a term can be critical to the way a case is managed. When the contractual relationship fails and the parties bring their dispute to the courts, the role of the law is to clear up the mess caused by breach. In the main the law achieves this good by ordering compensatory payments (damages) to be made to aggrieved parties. In some circumstances a right to terminate the contract is also recognised. One way in which the courts have approached the issue of which remedy is available is *term-based*. In other words, the right is related to the nature of the term broken and a distinction is made between major and minor terms. The first, known as conditions, trigger a right to terminate and claim damages if breached. In the case of lesser terms, known as warranties, breach does not allow for termination but only a claim for damages. From the mass of case law in this area, a condition has been variously described as an essential term or one that goes to the root of the contract, a breach of which reflects a substantial failure to perform the contract at all. By way of contrast, the Sale of Goods Act 1893 defined a warranty as a term which is 'merely collateral to the main purpose of the contract'. In short, a breach of essential or major terms allows for termination and damages, minor terms for only damages. Terms which could be either conditions *or* warranties depending on the consequences flowing from their breach have been variously described but are best known as *innominate*. This literally means that they have no name.

This appears to be a very straightforward approach but the question of how precisely a court, or businessperson, or their legal adviser goes about making the distinction between the major and the minor terms in a given contract remains. The judge's job is to construe or interpret the contract *as at the time it was made* and infer from it the possible intention of the parties. In *Bentsen v Taylor Sons and Co* (1893), Bowen LJ said that it was necessary to look at the contract in the light of the surrounding circumstances and make up one's mind whether the intention of the parties would best be carried out by treating the provision as a warranty or as a condition. This is as far as the courts have got in laying down guidelines for the predication or evaluation of terms, and it is clear that there is some degree of obscurity about how this approach to breach operates in practice.

In *Behn v Burness* (1863), in a deed dated 19 October 1860, it was agreed that the claimant's ship, 'now in the port of Amsterdam … and ready for the voyage, should, with all possible dispatch, proceed to Newport', where the defendant would load it with coal for Hong Kong. At that time, however, the vessel was, in fact, detained by bad weather at Niewdiep, 62 miles from Amsterdam, where it finally arrived on 23 October. When the vessel reached Newport, the charterer who had by then presumably made alternative arrangements, refused to load his coal and repudiated the contract. He was sued for wrongful termination by the shipowner. It was held that the repudiation was justified as Behn was in breach of an essential term which was the clause stating the 'whereabouts of the vessel' at the time of agreement. Williams J argued that the place of the ship at the date of the contract is vital information to the charterer on which they could make calculations about the likely time of the ship's arriving at the port of loading. He made clear that a statement is more or less important depending on the extent to which the object of the contract depends upon it. It was determined that for most charters, considering winds, markets and dependent contracts, the time of a ship's arrival to load was an essential fact. In short, the whereabouts of the vessel clause was a condition which had been broken by the claimant. In this particular case, this meant that the defendant was justified in terminating the contract.

This decision and other cases involving the breach of similar 'essential' terms in regular commercial use led to the understanding that such terms were always to be regarded as conditions. The 'once a condition, always a condition' result was applauded. It was seen as introducing a strong element of certainty into business contracts with the consequences of breaking such terms being readily apparent from the case law. Later, this development was reinforced in certain statutes. As we have seen, certain obligations of a seller of goods, such as the 'satisfactory quality' of those goods and their fitness for a particular purpose, are implied conditions by reason of the Sale of Goods Act. Breach of such an obligation gives the buyer a right to reject the goods as a matter of statute law. We have therefore reached a point where some terms are always to be classified as conditions on the basis of precedent or statutory authority.

However, an unsatisfactory feature of this position is revealed by the decision in *Arcos Ltd v Ronaasen & Son* (1933). In this case, a quantity of timber staves, described in the contract as being half-an-inch thick, was bought for the purpose of making cement barrels. Most of the staves delivered were nine-sixteenth inch thick. Although the discrepancy in no way impaired their suitability for the contract purpose, it was held that the buyer might nevertheless reject the timber. The seller was in breach of the implied condition, to be found in s 13 of the Sale of Goods Act 1893, that the goods delivered must correspond to the contract description. The fact that the buyer's motive in rejecting the goods was to allow himself the chance to buy elsewhere in a falling market did not affect the reasoning of the judges. The case clearly illustrates that breach of an 'essential' term can give a right to terminate even though performance is only marginally defective, the consequences for the 'injured' party are only slight and he is abusing the right to terminate. The situation has been rectified in part by a 1994 amendment to the Sale of Goods Act 1979 as regards sellers of goods who are dealing with buyers who are not dealing as consumers. The Act requires that if the seller's breach concerning description, satisfactory quality or fitness for purpose is so slight that it would be unreasonable for the buyer to reject the goods, the breach is not to be treated as a breach of condition but may be treated as a breach of warranty.

In 1962 the whole question of terms and breach was re-opened in the case of *Hong Kong Fir Shipping Co Ltd v Kawasaki Kishen Kaisha Ltd* (1962), where the 'term-based' approach outlined above was seriously challenged. In the leading judgment of the Court of Appeal, Diplock LJ stated that what was critical was not the nature of the term broken but the nature of the event arising from the breach. He argued that, if the consequences for the injured party were sufficiently serious then they should be entitled to terminate the contract. If they were not so serious, then they should only be able to claim damages. Diplock defined a sufficiently serious, breach as one which would deprive the victim of the breach of substantially the whole benefit which it was intended they should have obtained.

The facts of the case were that Kawasaki chartered a vessel from Hong Kong Fir for 24 months. The ship developed engine trouble and was laid up for repairs for 20 weeks out of the first seven months of the contract. Although it was made seaworthy at the end of that period, the charterers terminated the contract. It transpired that the main reason why Kawasaki did this was that freight rates had fallen dramatically and they could charter another vessel at a much lower rate. The owners Hong Kong Fir claimed damages for wrongful repudiation. The court held that Hong Kong Fir's breach of the seaworthiness clause had not given rise to consequences serious enough for Kawasaki to terminate. Amongst other things, the charterparty still had a further 17 of the original 24 months to run. As a result, it was determined that Kawasaki were only entitled to claim damages and Hong Kong Fir won the case.

On the basis of this 'seriousness of consequences' approach, the seaworthiness clause in this case only amounted to a warranty. However, had the court found the consequences of its breach to be such as to deprive Kawasaki of substantially the whole benefit from the contract, termination would have been justified and the clause would therefore have had the status of a condition. Diplock LJ put it this way:

> There are, however, many contractual undertakings of a complex character which cannot be categorised as being 'conditions' or 'warranties' ... of such undertakings all that can be predicated is that some breaches will and others will not give rise to an event which will deprive the party not in default of substantially the whole benefit which it was intended that he should obtain from the contract; and the legal consequences of the breach of such an undertaking, unless provided for expressly in the contract, depend upon the nature of the event to which the breach gives rise and do not follow automatically from a prior classification of the undertaking as a 'condition' or a 'warranty'. (p. 487)

He went on to argue that the emphasis in the earlier cases on the breach tended to obscure the fact that it was really the event resulting from the breach which relieved the other party of further performance of their obligations.

This approach to the problem of classifying terms is not necessarily as new as Diplock suggested. In another of 'the earlier cases', *Bettini v Gye* (1876), the court was at pains to look at the contract and the circumstances to see whether the particular term went to the root of the matter and rendered the performance of the rest of the contract a thing different in substance from what the parties had agreed. The court speculated at some length as to what the effect of the claimant's breach would have been if the contract had not been wrongfully terminated. It would therefore appear that, before the 'once a condition, always a condition' case law development, the remedy available might depend on the effect of the breach rather than solely on 'a prior classification' of the term broken. Citing other nineteenth-century cases, Peel and Treitel G (2007) endorse this point, speaking of a long-standing application of a general, open-textured rule under which the extent of the injured party's remedies depended on the seriousness of the breach (see also *Aerial Advertising Co v Bachelors Peas Ltd*, 1938). The majority of breach cases of this kind since the *Hong Kong Fir* decision have been decided according to the 'seriousness of consequences' approach, although in *The Mihalis Angelos* (1978), a majority of the Court of Appeal reverted to the 'once a condition, always a condition' approach in connection with a common clause relating to a charterparty.

Subsequent cases have had to address the issue of whether the parties are at liberty to determine what constitutes a condition and the nature of judicial discretion in this field. In *Schuler AG v Wickman Machine Tool Sales Ltd* (1974), the parties had themselves stipulated that a certain clause in their agreement was a condition. In that case, Schuler, a German company, made panel presses used mainly by car manufacturers. By a written agreement, they appointed Wickman as English agents and distributors for their products. One of the clauses of the contract, the only one to use the word 'condition', provided that it should 'be a condition of this agreement that' Wickman should send representatives to visit six very important customers once a week. Wickman was in breach of this clause, but Schuler did not at that time seek to end the contract and it was held that these breaches had been waived. Later Wickman were guilty of some very minor breaches of the clause and Schuler terminated the agreement. On appeal from an arbitrator, Mocatta J held that the use of the word 'condition' meant that Schuler could terminate if there was any breach of that term, however slight and however long ago, provided only that it had not been waived.

Following further appeals, the House of Lords held that the parties could not have intended the agreement to mean that a failure by Wickman to make one out of a possible 1,400 visits could entail an immediate right to terminate the distributorship. But Lord Wilberforce dissented in strong terms. In his view, the clause was a condition. It was wrong to assume:

> ...that both parties to this contract adopted a standard of easygoing tolerance rather than one of aggressive, insistent punctuality and efficiency. This is not a assumption I am prepared to make, nor do I think myself entitled to impose the former standard upon the parties if their words indicate, as they plainly do, the latter. (p. 263)

These points were also considered by Edmund Davies LJ in the Court of Appeal who was also troubled by the tensions between party autonomy and judicial discretion:

> Is it a sufficient indication of the contracting parties' intention as to the grave manner in which the breach of one of their agreed terms is capable of being treated that they have described it as a 'condition'? Other expressions may be insufficient – to take but one example, the undertaking of an opera singer to be in London 'without fail' at least six days before the commencement of his engagement was held by Blackburn J in *Bettini v Gye* to give rise only to ... compensation in damages. But if a term is described as a 'condition', is that enough of itself to make clear what the innocent party's rights are if it be breached? (p. 1183–1184)

It has been argued that it is now clear that the common law allows the parties to a contract to indicate expressly the consequences to be attached to any particular breach. However, it may be that they cannot do this by merely pinning the labels 'condition' or 'warranty' to their clauses. They must also state the effect with sufficient clarity. Moreover, in default of such indication, it is for the court to decide the legal result of a breach.

More recently still, the matter was considered in *Cehave NV v Bremer Handelsge-sellschaft mbH* (1976). In this case, the Court of Appeal held that breach of a stipulation in a standard form contract that goods were 'shipped in good condition' did not entitle the buyer to reject the goods unless the extent of the breach went to the root of the contract. The facts were that part of a £100,000 shipment of citrus pulp pellets was not in good condition and the buyers purported to reject the whole consignment. It was found that the provision as to shipment in good condition was an 'intermediate term', the breach of which in this case did not justify the buyer's termination of the contract. His proper remedy was in damages for the amount by which the value of the goods was reduced by their damaged condition.

It would seem then that, by 1976, the 'seriousness of consequences' approach would, by weight of recent authority, push the 'term-based' solution into relative obscurity. Only in *The Mihalis Angelos* (1987) had the Court of Appeal regarded the interests of certainty, as established through a line of precedents, as paramount. In that case, Megaw LJ stressed that:

> One of the important elements of the law is predictability. At any rate in commercial law there are obvious and substantial advantages in having, where possible, a firm and definite rule for a particular class of legal relationships ... It is surely much better both for shipowners and charterers (and incidentally for their advisers) when a contractual obligation of this nature is under consideration – and still more when they are faced with the necessity of an urgent decision as to the effects of a suspected breach of it – to be able to say categorically: 'If a breach is proved, then the charterer can put an end to the contract'. (p. 205)

The argument that the 'seriousness of consequences' approach dilutes commercial certainty is often raised, but certainty in business is an elusive concept. Upon what data does a businessperson make the decision to 'throw up' a contract? A number of factors may affect their decision. What is the state of the market? What alternative ways of proceeding are available? What advice do they ask for and receive? Do they want to deal with this party again? Is a dispute or litigation likely to attract unwelcome publicity? If he or she is wrong, will the other party sue? What are the relative costs? Is paying damages less expensive than keeping the contract alive?

In 1976, a further clue as to the way the law would develop was seemingly given in the House of Lords by Lord Wilberforce in the case of *Reardon Smith Line Ltd v Hansen Tangen* (1976). He was of the opinion that some of the earlier cases, such as *Arcos Ltd v Ronaasen,* were 'excessively technical and due for fresh examination'. He continued:

> The general law of contract has developed along much more rational lines in attending to the nature and gravity of a breach or departure than in accepting rigid categories which do or do not automatically give a right to rescind, and if the choice were between extending cases under the Sale of Goods Act 1893 into other fields, or allowing more modern doctrine to infect those cases, my preference would be clear. (p. 627)

Nevertheless, in 1981 in *Bunge Corpn v Tradax Export SA*, the House of Lords reached a decision which, in line with *The Mihalis Angelos*, re-emphasised the requirements of commercial certainty. The facts of this case were that Tradex agreed to sell 15,000 tons of soya bean meal to Bunge. The first shipment was to be delivered in June, beginning on a day chosen by the buyers. The buyers were to give at least 15 days' notice of the ship's readiness to load. The notice was given four days late and Tradex alleged that this breach allowed them to terminate the contract as regards the June shipment. They argued that the clause as to notice was a *condition, any breach* of which justified termination. It was held, rejecting Bunge's claim that the term was 'innominate', that this time stipulation in a mercantile agreement was 'of the essence' and was indeed a condition in the sense alleged.

It would seem then that confusion continues about the where the balance lies between the 'term-based' approach which emphasises certainty and the *Hong Kong Fir* approach which emphasises flexibility. However, a close analysis of the case suggests that the following terms will be found to be conditions without recourse to the question of the seriousness of the consequences of the breach:

(i) Statutorily implied conditions, since an *Arcos* type of decision can now be avoided following the 1994 amendment of the Sale of Goods Act 1979.

(ii) A term which 'has to be performed by one party as a condition precedent to the ability of the other party to perform another term'. This might, for instance, include notice to enable loading to commence on time, as in *Bunge*. The key factor here would appear to be the strict need for *co-operation* between the parties as without it the contract will not work.

(iii) Other mercantile terms well-established as conditions by precedent.

(iv) Terms clearly and reasonably designated as conditions by the parties themselves in the contract; see also *Lombard North Central plc v Butterworth* (1987).

However, the law is far from settled and debate amongst the judiciary reveals a series of different concerns which may conflict with each other. Of these, perhaps the greatest tension exists between the view that the parties are in the best position to define the seriousness of a breach and the proposition that the terms of a contract should only be enforced where a breach is important enough to disrupt performance in a serious way. Alongside an emphasis on party autonomy and an emphasis on the paper deal, some members of the judiciary are clearly concerned that their intervention is *proportionate* to the harm caused. To do otherwise might be to allow the parties to avoid a contract when there has only been a technical breach which does not go to the heart of the agreement. We have already learnt in Chapter 4 that many technical breaches are often ignored by the parties to business agreements on a day-to-day basis where the overall purpose of the contract is still attainable. Approaches to these issues raise much more fundamental questions about the role of law and the judiciary in contract. It is suggested that those who adopt an overly formalistic approach to breach are in danger of ignoring the implicit underpinnings of business agreements by allowing technical breaches to justify avoidance of a contract that has become uncomfortable to one of the parties.

FUNDAMENTAL BREACH

From the mid-1950s onwards, a series of cases threw up a new category of breach, known as fundamental breach, which can be understood as the opposite of technical breach. A fundamental breach is one which has disastrous consequences for the innocent party. In other words, this means that, when the performance promised is compared with actual performance, they were deprived of all, or substantially all, they had bargained for. The key to fundamental breach lay in the fact that it was only encountered in exclusion clause cases. The reason for this was that it was created as a judicial device to defeat clauses as wide-ranging and unfair as the one which protected the defendant company in *L'Estrange v Graucob* (1934). In this case, the exclusion clause was in 'regrettably small print', in 'a part of the document where it easily escaped notice' and printed on brown paper. It read: 'any express or implied condition, statement or warranty, statutory or otherwise not stated herein is hereby excluded'.

Those in favour of promoting the idea of fundamental breach argued that, if the court was able to find what was called a 'radical departure' from the contemplated performance, as opposed to a serious misperformance of an agreed obligation, then a doctrine of fundamental breach could deny a supplier the protection of a clause which excluded liability for breach. The difficulty came in distinguishing fundamental breach which warranted such special measures from other types of breach.

In one case, *Karsales (Harrow) Ltd v Wallis* (1956), it was held that there was a fundamental breach where the agreement had been about the sale of a car in good running order which would not go *at all* when delivered. In that case, Wallis inspected and drove a second-hand Buick in excellent condition. He made arrangements to acquire it on hire purchase under an agreement that excluded liability for breach of conditions and warranties. The car was later towed to his house at night. Many parts had been replaced by old and defective ones. When Wallis refused to pay instalments for the car, he was sued! The court held that the breach was 'fundamental', Karsales could not rely on the exclusion clause and Wallis had a complete defence.

The doctrine of fundamental breach was brought to bear not only in supply of goods cases, but also in those relating to the provision of services and work and materials. However, a major legal controversy arose as to the way in which it operated. Some judges, notably Lord Denning, considered it to be a rule of law with the effect that once a fundamental breach was found, the clause, *no matter how it was worded, automatically* failed to protect its user from liability. Other judges laid down that the doctrine of fundamental breach operated as a rule of construction which required the judges to exercise discretion. This meant that the exclusion clause was not automatically extinguished by the breach, but stood to be read or construed in the light of the breach, even though it was rarely if ever taken to have been intended by the parties to be applicable to a fundamental breach.

In reality, the willingness of the court to find a fundamental breach meant that an unfair exclusion clause would have been defeated whichever approach was used. However, the controversy was more than a storm in a legal teacup and the distinction between the two approaches is important because it is only the rule of construction approach which accords with the long-established general rules relating to breach of contract. These rules lay down that a party faced by a serious breach, such as a breach of condition, has, as we have discussed, a *right* to treat the contract as at an end. In other words, they have an election: they may terminate and sue for damages or they may affirm the contract but nevertheless sue for damages. They may even ignore or waive the breach as seen in *Schuler v Wickman* above. It follows that, before a serious breach situation can give rise to termination of the contract, the injured party must, expressly or impliedly, elect to bring the contract to an end as regards unperformed primary obligations. The breach may be of such a nature that the question of election is made redundant. This means that, in practical terms, further performance is impossible.

The rule of law approach to fundamental breach distorted these rules by claiming that such a breach automatically deprived the wrongdoer of the benefit of his exclusion clause, the contract in which it was to be found having ceased to exist. After several differences of legal opinion, it is now settled, following the decision of the House of Lords in *Photo Production Ltd v Securicor Transport Ltd* (1980) and the passing of the Unfair Contract Terms Act 1977. To the extent that the concept of fundamental breach remains, the injured party's rights are the same as for other serious breach situations. So they include, for example, the right to elect to terminate or to affirm. To the extent that exclusion clauses are not invalidated by the 1977 Act, the question of whether they provide protection for suppliers of goods or services is one of *construction* of the clause and the contract containing it.

CONCLUDING REMARKS

In this chapter we have, once again, seen tensions emerge between judicial intervention and respect for the preferences of the parties. Whilst some have sought to introduce a sense of proportion into the consideration of the gravity of breach, others have been concerned to respect the parties' prescriptions as to what constitutes a sufficiently serious chasm to warrant the ending of a contract. Although these matters might appear relevant at the end of the contractual relationship, for lawyers they are matters which need clarifying from the outset, if planning of risks and benefits is to be clearly thought out in advance. In reality, the cases suggest that the parties are not always that clear at the offset of the contractual relationship about how things will work out in the event of a breach. For some, this suggests a lack of business acumen, for others a reduction of costs. Planning can be expensive in a business community where the emphasis may be on quick turnaround and subsequent deals.

REFERENCES AND FURTHER READING

Adams, J and Brownsword, R 'Contractual indemnity clauses' (1982) JBL 200.
Adams, J and Brownsword, R (2007) *Understanding Contract Law*, Sweet and Maxwell, London.
Bojczuk, W 'When is a condition not a condition?' (1987) JBL 353.
Brownsword, R, 'Retrieving reasons, retrieving rationality? A new look at the right to withdraw for breach of contract' (1992) 5 *Journal of Contract Law* 83.
Devlin, Lord 'The treatment of breach of contract' (1966) CLJ 192.
Greig, D 'Condition – or warranty?' (1973) 89 LQR 93.
Peel, E and Treitel, G (2007) Treitel's Law of Contract, Sweet and Maxwell, London.
Reynolds, F 'Discharge of contract by breach' (1981) 97 LQR 541.
Weir, T 'The buyer's right to reject defective goods' (1976) CLJ 33.

 QUESTIONS

(1) Can you think of any situations in 'The Sad Tale of Angie and Georgie' in which the legal right to terminate a contract may well be of no practical significance.

Continued

? | *QUESTIONS (Continued)*

(2) Appraise critically the following statements:
   (a) 'In penalising wickedness, the Hong Kong rule rewards the incom-
       petent; like other moralism it operates unfairly'.

   (b) 'When the right to reject depended on the nature of the term in the
       contract which was broken, the innocent party simply had to go to
       the filing cabinet, consult the contractual document and then decide
       whether the term broken was a very serious one or not'.

   (c) 'Many people put forward their contractor's breach as a ground
       of release when they actually want to quit for wholly different,
       and legally inadequate, reasons, such as a movement in market or
       exchange rate, or a change in their own requirements or resources.
       This may be good business, but it seems a poor show'. (Weir, 1976).

(3) 'For the most part, the relationships between the classification and
    the consequential approaches, their underlying principles, and the
    contractual ideologies are quite clear. The proportionality and bad
    faith principles are consumer-welfarist, and are currently served by the
    consequential approach. The certainty principle and the principle of
    sanctity of contract are market-individualist, and are better served by
    the classification approach' (Adams and Brownsword, 2007) Discuss.

CHAPTER 18

REMEDIES

INTRODUCTION

In the majority of disputes arising from a contract, it is clear that self-help remedies will most often be resorted to before the injured party considers their formal legal remedies. Self-help remedies have a number of economic advantages. They are cheaper, informal and quick. In the everyday world of business, they may also produce a powerful incentive to perform. Complaints and threats to reputation, the holding of the other party's belongings and realisation of a 'security', all pose a considerable risk to those who claim legitimate breach or hope that an illegitimate breach will not be actioned because of the financial consequences. These factors provide an important backdrop to our consideration of formal remedies and will continue to be relevant as we move on to a consideration of whether or not litigation is the appropriate dispute resolution mechanism.

It is also important to remember that the majority of commercial lawyers devote most of their time to transactional matters rather than to disputes. The essence of their work is clarifying their client's commercial objectives in connection with a transaction and translating them into an agreed form of contract. Part of the lawyer's role will be to ensure that, so far as is possible, adequate safeguards are built into the contract for their client in the event that things go wrong in the business relationship at a later stage. The lawyer's objective will be to ensure that, if such difficulties do arise, their client will have a sufficient armoury of legal arguments and remedies to enable them to deal with difficulties in a commercially sensible way. It is in this context that students need to appreciate the necessary overlap between prudent commercial planning by the lawyer and client and a proper appreciation of legal remedies.

It is only by understanding the legal nature of breach and the available legal remedies that parties can make express provision in their contract for particular situations that may arise and so avoid, or at least limit, the potential for full-scale litigation. It should be clear from earlier chapters that lawyers go beyond just specifying what constitutes performance in a contract. They also have to plan for changes in circumstance which might make performance difficult and to plan how disputes which arise should be managed.

CONTRACTUAL PLANNING

A well-structured contract will have addressed these issues at a number of levels. Firstly, the drafter may have been able to anticipate the possibility of particular circumstances arising and may have included a specific remedy or mechanism for addressing the problem. One obvious example of this is a 'cure notice' procedure by which the party not in default delivers to the defaulting party a notice specifying the particular breaches complained of and requiring the defaulting party to remedy those breaches within a specified period. As we mention later in this chapter, it is also open to the parties to agree and include in the contract a specified financial penalty in the event of a particular breach occurring. Secondly, where the contract provides no clear answer to the particular breach of which complaint is made, it may contain an escalation procedure by which the parties are required to adopt a number of dispute resolution procedures aimed at securing a speedy settlement of the dispute at modest cost. We deal with such procedures in the next chapter. The final layers of planning are the contractual provisions concerned with exclusion and limitation of liability, liquidated damages and termination procedures.

Empirical studies of the use of contract in the commercial sphere have made clear that the majority of commercial contractors pay little heed to most contractual provisions during the performance of the contract. Case law in preceeding chapters demonstrates that the parties often stray from the original terms and conditions by varying the contract and that they often do so without satisfying the rules relating to consideration. These findings have been used by some to suggest that the formal contract is of little use in the lived world of contract. However, it has also been argued that, whilst this is true during trouble-free performance, the parties will revert to the contractual provisions if a problem arises and they are unable to resolve the problems by using self-help remedies such as re-negotiation of price or time scales. In such circumstances, it is the raft of contractual provisions outlined above and an understanding of the legal remedies available that will provide the foundations for a party's negotiating stance. For this reason, it is essential for both client and adviser to understand how the courts approach the issue of remedies.

Whilst commercial factors often take precedent over legal doctrine and process, it is clear that, when negotiating a settlement after breach, the parties commonly 'bargain in the shadow' of the law. Disputants can and do use the 'bargaining chips' created by contractual terms and legal precedent to bolster their position and add credibility to a claim that their position would be upheld by a court. The *threat* of litigation when used judiciously is, of itself, a powerful tool in the portfolio of the lawyer. Likewise, a proper understanding of the weaknesses in a party's position can inform that party's risk and cost analysis and thus perhaps facilitate an early settlement on commercially realistic terms. Whether or not litigation is used, it is important to know what remedies might be available.

There are three principal remedies for a breach of contract. These are specific performance, termination and damages. It will be seen that each of these respond to different needs. In some circumstances, what the injured party will want most is to bring the contractual relationship to an end as quickly as possible and move on. This is a particularly attractive option where there has been a complete breakdown in trust or it makes better business sense to find another supplier or purchaser. In other cases the injured party might want to insist on performance of contractual obligations. This situation might arise where the party in breach is a specialist, is supplying a rare commodity or has agreed to perform a service at a low cost. In each of these examples termination is not appropriate because the contract is special in some way and cannot easily be replicated. In a third scenario the injured party may need to be compensated for financial losses which have been suffered as a result of the breach. In the remainder of this chapter, we will go on to consider how the three principal remedies available for breach of contract address these various needs.

SPECIFIC PERFORMANCE

When the court issues an order for specific performance, it directs one of the parties to perform its obligations as specified in the contract. Such a remedy may appear to be a very natural one in response to breach of an obligation freely entered into by the party in breach. However, in English law, the remedy of specific performance is rarely granted. This is because it is generally unrealistic to speak of compelling performance in cases where one party is refusing to perform, has so managed their affairs as to make performance out of the question, or has broken the contract in a serious way. As a result, specific performance tends to be granted only where it is realistic to do so and damages are considered to be an inadequate remedy. For example, the remedy will not be granted for contracts for the sale of goods which are readily available elsewhere in the market, but it will be granted where the contractual subject matter is land, property, or other things which fall within the concept of 'commercial uniqueness'.

In *Perry & Co v British Railways Board* (1980), Perry obtained an order during the steel strike of 1980, that the Railways Board deliver a quantity of steel owned by him under contract. At the time of the case, steel was very difficult to obtain. Frightened of strike action, the Railways Board had refused to allow it to be moved. In this case it was said that damages would be an inadequate remedy because they would be 'a poor consolation if the failure of supplies forces a trader to lay off staff and disappoint his customers'. Similarly, the decision in *Sky Petroleum Ltd v VIP Petroleum Ltd* (1974) was made at a time when there was a petrol shortage. As a result Sky, who had contracted to take all their petrol from VIP, was granted an interim injunction to stop VIP withholding supplies. This amounted to temporary specific performance of a contract for the sale of goods. Although there were normally alternative sources of supply, this was not the case at the time as the market had failed.

Traditionally, the courts have also refused to enforce a contract under which one party is bound by *continuous duties*. This is because the performance of such contracts might require constant supervision by the court. However, in some such cases specific performance has been ordered and it has been suggested that the difficulty of supervision is sometimes exaggerated. There are various devices that the court can adopt to overcome such difficulty, such as appointing a receiver and manager, Moreover, there are several judicial statements in recent cases to suggest that 'constant supervision' is no longer a bar to specific performance but merely a factor to be taken into account. There has also been some indication of an increased willingness by the courts to sanction the use of this remedy, although some doubt has been cast on this change in attitude by the case of *Co-operative Insurance Society Ltd v Argyll Stores (Holdings) Ltd* (1998). However, the decision of the House of Lords in that case has itself been subject to criticism. As things stand, it would seem that the standard question 'are damages an adequate remedy?' might be rewritten to allow for consideration of whether it is just, in all the circumstances, that a claimant should be confined to a remedy in damages?

TERMINATION OF THE CONTRACT

Depending upon the nature of the contractual term breached and the consequences of the breach, the innocent party may be entitled to terminate the contract. This can be done in addition to a claim for damages. The right to do so may be contained in a contractual term or as a matter of general law. The right to terminate a contract is carefully regulated. The judiciary have shown themselves concerned to ensure that the 'engines of industry' are slowed as little as possible by breach situations. As a result, it has traditionally given weight to a requirement that the injured party could only terminate a contract following a serious breach and, if it did so, it had a duty to mitigate its loss.

Termination is not a straightforward remedy and must be undertaken with great care if the situation is not to be made even worse. As a first step, the innocent party and their lawyer will need to check the contract carefully to see if it contains express provision for early termination in the event of a breach. Such provisions may restrict or impose conditions upon the right to terminate or may provide a contractual procedure for termination that will need to be implemented in tandem with other rights. If a contractual provision for termination appears to be the safest route, there may be procedures such as service of a cure notice that will need to be followed to make the termination effective. A failure to do so may expose the innocent party to an argument by the defaulting party that the termination is ineffective.

Even an apparently clear provision in a contract giving a right to terminate may not be all it seems. In *Rice v Great Yarmouth Borough Council* (2000), a council sought to exercise a right of termination by reason of a contractor's various breaches of a contract for the provision of leisure management and grounds maintenance services. The right of termination for breach was expressed in the following very wide terms: '… if the contractor… commits a breach of any of its obligations under the contract… the council may… terminate the contractor's employment under the contract by notice in writing having immediate effect'. However, the Court of Appeal found that only a repudiatory breach or an accumulation of breaches that as a whole could properly be described as repudiatory could justify termination. In the Court of Appeal, Hale LJJ described the circumstances in which repudiatory breach could be found by the courts and in doing so reminded us that the courts do not easily set aside contracts:

> As the judge indicated, there are in effect three catefories: (1) those cases in which the parties have agreed either that the term is so important that any breach will justify termination or that the particular breach is so important that it will justify termination; (2) those contractors who simply walk away from their obligations thus clearly indicating an intention no longer to be bound; and (3) those cases in which the cumulative effect of the breaches which have taken place is sufficiently serious to justify the innocent party in bringing the contract to a premature end…. It is clear that the test of what is sufficiently serious to bring the case within the third of these categories is severe. (paras 35–36)

The court expressed concern that the council appeared to visit the same draconian consequences upon any breach, however small, so long as it was a technical breach of the contract. The court found that the breaches relied upon by the council were found to be insufficiently serious on either an individual or cumulative basis and, as a result, would not allow termination. The breaches did not substantially deny the council the benefit of the contract.

It is also clear that the parties should communicate their concerns to each other prior to a notice to terminate being issued. This was the position in *Anglo Group Plc v Winther Browne, & Co Limited* (2000) in which Winther Browne, by means of a third-party leasing agreement, purchased a computer system from a supplier. Winther Browne defaulted on payments due and the leasing company sued claiming that Winther Browne had repudiated the contract. Winther Browne claimed that there were defects in the system and counterclaimed for loss of profits and wasted salaries. The court found that contracts for the design and installation of computer systems required parties actively to co-operate with each other. Implied into the contract between Winther Browne and the supplier was a term requiring Winther Browne to communicate its needs clearly to the supplier and that the parties work together to resolve problems. The defects in the system had not been proven to constitute fundamental breaches of contract entitling Winther Browne to repudiate the contract. The suppler had performed substantially what it had contracted to do and Winther Browne had not fully co-operated in helping to resolve problems that had arisen.

A decision to terminate has to be properly communicated to the party in breach. The right to terminate may be lost if, in the meantime, the innocent party demonstrates an intention to continue with the contract. This might be the case, for example, if they place an order for additional services or make an advance payment of charges due under the contract. If the innocent party gets it wrong and purports to terminate in circumstances where, as a matter of law, it was not entitled to do so, the party in breach may be able to treat such 'wrongful' termination as a basis upon which it can then legitimately terminate the contract.

Where an ineffective termination by the innocent party enables the defaulting party to terminate, the end result (termination of the contract) is clearly the same. However, there may be very serious financial consequences for the innocent party. If the party in breach is struggling to meet its obligations or can only do so on an uneconomic basis, it may like nothing better than for the innocent party to terminate in circumstances where it may not have been entitled to do so. Not only will the defaulting party have escaped future performance under the contract but it may also have a claim against the innocent party for damages for wrongful termination. Even the opportunity for the defaulting party to raise such an argument will enhance its position in any subsequent negotiations for settlement that may take place.

These matters are intended to illustrate the many legal difficulties that may beset a party thinking of exercising a right of termination. But in reality, the parties will also have to deal with the many commercial issues that may arise. If a party terminates a contract for the supply of manufacturing parts, will it be able to find an alternative supplier at a competitive price or honour its contracts with a third party for the supply of the finished item? They may well have a remedy in damages in relation to such problems but this may be of little comfort in the short term or in the context of its reputation in the marketplace. As a result of these various factors, even where a right of termination exists, it is for many businesspeople a remedy of last resort. It is in this context that the remedy of damages assumes an even greater importance since it may, in practice, be the only remedy sought by the innocent party.

DAMAGES

A breach of contract gives the innocent party the right to claim damages to compensate them for any loss caused by the breach. This is subject only to restrictions imposed by any exclusion or limitation of liability provisions contained in the contract. By the mid-nineteenth century, damages had come to be regarded as the acceptable form of 'insurance' against the risk of default by a contracting party. Operating within the context of a market economy, the basic aim of the law was to ensure that a party was compensated for loss for which a financial value could be found. Within the business community, breach is not always an unqualified wrong. There are times when it can be economically efficient to breach a contract, such as when a better deal comes along. As a result, as the law of contract developed, market principles demanded that the parties be given a choice of either performing their obligations or compensating the other party for the loss which arose as a result of the breach. It would seem that the option of breach is the ultimate sign of freedom of contract.

The courts expect that a victim of breach mitigates their loss as far as is reasonable. The injured party's 'duty' to mitigate the loss means that it will not be compensated for loss which it could have avoided by taking reasonable steps; see Viscount Haldane LC in *British Westinghouse Electric and Manufacturing Co Ltd v Underground Electric Railways Co of London Ltd*, 1912). So, for example, where a seller fails to deliver goods, the buyer must immediately or within a reasonable time go into the market and secure substitute equivalent goods. Its damages will then be assessed on the basis of the difference if any between the contract price and the market price. Moreover, the buyer cannot delay at a time of a rising market. An early illustration of the market price rule arose in the case of *Gainsford v Carroll* (1824). This case concerned a seller who failed to deliver a quantity of bacon as agreed. It was held that the buyer, having terminated the contract, ought to have gone into the market at once for a replacement supply. As he had failed to do this, he could not recover damages in respect of the increase in the market price after that time. He could only recover damages equal to the difference between the contract price and the market price at the date of the breach.

THE NATURE OF LOSS OR DAMAGE

The statement that the injured party may recover damages for the loss sustained as a result of the breach obscures as much as it reveals. In fact, we have it on judicial authority that the law relating to damages is 'a branch of the law in which one is less guided by authority laying down definite principles than in almost any other matter one can consider' (Atkins LJ in *The Susquehanna*, 1925, p. 210). Since 1925 when this statement was made, the law of damages has moved no nearer to 'definite principles'. One matter that lawyers have sought to have clarified is the *kind* of damage or loss for which the injured party is entitled to recover compensation.

The traditional approach to this question is to say that the law protects the expectations created by the contract. Damages are therefore awarded to put the injured party, so far as money can do it, in the same position as if the contract had been properly performed (see the judgment of Parke J in *Robinson v Harman*, 1848). According to this scheme, the injured party is entitled to damages for the loss of its bargain so that their expectations arising from the contract are protected. These damages are called *expectation damages*. An alternative view, which is being increasingly applied, is that some situations require that, if the injured party is to obtain adequate compensation, it is necessary to put them back in the position in which they would have been in had the contract never been made. These damages are referred to as *reliance damages*. Here the intention is to put the innocent party into the position they would have been in if they had not entered into the contract. It will be remembered from the chapter on misrepresentation that this is a standard which has traditionally been associated with tortious remedies rather than contractual ones. In broad terms, damages calculated on this basis comprise the wasted expenditure incurred in reliance on the contract. This is not limited to expenditure incurred after the contract was concluded. The innocent party can also claim expenditure incurred before the contract was entered into provided it was within the reasonable contemplation of the parties that it would be likely to be wasted as a result of the other party's breach. We will return to this subject later.

The two approaches mentioned above are illustrated in diagrammatic form in Figure 18.1.

Figure 18.1: Expectation and reliance damages

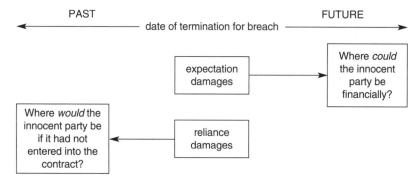

EXPECTATION DAMAGES

An award of damages to compensate the injured party for loss of the benefit they would have secured had the contract been properly performed may require a relatively straightforward calculation of lost profits. This would be the case for example if a manufacturer did not deliver the goods promised to a shop. In other cases, such as where there has been defective delivery of some sort, the position may not be so simple. Broadly speaking there are two ways of measuring expectation damages. Firstly, they may be measured by reference to the cost of curing of the defective performance. Secondly, they may be assessed by reference to the reduced value of what has been 'delivered'. In some cases, the two different approaches will produce the same result, in others they will be very different. The view a court will take as to the correct measure of loss will depend very much on the individual circumstances of the case.

The distinction between the two measures is very well illustrated in a case concerning a swimming pool. In *Ruxley Electronics and Construction Limited v Forsyth* (1996), builders were asked to build a swimming pool. The agreed depth was to be seven foot six inches but, when the builders completed the swimming pool, it was only six feet deep. There was nothing else wrong with it. The impact on the value of the pool was assessed at nil. The cost of correcting the breach, which was only possible by demolishing the pool and building a new one, was £21,560. In considering the question of which of the two approaches to measurement of damages was the correct one, the House of Lords held that it would not be reasonable for the owner of the pool to recover the cost of cure damages because the cost of carrying out the corrective work was out of all proportion to the benefit that he would obtain. In their view, the correct measure was the diminution in value, even in a case where such value was nil. A finding by the original trial judge that the pool owner was entitled to damages for 'loss of amenity' or the disappointment experienced in not getting a pool of the dimensions specified of £2,500 was allowed to stand.

The same principles will apply whether the claim is a large or a small one. For example, in *Sabir v Tiny Computers* (1999), Mr Sabir purchased a computer from Tiny Computers but sought to reject it seven months later on the basis that it was crashing more often than was acceptable. He brought an action against Tiny for damages for breach of contract. Even though it was found that an upgrade from Windows 95 to Windows 98 that Mr Sabir had undertaken without consulting Tiny had contributed 50 per cent to the problem, Mr Sabir was held to be entitled to damages for loss occasioned by faults in the machine not attributable to the upgraded software. The modest award of damages of £670 was made up of the cost of telephone calls between Mr Sabir and Tiny, compensation for loss of use, diminution in value of the computer and reimbursement of the cost of repair.

The case of *Pegler v Wang* (2000) involved much larger financial claims. This concerned a dispute in relation to a contract between Wang and Pegler, a manufacturer of engineers' and plumbers' brassware, under which Wang was to provide computer hardware, software and related services designed to improve Pegler's business efficiency. The total price agreed was £1,198,130 plus £235,000 each year for three years to cover maintenance. Wang's performance was extremely poor and the parties ultimately abandoned the contract. Pegler served formal notice of breach and required Wang to remedy its various breaches but Wang took no steps to comply. Pegler treated Wang's failure to do so as a repudiation of the contract which they relied on to bring the contract to an end. At the same time, they exercised a contractual right of termination. Pegler used third parties to provide the services it needed and issued proceedings against Wang, claiming damages of nearly £23 million. Pegler eventually admitted liability and the trial of the claim was principally concerned with examination of the damages claimed. Pegler was awarded £9 million. The heads of loss included lost sales, lost opportunity to increase margins, lost opportunity to make staff cost savings, the cost of replacement systems and consultancy services, lost opportunity to reduce finished stock held, the ability to negotiate improved purchasing terms and wasted management time.

RELIANCE DAMAGES

It has already been indicated that, in certain circumstances, an alternative approach to assessment of damages, namely the reliance model, may be adopted. If expectation damages are claimed, the claimant will be expected to give satisfactory evidence of the value of their expectations. If this is not possible, a reliance claim may be appropriate. This is illustrated in the case of *Anglia Television Ltd v Reed* (1972) which concerned a situation in which an actor failed to honour his contract with a TV company to appear in a film. The company was unable to find a substitute and the film was never made. It could not say what its profits on the project would have been and chose instead to make a wasted expenditure claim. The judge found that the TV company was entitled to recover wasted expenditure on fees paid to the director, designer and stage manager both *before* and after the contract had been entered into on the basis that the actor must have known perfectly well that such expenditure was likely to be incurred and would be wasted if he broke his contract. Damages awarded on this basis put the innocent party back into the position they would have been in if they had never made the contract.

A further example of this approach is the case of *The Salvage Association v CAP Financial Services Ltd* (1995) which concerned a contract for the development of new accounting software. When it became clear that the supplier was failing to sort out serious problems in the system in time to meet an agreed deadline for completion of the project, the customer exercised a right of termination and engaged another company to design a replacement system from scratch. The customer succeeded in recovering from the supplier £291,388 paid under the two development and implementation contracts entered into. In addition, it recovered £231,866 wasted expenditure. This was made up of payments made to a bureau facility for use of terminal time, wasted computer stationery, payment to consultants and payments to an independent third party in connection with testing. In addition, an award of £139,672 for wasted management time that could have been put to productive use in connection with other activities was made.

Reliance damages may be appropriate in relation to certain types of contract that require major 'up front' expenditure. It is, however, important to distinguish between costs incurred in connection with the project which may have been entirely wasted and costs that have provided some value even if the contract fails. For example, work undertaken may relate to steps that will not need to be undertaken again in making a replacement contract, such as the drafting of materials for a call to tender. In addition, what the claiming party cannot do is to use the reliance measure of loss in an attempt to escape the consequences of a poor commercial bargain. This proviso is illustrated by the case of *C and P Haulage Co Ltd v Middleton* (1983) where the claimant had been granted a licence to occupy premises for renewable periods of six months. The owner of the property acted in breach of contract by evicting the claimant from the property 10 weeks prior to the end of the six-month period. The claimant was able to work from home during that 10-week period and therefore suffered no loss of business. He did, however, bring a claim for the cost of the improvements he had made to the property. The court held that this was not recoverable because the loss flowed did not flow the breach. The claimant had made improvements to the property despite a contractual term in which he had agreed not to remove fixtures. Therefore, even if there had not been a wrongful eviction, the loss would still have been suffered because of the terms agreed; for a review of the cases on reliance loss, see *CCC Films (London) Ltd v Impact Quadrant Films Ltd* (1985). A further factor to bear in mind is that the claimant will not be entitled to any element of double recovery. They cannot, for example, claim both the cost of raw materials and the loss of profits on sale of the finished goods that they had expected to sell to the party in breach.

REMOTENESS OF LOSS

A breach of contract may initiate a course of events which results in loss to the claimant but the law will not necessarily hold the defendant liable for all the loss that flows from the breach. It may regard part of the loss as being too 'remote'. The principal justification for not permitting recovery of all loss is that, if it were to be permitted, the risk of entering into a contract might be considered so great that parties might be discouraged from doing so or, even in the event that they were prepared to proceed, that they would do so only on very onerous terms. The remoteness rule places a limit on damages, as does the rule on mitigation referred to below.

The basic test of remoteness, laid down in *Hadley v Baxendale* (1854), is whether the loss was within the reasonable contemplation of the parties. That case involved a flour mill which was driven by a steam engine. The engine came to a standstill owing to a broken crankshaft and the owner of the mill had to send the shaft to the makers as a pattern for a new one. The makers, in breach of contract, delayed delivery of the new shaft, which the mill owner did not receive until five days after he would otherwise have done. The mill being idle during this period, the owner claimed for loss of profits occasioned by the delay. It was found by Baron Alderson that:

> Where two parties have made a contract which one of them has broken, the damages
> ... should be such as may fairly and reasonably be considered either arising naturally,
> i.e. according to the usual course of things, from such breach of contract itself, or such
> as may reasonably be supposed to have been in the contemplation of both parties, at the
> time they made the contract, as the probable result of the breach. (p. 465)

It was held that the stoppage did not arise in 'the usual course of things' but was the result of special circumstances, namely the fact that the mill owner had only one crankshaft. This was not considered to be within the reasonable contemplation of the carrier at the time the contract was made. The maker of the shaft was therefore not liable for the loss of profits; he was only liable for nominal damages.

It is important to note that everyone is assumed *to know* the usual course of things and to know the consequences of breach in such circumstances. Knowledge of special circumstances, however, must be shown to be actual knowledge in order to attract liability for special loss. In *Hadley*, the miller's special circumstances militated against the application of the first limb of the remoteness rule and his failure to communicate his lack of a spare crankshaft to the carrier meant that he was not covered by the second limb either. It has been said of this case that the court implied that the optimal mill owner would not allow himself to be caught without a spare. In other words the courts expect that avoidable consequences must be avoided by those with power to avoid them. It would distort the market system to allow an offender against this principle to cast their losses upon another party, since a market system required the penalties for bad planning of enterprise to fall upon those who planned badly. Alternatively, it may be said that the court considered it to be unfair to impose such a wide liability for damages upon a carrier unless he or she was aware of the circumstances and had the opportunity to settle special terms.

As a result of *Hadley*, a party looking for compensation must now seek to bring its claim to compensation within one of the two limbs of the test mentioned in that case. The first possibility is that the loss occurred 'naturally'. The proper meaning of 'naturally' is something that has been expressed in the cases in many different ways. For example, it has been described as being 'in the usual course of events', 'a serious possibility' or 'a real danger'. In the case of *Koufos v Czarnikov* (1969), sugar merchants chartered a ship to carry some sugar from Constanza to Basrah.

In breach of contract, the shipowner made a number of detours along the way which resulted in the sugar arriving at its destination nine days later than would otherwise have been the case. During that nine-day period, the price of sugar on the Basrah market had fallen and the merchant therefore achieved a lower price on sale. The court found that it must have been within the common contemplation of both parties that, if there was a delay in delivery, it was 'not unlikely' that there would be a decline in the price of the goods during that period. In other words, it was a natural consequence.

The second possibility is that the claimant must demonstrate that the loss was within the reasonable contemplation of the parties at the time the contracts was made. The notion of reasonable contemplation has also caused problems of interpretation. Words such as 'loss', 'reasonable contemplation' and 'communication' are capable of manipulation, and in the modern business world, it may more readily be assumed than was the case when *Hadley* was decided, that a party has a fair knowledge of another's operations and techniques. This is not always true, however, as is well illustrated by the case of *Balfour Beatty v Scottish Power plc* (1994). Balfour Beatty had entered into a contract with the local electricity board for the supply of electricity to a concrete batching plant used in connection with the construction of an aqueduct. The electricity company was not aware that the construction work required a continuous pour of concrete and, in breach of contract, the supply of electricity was interrupted. As a result, a substantial part of the construction had to be demolished and rebuilt. The court found that the electricity company could not be expected to be aware of construction manufacturing processes, such as the need for continuous pour, and, so the damage suffered as a result of the failure in supply could not be said to have been within the reasonable contemplation of the company.

It is also true that a party cannot be expected to know details of the other party's business strategy unless this has been clearly communicated to them. This is demonstrated by the case of *Amstrad plc v Seagate Technology Inc* (1998). This concerned a contract between Amstrad, a major manufacturer and supplier of IBM-compatible personal computers aimed at the lower end of the market, and Seagate, which at the time was the biggest manufacturer of hard disk drives for such computers. Amstrad decided to launch a new range of upmarket models, with enhanced disk drives. It bought 56,000 hard disk drives from Seagate for the new range at a cost of $17 million. The launch of the new range was unsuccessful, largely because of major problems with the disk drives, which meant that users were unable to retrieve data. Amstrad was found to be entitled to receive damages for lost and delayed sales of the new range and for wasted costs, but was not entitled to recover any damages for loss of sales of a successor range of personal computers planned by Amstrad because such losses were not within the reasonable contemplation of the parties at the time the contract was made. These issues clearly have implications for contractual planning. The more information a party possesses regarding the risks attached to contract performance, the better opportunity it has to modify its terms. Actual knowledge of 'special circumstances' might, for example, lead or enable a party to increase its price, exclude the risk or insure against its occurrence.

The case of *Victoria Laundry (Windsor) Ltd v Newman Industries Ltd* (1949) is often used to illustrate the distinction between losses that flow naturally from the breach and those which must be categorised as 'special' losses. In that case, the defaulting party, an engineering company, had agreed to immediate delivery of a boiler to the claimant laundry business. The defendant did not know that the boiler was needed to extend the business. It was delivered five months late and the claimant sued for loss of profits. The court found that the claimant was entitled to compensation for loss of normal profits which were an entirely natural consequence of late delivery. The court did not accept that the claimant should be entitled to recover losses under especially lucrative contracts that it had just entered into with the government which it could not perform without the new boiler. The defendant did not know about these contracts and, as a result, the loss was not within the reasonable contemplation of the parties.

These decisions are not without their critics. It has been suggested that the law should not ignore the extent of the loss if it is to achieve fair restrictions on recovery. In a commercial contract, the *kind* of loss will nearly always be within the contemplation of the parties. For example, in the *Victoria Laundry* case, the loss under the normal contracts and under the lucrative contracts was the same in nature. It was only the amount of profit under the lucrative contracts that was exceptional and it could be argued that it is legitimate to distinguish between ordinary and exceptional losses in relation to both direct and consequential losses.

NON-PECUNIARY LOSS: DISAPPOINTMENT AND DISTRESS

Other factors have operated in recent years to widen the scope of recoverable loss in the form of damages. It has for many years been clear that, where a breach causes personal injury, an award of damages can go beyond pure economic loss and take account of pain and suffering. This was the case in *Godley v Perry* (1960), in which Godley bought a catapult which broke and, as a result, lost an eye. More significantly, inroads have been made into the old rule that contract damages could not be awarded for injured feelings. In part this has come about as a result of developments in negligence cases and the growth of consumer protection. In *Jarvis v Swan's Tours Ltd* (1973), Jarvis booked a winter holiday in the Alps with Swan Tours, whose brochure listed many attractions. The holiday fell far short of Jarvis's expectations and, in the second week, he was the sole visitor. On appeal on the issue of damages, the award was increased from £32 to £125. The court decided that 'damages can be given for the disappointment, the distress, the upset and frustration caused by the breach'. Similarly, in *Farley v Skinner* (2002) the House of Lords upheld an award of £10,000 for non-pecuniary losses to the purchaser of a house near an airport who had asked their surveyor to investigate whether the house would be affected by aircraft noise. The purchaser had gone ahead with the transaction on the basis of the surveyor's assurance that the property was unlikely to be affected. It was held by the court that the award of damages was justified either because a major or important part of the contract was to 'give pleasure, relaxation or peace of mind' or as compensation for 'inconvenience and discomfort'.

LIQUIDATED DAMAGES

In the opening section of this chapter we referred to the planning function of lawyers and it is to this point that we now return. Detailed planning of a contractual relationship can allow the parties to avoid costly disputes and litigation should a breach occur. One means at their disposal is the inclusion in the agreement of a clause providing for a fixed or calculable sum to be paid on the occurrence of a possible breach. For example, a building contract may provide that 'the contractor shall pay the building owner £500 per week or part thereof for delay in completion of the works'. It was this sort of clause that caused the commercial pressure that placed the parties in *Williams v Roffey and Nichols (Contractors) Ltd* (1991) in so much trouble.

Such a clause usually indicates the parties' willingness to avoid litigation over questions such as remoteness of loss and assessment of damages when the fact of non-compliance with the contract is not in dispute. However, the party in default may resist the operation of the clause and plead that it is an unenforceable *penalty*. If the court decides that the sum fixed is a 'genuine pre-estimate' of the actual loss likely to be suffered by the injured party in the event of the specified breach, then it is recoverable, whatever the actual loss. In these cases, the sum due is known as 'liquidated damages'. These can be compared with 'unliquidated damages' of the nature discussed above which can only be quantified by the Court after a breach has occurred.

A liquidated damages clause must be distinguished from both a limitation of liability clause and a penalty clause, neither of which are genuine pre-estimates of loss. The objective of a limitation of liability clause is to place an upper limit on the amount of damages recoverable by one or both parties. The limit agreed often has little connection to the possible losses that may be suffered as a result of a breach of contract. It is very much determined by commercial expediency, the need for certainty and the relative bargaining strength of each party. This is not to deny that a liquidated damages clause may in practice limit liability where actual loss exceeds the agreed figure, but its object is to benefit both parties by avoiding litigation on the matter. The essence of such a clause is that the stipulated figure can be seen as a genuine pre-estimate of loss. It is therefore essential that the sum assessed should be reasonable in relation to the damage anticipated and to all known facts, even though a precise calculation is not possible at the time the contract is planned or formed. If the sum fixed is obviously extravagant and unconscionable in comparison with the greatest loss which the injured party could suffer as a result of the breach, then it is viewed by the courts as a penalty. Such a sum is not recoverable, although the injured party can recover on the basis of unliquidated damages for actual loss.

The basis of the law relating to liquidated damages was laid down by Lord Dunedin in *Dunlop Pneumatic Tyre Co Ltd v New Garage and Motor Co Ltd* (1915). More recently, in *Robophone Facilities Ltd v Blank* (1966), Blank agreed to rent one of Robophone's telephone answering machines for seven years at £17 11s per quarter. A clause in the agreement stated that, if it was terminated for any reason, Blank was to pay Robophone 'all rentals accrued due and also by way of liquidated or agreed damages a sum equal to 50 per cent of the total of the rentals which would thereafter have become payable'. Blank cancelled the agreement before the machine was installed. It was held that Robophone could recover agreed damages of £245 11s. Since Robophone's facilities for supplying the machines exceeded and were likely to continue to exceed the demand, they were entitled to recover their loss of profit.

RESTITUTION

There is one further approach that may be adopted in appropriate circumstances in place of, or in addition to, damages. This is a claim in restitution. This may arise, for example, where the party in breach has wholly failed to perform their part of the contract. If a seller agrees to deliver goods to a buyer for which the buyer has paid in advance and the seller then fails to deliver, they must restore what they have gained to the buyer. A restitutionary claim may also arise where the party in breach has, as a result of the breach, obtained an unjust benefit which they would not otherwise have had. This topic has received recent judicial attention and, along with restitutionary claims in the event of a partial failure of consideration, is a fast developing area of law. Examples of how it can be used in quasi-contractual claims are indicated in Chapter 9.

CONCLUDING REMARKS

In this chapter we have looked at the remedies available to parties who believe they have suffered from a breach of contract. In this volume the decision has been made to place the chapter on remedies at the back of the book. However, in some courses, students will be asked to look at remedies before they study anything else. This is because it is important always to have in mind when reading cases what it is the parties wish to achieve. When considering extra-legal and self-help remedies, the emphasis may be on a host of different things that the parties want to achieve. But the courts have limited measures at hand to help put things right for the parties. We have seen in this chapter that the appropriate legal remedy is often dependent on the particular facts of a case. As a result, students should be encouraged to look closely at a fact pattern as well as the law in approaching this topic.

REFERENCES AND FURTHER READING

Barton, J 'The economic basis of damages for breach of contract' (1972) 1 *Journal of Legal Studies* 277.

Burrows, A 'Mental distress damages in contract – a decade of change' (1984) LMCLQ 119.

Burrows, A 'Specific performance at the crossroads' (1984) 4 *Legal Studies* 102.

Burrows, A (1993) *The Law of Restitution*, Butterworths, London.

Burrows, A (1994) *Remedies for Torts and Breach of Contract*, Butterworths, London.

Carter, J (1995) 'Suspending contract performance for breach' in Beatson, J and Friedmann, D (eds) *Good Faith and Fault in Contract Law*, Clarendon, Oxford.

Danzig, R 'Hadley v Baxendale: a study in the industrialization of the law (1975) 4 *Journal of Legal Studies* 249.

Harris, D, Campbell, D and Halson, R (2002) *Remedies in Contract and Tort*, 2nd edn, LexisNexis Butterworths, London.

Law Commission (1983) *Law of Contract: Pecuniary Restitution on Breach of Contract*, Report No 121, Law Commission, London.

Opeskin, B 'Damages for breach of contract terminated under express terms' (1990) 107 LQR 293.

Owen, M 'Some aspects of the recovery of reliance damages in the law of contract' (1984) 4 *Oxford Journal of Legal Studies* 393.

Tillotson, J 'The Portuguese bank note case: legal, economic and financial approaches to the measure of damages in contract' (1994) *68 Australian Law Journal* 93.

? **QUESTIONS**

(1) Angie and Georgie are clearly in a mess! Imagine that you have set up a series of meetings between Angie and Georgie and the following people:

(a) Mister C;

(b) Chelsea;

(c) Orange Peril;

(d) Wacky Machine Company and Ned;

(e) Dipti;

(f) Marcus;

(g) Monkish Soup Company;

(h) Claude;

(i) Kirsteen;

(j) St Ives Bank;

(k) The multi-storey car park.

What do you think they need to ask for in each of these meetings to improve their situation? Are the other parties in a position to provide what they want? How much of what they want can be translated into claims for specific performance or damages?

(2) How many actions for breach of contract can you identify in 'The Sad Tale of Angie and Georgie'? How would you advise Angie and Georgie to proceed as (a) a lawyer, (b) a friend?

(3) Draw up a schedule of damages that you think Angie and Georgie could claim.

CHAPTER 19

DISPUTE RESOLUTION

INTRODUCTION

At first glance, recourse to the courts appears to be the obvious means by which a party to a contract can enforce their contractual rights in the event of default or non-compliance by the other party. However, in practice, a whole host of factors may militate against the commencement of litigation as a means of securing enforcement. In this chapter we consider the various ways in which the parties to a contract might go about resolving their dispute. In an introductory text of this kind, it is not possible to describe the full range of dispute resolution techniques employed by parties in disagreements about a contract. As a result, some processes, such as early neutral evaluation and the mini-trial, can only be mentioned in passing. What we are able to do is to focus on the three forms of dispute resolution most discussed in legal circles: litigation, arbitration and mediation.

DISTASTE FOR LITIGATION

During the course of studying for your law degree you will spend thousands of hours reading the judgments of our superior courts. Legal education is renowned for its court-centric approach and this is inevitable given the emphasis placed on doctrine in subjects such as contract. But most research on disputes demonstrates that cases which are litigated, let alone reach the Court of Appeal or House of Lords, are atypical. There are a number of reasons for this. Perhaps, most importantly, the pursuit of litigation can involve an immense commitment of resources, both in legal costs and management time. For the commercial party, even if the claim is successful, not all of the costs will be recovered and time spent by personnel in protracted preparation for litigation might be better spent devoted to core business.

Successive empirical studies of contractual practice have demonstrated that few disputants in the commercial sector even consider going to a lawyer to help them resolve contractual disputes. This is because the use of litigation to resolve disputes is seen as costly in terms of financial outlay, reputation and commercial relationships. Even when they do approach lawyers, Macaulay (1963) found that disputants in the commercial sector rarely resort to litigation. In their study of the engineering industry, Beale and Dugdale (1975) found that, even where a liquidated damages clause for late delivery was in a contract, buyers were loath to use it on breach to obtain compensation. To their mind, the key purpose of such causes was to encourage the setting of realistic delivery dates. Their study found that frequent citation of contractual terms actually served to destroy the relationship rather than make it more efficient. Lewis (1982) found that the parties were much more likely to use non-contractual remedies when disputes arise such as peer pressure, re-negotiation or the threat of withdrawal of future business. Some of these self-help remedies are evident from the cases that do end up in court. The first reaction of the contractor and sub-contractor in *Williams v Roffey* was not to litigate but to re-negotiate the terms of the contract so that completion of the building project could be achieved.

Even where the parties are disposed to litigate, there are a number of structural barriers to using the courts. The delay involved in obtaining a judgment and the inevitable commercial consequences of this. Even having obtained a judgment, the defaulting party may have insufficient assets to pay damages. There are also the uncertainties associated with litigation. Whatever the rights and wrongs of the case, there may be insufficient evidence fully to support a claim and the risk of losing. As any litigator will tell you, there is no such thing as a certain case. However strong your claim, you may have the misfortune to meet a judge who does not agree with your assessment of the case. For consumers, these same factors come into play but are exacerbated by worry caused by involvement in stressful and unfamiliar litigation procedures. These various factors have led many researchers to suggest that many disputants react to a grievance by 'lumping it' and cutting their losses.

Costs and the 'win or lose' nature of litigation have also led the business community, from the late nineteenth century onwards, towards *increased self-regulation* as regards contractual disputes. Various techniques have been adopted by the business community in advance of disputes to avoid entering the litigation arena. At the mid- to high-value end of commercial transactions, contracts have become increasingly more sophisticated as lawyers seek to avoid ambiguity and so reduce the scope for dispute. Most contracts for large-scale projects now contain carefully drafted exclusion and limitation of liability provisions, geared to risk management. In addition, liquidated damages provisions which regulate the amount of compensation to be paid on occurrence of a specified breach are commonplace. This means that disputes can be settled quickly and contractual performance completed with minimal delay.

The adoption in commercial contracts of 'escalation procedures' is also designed to contain disputes and encourage their settlement at an early stage. Such provisions will generally provide for representatives on both sides to engage in negotiations about a dispute which has arisen within a specified time period. If discussions fail, the matter is referred to senior management, perhaps in the form of a mini-trial (see below) and, if that is unsuccessful, then to mediation. Only if all of these various processes fail will the parties resort to litigation or another form of adjudication.

The conclusion to be drawn from the above factors is that, in making a decision as to whether or not to pursue a legal claim following a breach of contract, a variety of factors will have to be taken into account. Figure 19.1 summarises the most important of these considerations. Whilst not exhaustive, Figure 19.1 illustrates that, in the real world, contractual provisions cannot be determinative of how a breach of contract is resolved. This is because it is only in an adjudicatory process, such as litigation, that these principles will be given priority. In light of the various factors mentioned above it should not be assumed that bringing legal proceedings is possible or even desirable in the majority of cases.

To the extent that an aggrieved party concludes that they *do* wish to pursue a claim, they must next give consideration to the best means of doing so. As explained in the opening paragraphs of this chapter, the natural inclination of most businesspeople will be to look for a quicker and cheaper form of dispute resolution than that offered by the courts, although in some circumstances the litigation process may still offer advantages over other forms of procedures. We will now turn to consider the various

Figure 19.1: Deciding whether to make a legal claim

The strength of the legal case	Is there sufficient documentary and oral evidence to establish the facts necessary to support the claim? Will the witnesses of fact make credible witnesses? How will they stand up to cross-examination? Are relevant witnesses still employed? If they have moved on will they be willing/interested in assisting in preparation of the case?
	Will it be possible to obtain the expert evidence necessary to support technical points needed to prove the claim?
	If successful in establishing the facts relied upon, what is the percentage chance of success of the legal arguments succeeding?
Financial factors	What is the value of the claim compared to the legal costs involved in pursuing it?
	What is the value of the management time that will be involved in preparation of the legal case? Can we afford to divert this time away from our business?
	What percentage of legal costs can be recovered from the other party in the event the claim is successful? What is the likely amount of legal costs that will be payable to the other party in the event that the claim is unsuccessful? Is insurance cover available in relation to costs exposure? If so, what is the amount of the premium payable?
Commercial factors	Are we likely to want to do business with this party again?
	Will our reputation in the marketplace be damaged by pursuing a claim?
	Will litigation attract adverse or unwanted publicity?
	Will an adverse decision by the court produce a binding precedent that may have 'knock-on' consequences in relation to other contracts on similar terms?
	What are our commercial objectives in relation to the claim? Can we achieve these by other means or perhaps more quickly/ cheaply by using some other form of dispute resolution process?
Other	Litigation risk – whatever the apparent strength of the claim it is impossible to predict with certainty the decision the judge will make.
	Litigation is a destructive and stressful process. Do we have sufficientresources and commitment?

forms of dispute resolution process available, what is involved in using them and the factors that may influence a party in deciding whether to adopt a particular procedure.

VOLUNTARY AND MANDATORY PROCEDURES

Before looking at the range of dispute resolution procedures available, it is very important to understand the distinction between mandatory and voluntary procedures. The best example is litigation in which the parties must comply with the judgment imposed on them by a judge. Subject to certain limitations, an aggrieved party always has the right to take their claim to the court and the court will nearly always have the necessary authority over the defending party to compel it to submit to its authority. Similarly, many contracts contain an agreement to submit disputes to arbitration and to comply with the decision of the arbitrator. The basis of the tribunal's power will be the parties' prior agreement to submit a dispute to an arbitrator for determination. Mandatory procedures necessarily involve the appointment of an independent third party charged with determining the 'correct' legal position on the matters in dispute between the parties. Subject to any right of appeal that may exist, such decision is binding on the parties, that is in general terms they have no choice but to accept the decision. If the losing party fails to comply with the decision, the successful party will be entitled to look to the court to assist in enforcement.

By way of contrast, voluntary procedures are much more flexible and enable parties to keep their options open while exploring the possibility of compromise. They tend to be aimed at bringing the parties to an agreement on how the dispute is to be resolved. A prime example is mediation which seeks to facilitate the parties coming to their own agreement. As a general rule, voluntary procedures are conducted on a without prejudice basis, that is communications between the parties and documents created for the purposes of the procedure cannot be relied upon should the case go to court. If at the end of a voluntary procedure the parties are unable to reach terms of settlement which each feels that it can accept, they are free to walk away from the process without having prejudiced their legal position in any way.

A further important distinction lies in the nature of the remedy that may be achieved through each of these two categories of process. Where a dispute is referred for mandatory or binding determination to a third party acting in a judicial or quasi-judicial capacity, the role of the parties to the dispute is strictly limited. They have no control over the outcome of the process because that aspect is determined by the third party. Moreover, the third party charged with such responsibility is confined to adjudicating upon the specific issues referred to them and in strict accordance with the legal merits of the case. Many voluntary procedures, on the other hand, involve active participation by the parties in the formulation of an agreed outcome, the form of which often embraces matters which may be unconnected with the formal legal issues in dispute. They may, however, enable a commercially viable solution to be achieved.

FORMS OF DISPUTE RESOLUTION

As a result of growing concerns about the efficiency and effectiveness of litigation, a substantial overhaul of the civil justice system has taken place in the last two decades. This has been brought about by a combination of private enterprise, government intervention and industry pressure and has gone some way to meeting the concerns of the commercial sector. These changes have occurred in tandem with an increase in the range of dispute resolution procedures available to parties. The result is that the emphasis in modern dispute resolution is on selection of the best process to achieve a favourable outcome by the most efficient means. As already discussed, this is not the same thing as securing proper application of contractual principles in order to prove a good legal case. For most businesspeople, a favourable outcome is defined in terms of their commercial objectives and financial cost.

LITIGATION

Where resort to binding determination by a third party cannot be avoided, litigation remains the last port of call. In common with other forms of adjudication like arbitration, it involves a neutral third party listening to the arguments of two opponents and, on the basis of the evidence presented, determining which of the two best explains the legal position. It follows that adjudication produces a winner and a loser and that, in this country at least, the approach to the presentation of evidence is an adversarial one. It is also important to stress that adjudication is undertaken by someone with the authority to *impose* a decision upon the parties.

The landscape of court-based adjudication is, however, significantly different to how it was 10 years ago. This is because of the radical changes made to civil litigation as a result of the Woolf reforms. The aims of this review were to address the key problems of cost, delay and complexity of proceedings. After extensive consultation, Lord Woolf published his final report which led to new Civil Procedure Rules (CPR) which became law in April 1999. The reforms were driven by a perceived need to offer appropriate legal procedures at reasonable costs which are *proportionate* to the case and to deal with cases with reasonable speed. However, in reality, it remains an inescapable truth that parties with deep pockets, assisted by able lawyers, can exert considerable procedural and commercial pressure within the litigation landscape. This reinforces the fact that, however far the reforms may have improved procedures, litigation remains very much a process of last resort.

A number of key elements of the reforms are particularly worthy of note. Firstly, with effect from April 2003, the CPR imposed on all parties to a dispute an obligation to comply with pre-action protocols aimed at avoiding the premature commencement of litigation. These protocols also encouraged an informed dialogue that is more likely to lead to a settlement of the claim. The pre-action procedures require the party making the claim to deliver sufficient information to the other party to enable them to understand and investigate the claim. In response, the defendant must send the claimant all essential documents upon which they rely. Thus, in relation to a breach of contract claim, claimants will be required to indicate with reasonable detail the terms of the contract upon which they rely, the breaches they say have been committed by the defendants and the nature and amount of their financial loss. This then gives defendants an opportunity to assess at an early stage whether there is substance in the claims made by the claimants and, if they do not accept the validity of all or any of the claims, to respond to the claimants explaining in detail why this is so.

In this way, the parties ought to be relatively well placed to assess the strengths and weaknesses of their positions and to decide whether a claim or defence is likely to succeed. An early 'reality check' can be extremely effective in facilitating meaningful negotiations that may avoid the need for the claim to be taken any further. The objective is to compel a party to be completely 'upfront' about the nature of its claim or defence at a much earlier stage in the proceedings than has traditionally been the case.

Another important development has been that defended claims can now be allocated to one of three tracks: the small claims track, the fast track and the multi-track. The objective of this system is to ensure that every claim is dealt with by the fastest and most cost-effective procedure appropriate. The small claims track is the normal track for any claim which has a financial value of less than £5,000 and is exclusive to the County Court. This will be the track appropriate for most small contractual claims, for example, the sale of faulty consumer goods or a dispute about the quality of minor building works. The fast track is an innovation brought about by the Woolf reforms and is the normal track for claims valued between £5,000 and £15,000. The fast track is intended as a limited procedure designed to take to trial, within a short but reasonable timescale, straightforward claims that do not require the more complex procedures of the multi-track and that can be dealt with by a trial lasting not more than one day. The multi-track is for more complex, high-value claims for which one of the other two tracks are not appropriate.

It is now the court, rather than the parties, that dictates the procedure and timetable to be adopted. The court rules contain a list of 12 factors which go to make up effective case management. These include encouraging the parties to co-operate with each other in the conduct of proceedings, deciding the order in which issues are to be resolved, considering whether the cost of a particular step justifies the cost of taking it and fixing timetables, or otherwise controlling the progress of the case. In the past, the role of judges in preparation for trial has been much more responsive. Under CPR, the judge will now take a more proactive role in managing the case. The judge will be looking to see that the most time- and cost-effective procedures are adopted, and should look to the parties to justify any proposed departure from these.

ALTERNATIVE (OR APPROPRIATE) DISPUTE RESOLUTION

The courts now actively promote the use of alternative dispute resolution (ADR) as a means of resolving claims without the need for a trial. Pre-action protocols require those thinking of litigating their dispute to indicate whether they are prepared to participate in such procedures. In addition, active case management by the courts in the post-Woolf environment has meant that the parties are now encouraged to use ADR procedures if the court considers it appropriate. Perhaps most significantly, in appropriate cases, the court's powers in relation to costs enable it to penalise a party that has adopted an unreasonable position in refusing the use of ADR. The need for such sanctions arises as a result of the reluctance of some parties and their advisers to participate in, or even consider the use of, mediation or other forms of ADR. The reasons for such reluctance are varied, ranging from an unwillingness on the part of lawyers to engage in a process with which they have no familiarity or confidence, to a level of animosity between the parties that causes them to refuse to consider any form of out-of-court negotiation. In introducing sanctions for failure to consider ADR, the court makes it essential for lawyers to discuss the possibility of ADR and to ensure that their clients understand the possible costs consequences if such an approach is not at least explored.

The possible imposition of costs sanctions raises the question of what constitutes unreasonable conduct. How far does a party have to go in order to establish that they have acted reasonably? Do they have to accept an offer of mediation in all cases even if they believe that the process will be a complete waste of time? This issue has been considered by the courts in a number of recent cases. In *Dunnett v Railtrack plc* (2002) Railtrack succeeded in defending an appeal brought by Dunnett. As a result they would normally expect to recover its costs. Instead, the Court of Appeal decided to penalise Railtrack by making no order for costs, which meant that Railtrack had to pay the costs of bringing the action. The basis for the court's decision was Railtrack's rejection of an offer by Dunnet to take the dispute to mediation. The court indicated that, if a party rejected ADR out of hand when it had been suggested by the court, it would suffer the consequences when the question of costs came to be decided. The court emphasised that the parties themselves also had a duty to consider whether ADR was a possible remedy. The later case of *Hurst v Leeming* (2003) gave further guidance as to acceptable reasons for refusing mediation. It was held that the already high costs of the case, the serious nature of the other party's allegations, or one party's subjective view of the merits of the other's cases were not valid reasons to reject mediation. A reasoned conclusion that there was no real prospect of success in a mediation *was* a valid reason for refusal but the hurdle to overcome in relying on this ground was considered to be high; see also *P4 Ltd v Unite Integrated Solutions plc* (2006).

Two later cases have, however, emphasised that a refusal to mediate is not fatal. In *Valentine v Allen* (2003), Valentine argued that Allen should not be entitled to the costs of successfully resisting his appeal in the usual way because they had rejected two separate offers of mediation. The Court of Appeal pointed out, however, that before the appeal, Allen had made offers of settlement which were reasonable and generous. The parties had met to discuss settlement and the respondents' solicitors had entered into considerable correspondence in an effort to try to settle the case, even offering a 'round the table' meeting. The Court of Appeal held that the respondents had acted reasonably and it was not appropriate to deny Allen his costs.

In *Corenso (UK) Ltd v Burnden Group Plc* (2003), the judge found that neither party could be blamed for a failure to mediate. Various methods of ADR had been suggested, negotiations had been attempted and it was clear that the parties were prepared to attempt to resolve the matter without going to court. The judge emphasised that a party's obligation is to attempt to resolve the dispute by using ADR, of which mediation is only one form. Mediation would only be appropriate in some cases and, so long as the parties had shown a genuine and constructive willingness to try to settle the dispute, a party would not be penalised because it had not agreed to go along with a particular form of ADR proposed by the other side. The lesson to be drawn from these cases is that the obligation to consider ADR is not an inflexible one and that each case must be carefully considered on its individual facts. That said, it is a brave litigant who will now dismiss an offer of ADR out of hand.

EXPERT DETERMINATION

The Woolf reforms have sought to encourage the use of ADR but, in truth, alternatives to litigation in the form of private dispute resolution procedures have existed and been used extensively for many years by the business community. Until recent years, however, these have for the most part taken the form of binding procedures such as arbitration and expert determination. For example, arbitration is often used to resolve re-insurance disputes and commercial leases frequently incorporate an expert determination procedure in relation to disagreements arising on rent review. Clauses allowing for referral of disputes to such processes frequently appear in standard form contracts. In other instances, such as the private adjudicatory scheme introduced for the construction industry in the Housing Grants, Construction and Regeneration Act 1996, standard procedures are implied where the contract is silent on the matter.

An expert determination occurs when the parties agree to refer a dispute to a neutral third party with a particular technical expertise who will apply that knowledge when *adjudicating* the matters in dispute. The exercise is very often done on paper without a hearing. Each party will provide the expert with written submissions setting out its case and supported by relevant documents. There may be an opportunity for each party to reply to the submissions made by their opponent and the expert will then make its decision. With some limited exceptions, the decision of the expert is final and binding. There is no appeal.

The advantages of the process are that, because of the procedure adopted, the cost and, perhaps more importantly, the delay involved can be significantly less than most other forms of binding dispute resolution. An expert determination is a particularly useful option where a dispute is concerned solely with a technical issue. For example, did work performed by an IT contractor comply with a technical specification or has a financial calculation been undertaken correctly? In these circumstances, expert determination by an engineer or accountant may be by far the best route for parties to adopt. A third-party expert will be familiar with industry norms and practices, and can thereby bring useful background knowledge to the dispute that will aid speedy and cost-effective resolution. Expert determination is routinely used in certain industry sectors. For example, it is commonly used to determine a revised rent on implementation of a rent review clause in a commercial lease. It is also used in certain types of agreement, such as completion accounts in a share sale agreement.

Arbitration is one of the most popular forms of expert determination. Indeed, it is so common that many have argued that it is no longer an 'alternative' but the norm. This form of dispute resolution is a private adjudicatory process by which parties appoint a third party to make a binding determination in relation to matters in dispute between them. The parties are free to name an arbitrator they wish to use in advance or allow a professional body such as the Institute of Arbitrators to select one. There is also a considerable amount of flexibility as regards venue and procedural rules. An agreement to arbitrate disputes may be included in the parties' contract in the form of an arbitration clause. Alternatively, it may be entered into after a dispute has arisen as a 'submission agreement'. An arbitration agreement is itself a contract and subject to the same rules as to validity, construction and enforceability as other contracts. For example, if a particular issue in dispute between the parties does not fall within the description of matters referred to arbitration, the arbitrator will have no power to deal with it even if requested to do so by one of the parties.

Commentators have identified a number of advantages of arbitration over litigation. Of these, finality and speed have been shown to be particularly important in the commercial sector. In broad terms, parties are free to opt out of any right of appeal against the arbitrator's determination and, even where they do not agree to do so, in most jurisdictions the grounds for appeal to the local courts will be extremely limited. In this way, the process meets the needs of business people to achieve certainty of outcome at the earliest date possible and thus allow them to move on in their business. Various business decisions may be held up while a company waits to find out whether it will be found liable to pay a substantial capital sum, or if it has the right to sell products on to a third party. A further factor is that the cost of taking a dispute through various levels of appeal can be substantial. As a consequence, the parties' businesses may be deprived of much needed resources. However, the benefits of finality naturally carry a cost. The 'advantage' of having no right of appeal is not one that will necessarily be recognised by the losing party to the dispute. In very general terms, when the parties have appointed a robust arbitrator, a determination may be obtained in a much shorter timeframe than would be the case were the dispute to be litigated.

Arbitration also has the advantage of being a private dispute process and under most systems of law is a more confidential procedure than litigation. The proceedings are held in private and under English law there is an implied obligation on both parties not to disclose events in the arbitration room or to use for their own purpose documents prepared for the arbitration process. These factors are very important in the commercial sector, as it may be desirable for the dispute not to attract publicity. One of the parties may be seeking to expand their business and may feel that their reputation may be damaged. In the alternative, the dispute may relate to sensitive technical information or business strategies that the parties prefer should remain confidential.

The parties to an arbitration also have a much greater degree of control over the choice of arbitrator than the parties to litigation will have over the selection of a judge hearing a case. It is possible to specify in the arbitration agreement appropriate qualifications which an arbitrator appointed under the contract should have and these can be tailored to meet the particular type of dispute or issues arising. So, for instance, contractual disputes concerning issues of foreign law may result in the appointment of a panel of arbitrators of whom one has a legal qualification in that jurisdiction. Given the growth of international trade in recent decades, such requirements could prove critical to success. The arbitration process also allows for greater procedural flexibility than may be the case in relation to many court processes and procedures can be tailored to the particular needs of the dispute. Moreover, the parties will have the comfort of being involved in the choice of arbitrator and can therefore select someone in whom they have confidence and trust rather than relying on the judgment of an unknown judge.

In an ideal world, when parties from different jurisdictions negotiate a dispute resolution provision in a contract, their objective will be to find a form of provision with which they both feel comfortable. For many parties, the first choice will be litigation before their home courts but this leaves the other party at risk of feeling that they are at a disadvantage. In such situations, the parties may be prepared to consider that the dispute be referred to arbitration in a third jurisdiction is something that the parties are prepared to consider. Although the arbitration will take place in a jurisdiction foreign to the parties, the experience will at least be mutual.

Another key benefit relates to enforcement. While important steps have been taken over the last few decades in relation to international agreements governing reciprocal enforcement of foreign court-based judgments on harmonised terms, the position is still rather patchy at a global level, although there are some very good regional regimes. Examples include the Brussels and Lugano Conventions relating to European disputes. Most trading nations are parties to the New York Convention on the Recognition and Enforcement of Arbitration Awards 1958. The principle underlying the convention is that an award made in any state will be recognised and enforced by any other state which is a party to the convention provided that the award satisfies certain basic conditions. The formalities required for obtaining the recognition and enforcement of convention awards are relatively straightforward and the convention does not permit any review on the merits of an award to which it applies.

Arbitration also has a number of disadvantages. Somewhat surprisingly, the cost of arbitration can be significantly higher than litigation. The parties will have to pay the arbitrator's fees whereas a judge comes free. The parties will also have to provide a suite of rooms for the hearing, together with appropriate support services such as transcription and secretarial services. If there is a panel of three arbitrators and a lengthy hearing in a foreign venue, these may be considerable.

MEDIATION

The use of mediation to resolve commercial disputes has increased significantly in recent years in response to the changes introduced by the Civil Procedure Rules. The Centre for Effective Dispute Resolution has claimed that, in 2006–7, there was a 33 per cent increase in the number that took place. A preference for mediation schemes over other forms of dispute resolution has been demonstrated by the British Marine Federation, the British Institute of Architectural Technologists and the Baltic and International Maritime Council. The Centre for Effective Dispute Resolution (CEDR), one of the country's largest mediation providers, claims that, in the 12 months between April 1999 and March 2000, they experienced a 141 per cent increase in the number of commercial disputes referred to them. In the following year, the organisation arranged 467 commercial mediations, of which commercial contract disputes accounted for 31 per cent of cases, some of which involved damages of between $1.1m and $8m.

In March 2001, the then Lord Chancellor's Department (LCD) announced that all government departments should seek to avoid litigation by using mediation and a year later the Office of Government Commerce published a dispute resolution guide for all those involved in the drafting of UK procurement contracts. At a European level, the European Commission's *Green Paper* on developing commercial mediation in the European Union was also published and adopted in 2002. The Insurance Mediation Directive of 2002 also supports this trend and seeks to ensure a high degree of professionalism and competence amongst intermediaries in insurance disputes.

Mediation is a private process in which the parties to a dispute come together for an agreed period to attempt to reach a resolution of their dispute with the help of a neutral third party. In a commercial setting, the parties are often accompanied by their lawyers, although this is less common in other spheres. If an agreement can be agreed, a settlement contract is signed. The process is a consensual one in the sense that the parties have chosen to mediate and have not been forced into the process in the same way they might be forced into litigation or contractually bound to refer to arbitration. If the parties cannot reach agreement, they are free to revert to what other form of process they think appropriate. All of the discussions and negotiations that take place during a mediation remain confidential and may not be disclosed to a judge or arbitrator who may later have to deal with the dispute.

In general terms, there are two forms of mediation which operate in the commercial sphere, although there are an increasing number of variations. These are, *facilitative* mediation in which the mediator assists the parties to formulate a settlement and *evaluative* mediation in which the mediator may assist the process by giving a non-binding view of the merits of the particular issues between the parties. It is also possible for parties to agree to med-arb, in which case the mediator, in the event the parties are unable to reach a settlement, will change role to become an arbitrator and in that capacity will then make a binding decision on the merits.

In contrast to adjudication, the role of the mediator is to encourage the parties to reach a result that best suits their needs rather than imposing one upon them. The mediation process usually opens with a joint meeting of the parties and mediator at which each party is given an opportunity to make a statement about its position but there is considerable flexibility about how the process can be organised. Frequently, the meeting will then break up into two camps or 'caucuses' and the mediator will embark upon a form of shuttle diplomacy, moving from party to party, trying to narrow issues, play 'devil's advocate' and assist the parties in identifying some common objectives. There are, however, no hard and fast rules about how the process should work. The essence of mediation is that it should be as responsive as possible to the needs of the parties and the particular dispute.

Mediation can be of considerable value in relation to commercial disputes, particularly where the number of companies operating in the particular industry sector is small or where the contractual relationship between the parties is a long-term one. In these circumstances, for obvious reasons, it is in both parties' interests to find a solution that will enable them to continue working together. This factor can assist the mediator in trying to establish some common ground upon which a settlement can be reached. They will often try to explore with the parties factors outside of the formal legal issues to see if there are commercial matters not directly connected with the dispute but which may assist the parties in reaching a commercial compromise acceptable on both sides. For example, one party may owe the other a payment under their contract but be suffering from a cash flow problem. An agreement in which the amount paid is reduced but the paying party commits itself to placing a new order for additional work may well be acceptable to both parties, and may allow them to preserve the relationship more or less intact. As a result mediation clauses in commercial agreements are now becoming much more common.

Commercial entities have become much more receptive to the idea of mediation. Its attractions for the businessperson are clear. In addition to the obvious savings in costs, it enables them to exercise some degree of control over the outcome of the dispute, it avoids the considerable waste of management time involved in the litigation or arbitration process and can salvage a valuable business relationship. Where parties have already embarked upon litigation, mediation can also serve as a valuable opportunity to undertake a 'reality check' on their position. Most legal advisers will ensure that, when the mediation takes place, their client has detailed information on the key factors that should inform their approach to settlement. These will almost certainly include details of legal costs incurred to date and legal costs likely to be incurred in taking the dispute to trial. A second important factor will be an analysis of possible outcomes at trial and net financial consequences in relation to each. The percentage chance of success and net financial outcome are matters to which most businesspeople will readily relate and in the context of which they can make informed decisions in relation to their negotiating position in the mediation.

Figure 19.2 illustrates the sort of cost–benefit–risk analysis that a party, with the assistance of its lawyers, will be undertaking in preparation for and during a mediation. In the example given, the percentage chance of success of litigation is high and a party in this position may well feel relatively comfortable in taking the claim to trial should a mediation fail to produce a satisfactory outcome. However, even in a case as strong as

Figure 19.2:   Analysis of litigation factors prior to mediation

key factors	
costs incurred to date	£20,000
additional costs likely to be incurred to date of trial	£50,000
total costs likely to be incurred by the other side in taking the matter to trial (some guidance on this can be gleaned from the forecast of costs which each party is obliged to file withthe court)	£80,000
percentage chance of success in litigation	70%
value of claim	£200,000
possible scenarios	
success attrial: 1 recover amount claimed (£200,000) 2 obtain an order for costs resulting in a recovery, following an assessment of costs by the court, of approximately 60–70% of actual costs in curred (£45,500)	net outcome: receive £175,500
lose at trial: 1 recover nothing 2 bear 100% of own costs (£70,000) 3 subject to an order for payment of costs to the other side resulting in a payment out of approximately 60–70% of opponent's actualcosts (£52,000)	net outcome: pay out £122,000

this, the 25 per cent possibility of a nil recovery and payment of an opponent's costs in the order of £50,000 is something that will cause pause for thought. Clearly, were the percentage chances of success to be significantly lower, the incentive to find a solution in the mediation will be that much greater. In complex cases, such analyses are not always straightforward. There may be several different issues with different risk–cost factors attached to each. The range of permutations may be considerable and the lawyer will have to focus in on the most likely scenarios in order to determine a negotiating strategy with their client. One of the goals of the mediator will be to find a position where, for each party, the risk–benefit of proceeding to trial is less attractive than the proposal on the table in the mediation.

CONCLUDING REMARKS

It is clear that, in recent years, the state has made efforts to devolve power for management of disputes to the parties. Disputes which previously would have plodded through the litigation system are now more commonly referred to alternative forms of dispute resolutions and the amount of cases reaching trial has reduced significantly as a result. In the business sector, there has long been a desire to manage disputes more effectively and thus avoid the trials and tribulations of litigation. The net result of this is that, where used appropriately, dispute resolution procedures can be seen as an extension of routine business activity as parties seek to renegotiate their position on the basis of familiar commercial factors such as risk, trust and cost. The role of the lawyer will be as much to assist clients in finding the most appropriate form of dispute resolution process as to advise on the legal merits of the case.

Our factor discussed in the context of mediation leads us back to some of the key themes introduced at the beginning of the book and referred to throughout. Mediators are far from alone in arguing for a relational and contextualised understanding of contracts and disputes which arise because of them. Socio-legal researchers have identified a number of ways in which the judiciary has failed to understand, or respond to, the needs of contracting parties, especially those involved in long-term relationships and we have argued that the law of contract is facing something of a legitimation crisis as a result. A succession of empirical studies have demonstrated that formal law is frequently ignored or circumvented by contracting parties because of its inability to reflect the needs of the contracting parties and nuances of their relationship. For some, formal law has become more or less irrelevant to the performance of long-term contracts because of its reliance on individual self-interest and economic rationality at the cost of more widely accepted notions of common interest and flexibility, such as those espoused by many feminist writers.

This state of affairs has led academics to call for the architects of the law and legal system to devise doctrines and processes which give adequate expression to relationships guided by the knowledge acquired about their empirical character. It could be argued that these concerns begin to be addressed in the post-Woolf environment. In common with many mediators, modern contract theorists are much more likely than their forebears to advocate a return to models of contract that address communication between networked subjects. They have argued that many commercial contractual relationships are better understood as involving long-term bonds, in which concerns about reputation, interdependence and co-operation are high.

REFERENCES AND FURTHER READING

Beale, H and Dugdale, T 'Contracts between businessmen: planning and the use of contractual remedies' (1975) 2 *British Journal of Law and Society* 45.

Brown, H and Marriot, A (2002) *ADR Principles and Practice*, Sweet and Maxwell, London.

Campbell, D (2003) 'Forbearance, alternative dispute resolution and settlement' in Collins, H *The Law of Contract*, LexisNexis, Butterworths, London.

Galanter, M 'Worlds of deals: using negotiations teach about legal process' (1984) 34 *Journal of Legal Education* 268.

Genn, H (1998) *Final Report to the Lord Chancellor on the County Court Pilot Scheme*, Lord Chancellor's Department, London.

Genn, H (2007) *Twisting Arms: Court Referred and Court Linked Mediation Under Judicial Pressure*, Ministry of Justice, London.

Harris, D, Campbell, D and Halson, R (2002) *Remedies in Contract and Tort*, 2nd edn, LexisNexis Butterworths, London.

Lewis, R 'Contracts between businessmen: reform of the law of firm offers and an empirical study of tendering practices in the building industry' (1982) 9 *Journal of Law and Society* 153.

Macaulay, S 'Non-contractual relations in business – a preliminary study' (1963) 28 *American Sociological Review* 55.

Mulcahy, L (2004) 'Bargaining in the shadow of the flaws? The feminisation of dispute resolution' in Mulcahy, L and Wheeler, S (eds) *Feminist Perspectives on Contract Law*, Cavendish, London.

Palmer, M and Roberts, S (2005) *Dispute Processes: ADR and the primary forms of decision making*, Cambridge Uiversity Press, Cambridge.

Woolf, Lord (1994) *Access to Justice: Interim report*, HMSO, London.

Woolf, Lord (1996) *Access to Justice: Final report*, HMSO, London.

? QUESTIONS

(1) Look back at each of the disputes that Angie and Georgie have become embroiled in and identify which of the following dispute procedures is most likely to help them achieve what they want:

  (a) bilateral negotiation;

  (b) mediation;

  (c) arbitration;

  (d) court-based adjudication.

  Give reasons for your response.

(2) Can you find out how much each of the processes named in question (1) might cost? What costs other than lawyers' fees and third-party fees could you include in your list?

(3) Can you fill in the checklist in Figure 19.2 in relation to Angie and Georgie's dispute with Orange Peril? Is your conclusion that they should mediate or not?

(4) Appraise critically the argument that the Woolf reforms of the civil litigation system pose a threat to the development of the common law.

(5) Can you discover 10 reasons why commercial arbitration is preferable to litigation in the field of international commerce?

INDEX